Artificial Intelligence, Automation and the Future of Competence at Work

Artificial intelligence and the autonomous robots of the Fourth Industrial Revolution will render certain jobs and competences obsolete but will also create new roles, which in turn will require new sets of skills. They will also transform how we produce, distribute and consume, as well as how we think. Rather than a linear understanding of evolutionary processes, we will develop a more interactive and circular interpretation.

This book offers a unique and holistic perspective on the future of work in the context of industry 4.0. It discusses the globalization of capital markets, how artificial intelligence can help organizations to be more competitive and the new role of leadership in this technological landscape.

The author argues that there are four categories of competences, which will be required to maintain the relevance of human skills and expertise in the innovation economy. The new jobs that come into being will lend themselves to a particular set of skills. General competences will be necessary for roles involving the 4Cs of communication, creativity, collaboration and change. Specific or STEM competences will be called for across the science, technology, engineering and mathematics sectors. Human competences will lend themselves to positions comprising the SELC framework of social, emotional, leadership and cultural skills. Critical or REVE competences will be in demand for roles embracing reflection, ethics, values and the environment.

This book provides a human-centric view of the current technological advancements of artificial intelligence and robotics and offers a positive outlook for human actors seeking continued relevance. It will appeal to scholars and students of the innovation economy, the knowledge society and the coming Fourth Industrial Revolution.

Jon-Arild Johannessen is Full Professor of Leadership at Kristiania University College, Norway.

Routledge Studies in the Economics of Innovation

The Routledge Studies in the Economics of Innovation series is our home for comprehensive yet accessible texts on the current thinking in the field. These cutting-edge, upper-level scholarly studies and edited collections bring together robust theories from a wide range of individual disciplines and provide in-depth studies of existing and emerging approaches to innovation, and the implications of such for the global economy.

The Dynamics of Local Innovation Systems
Structures, Networks and Processes
Eva Panetti

Innovation in Knowledge Intensive Business Services
The Digital Era
Anna Cabigiosu

The Impact of the Sharing Economy on Business and Society
Digital Transformation and the Rise of Platform Businesses
Edited by Abbas Strømmen-Bakhtiar and Evgueni Vinogradov

Automation, Innovation and Work
The Impact of Technological, Economic, and Social Singularity
Jon-Arild Johannessen and Helene Sætersdal

The Political Economy of Digital Automation
Measuring its Impact on Productivity, Economic Growth and Consumption
Sreenath Majumder and Anuradha SenGupta

Artificial Intelligence, Automation and the Future of Competence at Work
Jon-Arild Johannessen

For more information about this series, please visit: www.routledge.com/Routledge-Studies-in-the-Economics-of-Innovation/book-series/ECONINN

Artificial Intelligence, Automation and the Future of Competence at Work

Jon-Arild Johannessen

Routledge
Taylor & Francis Group
LONDON AND NEW YORK

First published 2021
by Routledge
2 Park Square, Milton Park, Abingdon, Oxon OX14 4RN

and by Routledge
52 Vanderbilt Avenue, New York, NY 10017

Routledge is an imprint of the Taylor & Francis Group, an informa business

British Library Cataloguing-in-Publication Data
A catalogue record for this book is available from the British Library

Library of Congress Cataloging-in-Publication Data
Names: Johannessen, Jon-Arild, author.
Title: Artificial intelligence, automation and the future of competence at work / Jon-Arild Johannessen.
Description: Abingdon, Oxon ; New York, NY : Routledge, 2021. | Series: Routledge studies in the economics of innovation | Includes bibliographical references and index.
Identifiers: LCCN 2020029650 (print) | LCCN 2020029651 (ebook) | ISBN 9780367640460 (hardback) | ISBN 9781003121923 (ebook)
Subjects: LCSH: Labor supply—Effect of automation on. | Automation—Economic aspects. | Artificial intelligence—Economic aspects. | Vocational qualifications. | Skilled labor—Effect of automation on.
Classification: LCC HD6331 .J637 2021 (print) | LCC HD6331 (ebook) | DDC 331.25—dc23
LC record available at https://lccn.loc.gov/2020029650
LC ebook record available at https://lccn.loc.gov/2020029651

ISBN: 978-0-367-64046-0 (hbk)
ISBN: 978-1-003-12192-3 (ebk)

Typeset in Times New Roman
by Apex CoVantage, LLC

Contents

Figures

1 Introduction

What competences will be in demand in the Fourth Industrial Revolution?

Key points in this book

1 New jobs will be created requiring various types of competences. Four categories of competences that will especially be in demand are general competences, specific competences, human competences and critical competences.

a) Jobs requiring general competences will be created in the following areas: communication, creativity, collaboration and change (the 4Cs).
b) Jobs requiring specific competences will be created in the following areas: science, technology, engineering and mathematics (STEM competences).
c) Jobs requiring human competences will be created in the following areas: social, emotional, leadership and cultural (SELC competences).
d) Jobs requiring critical competences will be created in the following areas: reflection, ethics, values and the environment (REVE competences).

2 A new technological paradigm will emerge.
3 A balanced competences paradigm will emerge.
4 To gain an understanding of changes in the future, it will be important to examine new trend lines, rather than just follow the media headlines.

Introduction

We are at the beginning of a new industrial revolution, the Fourth Industrial Revolution (Schwab, 2016). However, this revolution will not necessarily result in the whole world being seriously affected by ubiquitous intelligent robots and artificial intelligence[1] (Avent, 2017). Changes will occur very rapidly in some sectors, with serious consequences for workers whose jobs become redundant, while changes will take longer in other sectors (Lima, 2017). Things are happening very fast in some sectors, such as the auto industry. In other sectors, such as the educational sector, change will be more sluggish (Avent, 2017; Susskind & Susskind, 2015). In the future, it is probable that the more traditional educational institutions will continue to disseminate knowledge that was relevant to the Third Industrial Revolution, such as knowledge related to automation of production and digitization (Gaskarth, 2015). However, if traditional educational institutions are too slow to adapt to future changes, the market will probably replace some of the traditional educational models with other models, such as those adopted by private corporate universities (Johannessen, 2020a, 2020c; Barrow, 2019). In the health-care sector, technological competences will become a natural part of the curricula for training health-care personnel (Johannessen, 2018; Bleuler et al., 2017; Xie, 2017).

If humankind is to benefit from the new developments in the Fourth Industrial Revolution, we will need to develop other competences than just specific ones, such as critical competences. Among other points, critical competences are based on the knowledge needed to enable reflection on the ethical and value-related challenges of the new technological developments that we can observe emerging at the start of the Fourth Industrial Revolution (Johannessen, 2021). These critical competences also include the ability to 'see' patterns and understand what is happening to the environment, and the consequences this may have for people, organizations, society and the planet (Lima, 2017).

The intelligent robots and artificial intelligence of the Fourth Industrial Revolution will transform how we think: rather than a linear understanding of evolutionary processes, we will develop a more interactive and circular understanding (Schwab, 2016).

'Techno-evangelists', i.e. those who believe that technology will solve all the challenges we face, often express the view in various newspaper articles and books that specific competences (science, technological, engineering and mathematical – STEM) will be the only competences in demand in the Fourth Industrial Revolution (Svarre, 2019). However, we are of a different view. In addition to specific heavyweight, technological skills, we will also need more general competences. These competences will be in the areas of communications, creativity, collaboration and change.

If we do not adapt in step with changes in the external environment, we are at risk of rapidly emulating the fate of the frog in the following story. The story goes like this (Handy, 1995). A frog is put into a large cooking pot filled with cold water. The water is heated up extremely slowly. The frog acclimatizes to the gradually warming water, and as we all know, eventually basks itself to death. The other story about the frog goes like this: a live frog is put into a pot of boiling water. The frog reacts instantly by jumping out of the pot. We humans could rapidly share the fate of the frog in the pot of cold water, unless we adapt to changes taking place in our external environment. In this context, we might quote Russell Ackoff (1981: 2) and say, 'Plan or be planned for'. In other words, we should carve out our own futures and not simply adapt to what other people have planned for us. This is a story about gradual changes. In China, President Xi Jinping[2] warns that we should be more wary of the grey rhinos rather than the black swans. A 'black swan' is an unpredictable change in the economy, while a 'grey rhino' is a large, visible threat that goes ignored (as with the frog in the water that is gently heated). Nevertheless, we react to sudden and dramatic changes (a 'black swan') – or as illustrated in the story previously mentioned – the frog that jumps quickly out of the pot of boiling water (Handy, 2002).

If we consider the auto industry as an example, there can be no doubt that intelligent robots and artificial intelligence will lead to a new wave of automation (Ford, 2016). This will in turn lead to a greater demand for specific competences, which we refer to in this book as STEM competences[3] (Bruce & Crook, 2015; Brynjolfsson & McAfee, 2014). The transition from combustion engines to electric engines in vehicles will also boost the trend towards completely automated car factories, with no need for human workers on the production lines (Johannessen, 2019b).

Economic globalization is increasing simultaneously with the emergence of a new technological paradigm, which focuses on artificial intelligence and intelligent robots. Along with other forces opposed to economic globalization, National Populist parties around the globe are trying to dam up the river of economic globalization; but the dams will inevitably be broken down by the surging forces of the global knowledge and innovation economy (Boutrup, 2018). In simple terms, this means that there will also be a demand for more general competences. As mentioned earlier, these competences consist of communication, creativity, change and collaboration (the '4Cs') (Johannessen, 2020a, 2020c; Lima, 2017; Ford, 2016). These general competences, together with specific competences, will pose a new challenge of how to satisfy the demand for these expanding competences at the threshold of the Fourth Industrial Revolution. These two classes of competences can be described as the necessary competences that will be required in the Fourth Industrial Revolution.

The transition from the production of combustion engines to electric engines in the auto industry and the transition to green methods of production, distribution and consumption in the economy as a whole (Klein, 2019) will generate a demand for a third class of competences. We can describe this class of competences as human competences, which we can refer to as social, emotional, leadership and cultural competences (Johannessen, 2020a, 2020c; Goleman, 2018). The globalization of capital markets that started with the fall of the Berlin Wall and continued into the early twenty-first century with China's entry into capitalist markets further boosted demand for human competences (Johannessen, 2019a). The new intelligent robots and advanced artificial intelligence that will see the light of day in around approximately 2045, when singularity occurs (Johannessen, 2020a; Kurzweil, 2005, 2008) will further increase demand for human competences. Such a trend will demand competences that will be decisive for ensuring that lives of people are not reduced to a meaningless existence (Avent, 2017).

In addition to the social and emotional competences needed at the threshold of the Fourth Industrial Revolution, other human competences in demand will consist of competence in strong and enlightened leadership. We will need leaders who inspire confidence and who understand the approaching era, rather than leaders whose visions and plans for the future are based on narratives and knowledge that relate to the previous industrial era (Handy, 2002; Johannessen, 2019a). In addition to these three areas of competence within the human competences, we will also need cultural competence in the global economy, so that we can understand and engage with cultures in the global knowledge society (Handy, 2002; Johannessen, 2020c).

The change processes that are already taking place and that are being boosted by new technology will affect even the smallest communities. This will create a demand for critical competences, which will require every one of us to reflect on what we want from the impending changes. These critical competences can be referred to using the acronym REVE, which stands for reflection, ethics, values and environmental competences (Klein, 2019; Johannessen, 2020c, 2021). These critical competences will be decisive for the many challenges we will face in the future as we move towards singularity (Johannessen, 2020a; Kurzweil, 2008).

In addition to the four classes of competences discussed previously, there are what we term here 'service competences'. Examples of people with these competences are call-centre workers, hotel cleaners, hospital porters and so on. Many of these jobs will continue to be necessary for the foreseeable future. However, such workers will be poorly paid, and their competences will not be equal in status to those four classes of competences.

We have developed three 'case letters'[4] that illustrate different aspects of globalization and new technology. One of these case letters shows what will happen regarding some of these service competences.

Narratives

Case letter 1

Trawlers catch fish in the seas off Mehamn, a small fishing village in the far north of Norway. The fish are frozen on board the trawlers. Once frozen, the fish are sent to China for processing. In China, the fish are thawed, processed, put into attractive packaging and refrozen. Finally, the packaged fish is sent back for retail sale in places that include Mehamn. The fish that comes back to Mehamn from China costs consumers about NOK 1 less per kilo than if the fish had been processed in Mehamn. Of course, the price of the fish does not take account of environmental costs and the social costs of unemployment in Mehamn. People in general need to reflect on the ethical, environmental and social problems that such production processes inflict on individuals in a small community that is economically dependent on fish, on the environment and on the values on which our society should be based (Johannessen, 2020b).

Case letter 2

Swindon is a town in southwest England. Swindon will lose 3,500 jobs simply because the senior executives at the Honda Motor Company believe, for various reasons, that the production line should be shut down because it will be more profitable to relocate production to a low-cost country. This should provoke reflection on the green economy and also on ethical considerations relating to whether we should base our values on prioritizing profit over car-workers' welfare, as well as the consequences for the local community.[5]

Case letter 3

In 15 projects being run by the Danish pension company PFA, robots are sending automated responses to customer queries. One of the projects has involved training a robot to understand what customers really mean when submitting their queries. PFA receives more than 1,000 emails every day, and this figure is rising by 5–10 per cent each year. According to Daniel Hasselager Brevadt, director of artificial intelligence at PFA, very soon, within about one month, an artificially intelligent robot will respond to 20 per cent of all emails. Brevadt continues: 'We are obliged to think about new technologies and forms of service, because there is competition from abroad. I am slightly concerned about the competitiveness of the entire sector'.[6] The point of this short case letter is to emphasize that even within the service sector, people with competences that require relatively little education will be competed out of their jobs by artificial intelligence and intelligent robots.

Readers should note that this book focuses mainly on OECD countries, which we also refer to as the industrialized world. We focus on the competences that will be needed in these countries, and how they will be affected by the Fourth Industrial Revolution. That said, we should also be clear that globalization, new technologies and automation have brought about enormous social improvements in countries such as India and China, among others. In India, the percentage of the population living in poverty fell from 60 per cent to 22 per cent in the period from 1982 to 2012. Over the same period, projected longevity has risen from 49 to 66 years. We have seen a similar – even more positive – trend in China. In China, the percentage of the population living in poverty fell from 84 per cent to 13 per cent during the same period. Between 1982 and 2012, 600 million people in China emerged from poverty (Ross, 2016: 11).

Some narratives that exemplify competency challenges

In 2012, the Lindø shipyard on the island of Funen in Denmark closed down, leaving roughly 3,600 workers unemployed. By the end of 2018, the new robotics industry on the same island was now employing 3,600 workers. It is expected that the robotics industry on Funen will grow by 35 per cent over the next two years and that the number of employees will increase to roughly 4,500. Exports from the robotics industry cluster on Funen have almost doubled over the last few years. At the beginning of 2019, the Funen robotics industry cluster consisted of 129 companies and new companies are continuously being established. 'The problem is the lack of manpower', says the executive manager of Odense Robotics, one of the largest companies in the cluster; he adds, 'a lack of IT skills, competence, and engineers is causing a bottleneck'.[7]

The new Danish robotics industry is not confined to the Funen robotics cluster – many entrepreneurs throughout Denmark are working with the new robotics technology. One of these is Lasse Thomsen, who works in Aalborg in north Jutland. He has developed a robot that is used in the rehabilitation of patients in hospitals and nursing homes.[8] 'This robot functions as an aid to the staff of the hospitals', says Thomsen. The rehabilitation robot 'Robert', developed and constructed by Life Science Robotics, has been used to rehabilitate elderly patients at OUH (Odense University Hospital). The health-care sector will most probably be one of the largest customers for the production of such robots in the future. As the intelligence level of these robots increases, the scope of application will also increase.

Thomas Visti, another Danish robotics entrepreneur with an educational background in electronics and engineering, started Mobil Industrial Robots in 2014, which by 2018 had a turnover of DKK 200 million.[9]

Many believe the fast-growing robotics industry to be the new industrial 'gold mine', and this 'gold' is certainly shining brightly in the Danish robotics industry. However, it is the lack of the right expertise that may slow down the extraction of this 'gold'. Large international equity funds have spotted the opportunities for investment in the Danish robotics industry. For example the US technology giant Teradyne bought Universal Robots in 2015 for more than DKK 2 billion, despite the fact that the company only had a turnover of DKK 200 million at the time of purchase.[10] It is the expectations of the future possibilities in this robotics 'gold mine' that have attracted the large international equity funds. Consequently, the new 'gold' in Denmark is no longer the pig meat industry, with its bacon and other products, that have been successfully exported around the world for decades, but instead the expertise that is being developed in their robotics industry. In addition to the sale of Universal Robots, three years later Teradyne purchased Mobile Industrial Robots for DKK 1.7 billion, while turnover at the time of purchase was only DKK 70.5 million.[11]

The rapid growth in the robotics industry, and the fact that large international equity funds are acquiring many of these businesses, indicate that the robotics industry will change the entire production and distribution system, just as the Internet changed how people interact with each other (Lima, 2017). There are also many indications that the robotics industry in Funen, as well as in other similar clusters around the world, will develop robots that will change the way we learn (Susskind & Susskind, 2015). Already today, KUBO Robotics in the Funen robot cluster is developing a learning robot for children that will help them learn how to code robots. The new areas where robotics can be used in the future seem only to be limited by the imagination. When singularity becomes a fact in around 2045 (Johannessen, 2020a; Kurzweil, 2008), the robotics industry will most probably take off in the same way that the automotive industry took off with the invention of the internal combustion engine. If the robotics industry is linked to the New Green Deal (Stiglitz, 2019: 2),[12] this will provide many jobs, not only for skilled workers, but also for the unskilled and those with shorter educations.

Similar stories to the one described previously about the Funen robotics cluster in Denmark may be found all over the world. In her book, *The Great Tech*

Revolution: How China is Shaping our Future (2018), Christina Boutrup (2018) has described and analyzed the Chinese economy and the aim of the Chinese to become the world leader in the robotics industry. She writes about a new 'Silicon Valley', which is growing up in Beijing around the top universities of Tsinghua and Beida. The most important area of this new 'Silicon Valley' is the Zhongguancun Science Park (Boutrup, 2018: 43–44). By 2018, this technology cluster had several thousand companies specializing in biotechnology, software development, robotics and other high-tech fields. Boutrup comments that there are several innovation centres that focus on the robotization of various functions in social life, ranging from the use of robotics in supermarkets to 3D printers (Ibid., 44–56). 'Made in China 2025', China's strategic plan for future development, has the aim of making China the world leader in robotics by 2025, as well as in other high-tech industrial areas, such as computer chips, aviation, shipping, railways, electric vehicles, renewable energy, agricultural technology, strategically important minerals and biotechnology (Ibid.: 49). Boutrup (2018) also notes that China is well on its way to being able to compete globally in robotics technology.

Another indicator that only reinforces the future trends indicated by the story about the robotics cluster in Funen, and the development of Chinese technological expertise, is the prognosis for European automotive production. In a major report carried out by KPMG, an international cooperative, it is predicted that Europe's share of world automotive production will fall by 10 per cent over the next decade, from the present 15 per cent to 5 per cent in 2030.[13] This will mean a significant reduction in the need for labour in this industry in Europe. If we consider the fact that Made in China 2025 aims to greatly increase its electric vehicle production (Boutrup, 2018: 46), we can envisage the contours of the changes that will occur, regarding the global location of electric vehicle production, which does not bode well for future auto production in Europe. Today, this industry employs approximately 13.3 million workers, constituting 6.1 per cent of the European workforce. At the same time, the EU envisages growth in the industry. However, roughly 80 per cent of this growth will come from outside Europe.[14] What will happen is that the European factories will be further automated to keep sales and profits up and enable them to compete with China, among others. In turn, this will lead to a fall in demand for skilled and unskilled labour.

The transition from the production of internal combustion engines to electric engines in the automotive industry will result in the entire industry demanding completely different skills than before. In addition, the production of electric vehicles will need different raw materials, such as copper, which will create an increased global demand for copper, and as well as other minerals. In this context, it is worth noting that Made in China 2025 focuses especially on the production and use of strategically important minerals (Boutrup, 2018: 49).

Global developments have also posed special challenges for other parts of European industry. For example as mentioned previously, in Swindon, England, Honda has decided to close down car production by 2022 with the loss of 3,500 jobs, as well as the loss of as many jobs in the associated sub-industries. The closure may be attributed to changes in the global demand for cars. In China and the

US, which are the largest markets, Honda has a production of two million cars a year, while it only produces 150,000 cars in Swindon.[15]

The indicators that future competences will largely be focused on robotics technology, intelligent robots and artificial intelligence, can be found, among others, in Made in China 2025 (Boutrup, 2018). The strategic plan explicitly states that China aims to be the world's leader in robotics technology.[16] The US, Russia and the EU also have similar goals (Terney, 2018: 85–99). This clearly means that companies that are engaged in robotics activities, such as the industries in the Funen robotics cluster, and other similar clusters around the world, will need to develop their competences to compete with China's major investment in this technology. The upside for the Danish robotics cluster and other similar clusters is that the Chinese investments will lead to increasing demand for this expertise, something that will result in their expertise in robotics giving them a gilt-edged position in the high-tech market.

The examples we have described earlier suggest that the beginning of the Fourth Industrial Revolution will involve a global struggle for competences in STEM disciplines (science, technology, engineering and mathematics).

Description

As described previously, we have divided future competences into specific, general, human and critical competences. Critical competences will enable individuals to take action against the state, when the state invades and interferes with the private lives of its citizens without due cause, or when the state fails to deal with problems within its areas of responsibilities, such as social and environmental problems. For instance, governments have been widely criticized for their inability to deal with the climate crisis. Greta Thunberg, the young Swedish environmental activist on climate change, may be viewed as one such individual, who possesses a high degree of critical competences. This has been demonstrated by her efforts to bring to public attention the inability of governments to deal with the climate crisis. Among other things, she has led school strikes campaigning against the lack of governmental and international action to address the climate crisis. Due to her initiative, 'the school strike for climate' became an international movement.

In her book, *Eichmann in Jerusalem* (2006), Hannah Arendt emphasizes the right to have human rights. It is this right that Greta Thunberg exercises. However, it is not just a human right to be able to say something about a global development that is going in the wrong direction, but the duty of any critically minded citizen not to be a bystander to such developments. It is this duty associated with a human right that a person like Greta Thunberg is activating. For Hannah Arendt, the right to have rights is the most basic human right. Critical competences concern protecting and maintaining these human rights. The rebellion that Greta Thunberg stands for as an icon concerns the people's rebellion against the technocrats, against a political class that thinks in terms of goals and means, and which is governed by calculations and figures, weighing and measuring. Greta

Thunberg says that she and other young people do not have the time to wait until they are adults, to take over control of things that are going in the wrong direction. With their criticism of the establishment, they wish to take grassroots control. The school strikes aimed at taking a stance against the worsening climate crisis may be said to have the same critical approach as that of the Yellow Vests in France. It is a grassroots rebellion against a rule-based bureaucracy and a rigid political system. The actions of Greta Thunberg demonstrate that the individual in society is not superfluous and that it matters what each of us say and do. Greta Thunberg represents the individual's commitment against a rigid bureaucracy, and the elite's goals-and-means thinking.

It is against this background that Figure 1.1 has divided the competences needed in the Fourth Industrial Revolution into necessary and sufficient competences. The general competences (the 4Cs) and the specific competences (STEM) are necessary but not sufficient if society is going to develop in the direction that people want. It is here that critical competences, as demonstrated by somebody like Greta Thunberg, make themselves evident. She shows us that every one of us matters and that each individual has a responsibility and should be committed to taking that responsibility.

Greta Thunberg, the Yellow Vests, environmental activists and many other activist movements are up against the authorities' disregard for their views, movements and revolt.

The feeling of being able to say what you want, but not being taken seriously, is the Achilles's heel of the freedom of expression. You can say what you want, but

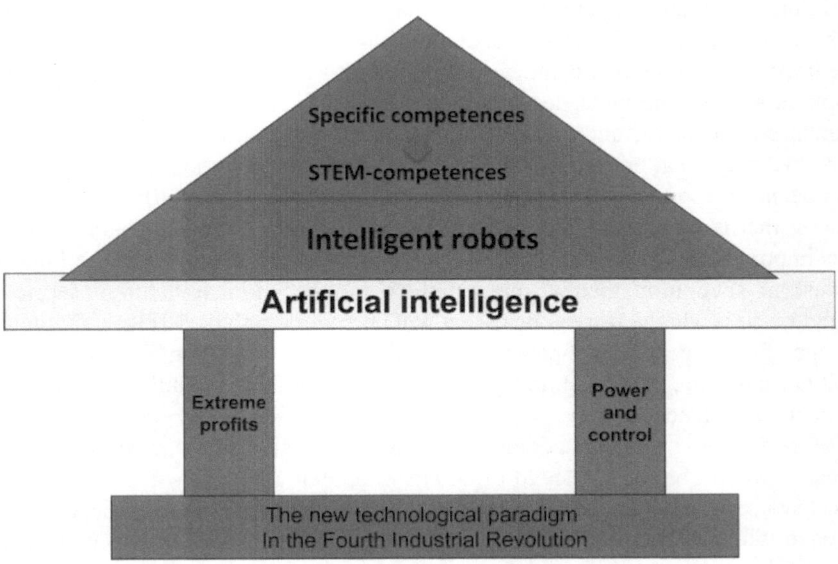

Figure 1.1 The new technological paradigm

the authorities do not take it seriously. Human rights, as expressed in national and international documents, such as the right to hold a school strike, mean nothing if that right is not linked to the obligation of governments to listen to their critics. If society does not recognize such critical competences, then this competence is worth nothing, that is to say it is no more than a safety valve that governments can use to cushion pressures and release tensions.

Critical competences are crucial to the legitimacy of governments among their populations. If governments ignore the views and opinions expressed by those citizens who possess critical competences, then they will most probably develop into arrogant rule-based bureaucracies, made up of technocrats and *political broiler*[17] elites.

Greta Thunberg's actions are an indication that it is not tomorrow when efforts should be made to tackle environmental problems but today. In this context, critical competences may be linked to social and emotional competences (SEC). It is these social and emotional competences, along with taking leadership in the culture of which one is part, which are expressed in the fact that each one of us should be a 'Greta Thunberg', and stand up for the values one believes in. What Greta Thunberg teaches us is that a real democracy is not simply about holding elections, but about the real will of the people, that is popular active participation in dealing with problems that are happening now.

You should care about things that you can do something about. This is what Greta Thunberg exemplifies in a good way by using her critical competences actively. At a time when intelligent robots and artificial intelligence are on everyone's lips, it is precisely social and critical competences that should be in demand, so that we do not enter the new age with history as our vision for the future. In addition to critical competences, which may be viewed as a type of moral compass, it is crucial that balance in social development is attained by emphasizing the importance of human competences. These competences are described in this book as social, emotional, leadership and cultural competences. Without these human competences, and critical competences as exemplified by Greta Thunberg, we may soon end up in a situation in which technological and innovative competences completely dominate our way of thinking. If the sufficient competences, that is the human and critical competences, are diminished and deemed less important in the development of knowledge as we move towards the Fourth Industrial Revolution, then we may run the risk of becoming a victim of Zapffe's paradox: 'It is what you are good at that will be your downfall'.[18] If we only focus on specific and general competences, then this may be our downfall, because we will not have integrated stabilizing mechanisms, that is by including human and critical competences.

More than ever, we need people who possess critical and human competences, because we are on the threshold of an era when being human will be put to the test (Svarre, 2019). The challenge is that intelligent robots and artificial intelligence will question our human way of being. More than ever, we will need good individuals, teams and communities who can perform well. However, this does not only mean performances that can be measured, counted and weighed in terms of economic and technological variables. What we will need primarily is someone in every culture who can take on the mantle of leadership to set a new course. This concerns people who possess human and critical competences. This is why we have included the example of Greta Thunberg. There is much to suggest that Greta Thunberg has struck emotional chords in each one of us, precisely because she speaks to something human in us at a time when advanced technology is increasingly pervading our lives. In other words, the young environmentalist Greta Thunberg speaks directly to our hearts, touching chords we thought we had forgotten. If we are to succeed as a society, we will need to develop a balanced competence profile, especially in a future when artificial intelligence and intelligent robots will come to permeate our lives. In other words, competences that do not necessarily immediately lead to increased earnings are perhaps the competences that will make earnings possible, that is critical and human competences.

Analysis

People's lives will be affected in the near future by the increased use and development of artificial intelligence, intelligent robots and intelligent informats[19] (Susskind & Susskind, 2015). For instance, we will witness an increased development and use of self-driving cars, diagnostic robots and robotic surgery in medicine, intelligent informats, drones used in fisheries and agriculture, robot lawyers and so on (Abd, 2017; Zhao et al., 2017). Whatever forms the development and use of the new intelligent technology take, it will dramatically affect people's everyday lives in many ways (Bleuler et al., 2017).

Many of the industrialized countries have plans to become world leaders in artificial intelligence by 2025–2035 (Wilson, 2017; Xie, 2017), including the US, China, Denmark and many of the EU countries. Of course, not every country can become the world leader. However, we do not intend to polemicize here by trying to figure out which country will actually take on the role of world leader. The point we are making is that development of this technology will be prioritized by both governments and businesses (Mataric, 2007). Therefore, many national governments will prioritize the STEM disciplines in order to facilitate developments within the field of artificial intelligence (Abd, 2017; Susskind & Susskind, 2015). However, artificial intelligence is not just something that belongs to the distant future but is something that is being used and developed in the present, and which will continue to be developed as we move towards the singularity, which will most probably occur in around 2045 (Johannessen, 2020a). The following thought experiment will attempt to show how we are already using this technology on a large scale and how it will quite probably be developed in the future.[20]

The thought experiment is about Per's daily routine, from the moment he wakes up until he arrives at the office in the morning. On waking up, Per checks an application on his phone that he uses to measure his heart rate and breathing, which also provides information about his sleeping rhythm. The application is based on artificial intelligence and machine learning. If we digress a little here and consider how such applications may be developed in the future, then it may be imagined that such an application can be connected to a small implant in the ear or finger. In this way, the application will be able to rapidly send all the relevant health data directly to a 'doctor', that in reality is an intelligent robot that 'knows' Per's health history. This intelligent robot will be connected to other intelligent robots, i.e. global informats. By the time Per has gotten out of bed, the application knows the state of Per's physical condition and recommends what he should eat and an exercise program for that particular day.

When Per wakes up and opens his eyes in the morning, the light in the bedroom slowly turns on, and soothing music fills the room. This is not so much a future scenario, but an application that some people already have in their homes today. In the near future, it may be imagined that the music will be intertwined with a voice informing Per about the state of the traffic on the route he uses to drive to work; the voice may recommend an alternative route so that Per can save some time and avoid getting stuck in a traffic jam. The GPS system in Per's car will automatically set to the alternative route after Per has approved the new route. Per is already able to speak to his 'smart' radio and 'smart' refrigerator today. Per's refrigerator has been programmed to sense what kinds of products are stored inside. It can determine if some food items need to be replenished and is able to send a message to the store Per uses which handles deliveries. Per's smart refrigerator is also able to connect with his smart microwave to facilitate the preparation of Per's evening meal. The 'internet of things' that makes such operations possible has already been implemented in some places and is likely to appear in many, if not all, homes in the near future. If we look a little more into the future, self-driving cars or drones will be able to deliver the products to Per's refrigerator. It may be imagined that the refrigerator is organized in such a way that it is connected to a type of capsule pipeline, so that the food is physically transported from a drone or a self-driving car to Per's refrigerator. That is the refrigerator may receive the delivery of the food without anyone physically opening the door of his refrigerator.

When Per has finished eating the breakfast that was recommended by the health application on his phone, he opens his email using a verbal command. Both his computer and his smart phone are installed with speech recognition software; this means that Per does not have to memorize various codes to login to his accounts and the various sites he uses. How many readers have to remember as many as ten to 15 codes to access various accounts and websites! In the near future, voice recognition software installed in various devices will become more widespread, possibly linked to fingerprint recognition. Anyone with some knowledge of crime detection will understand the security advantages of using a fingerprint in conjunction with voice recognition to open various accounts and websites. Although voice and fingerprint recognition software is available today, it is still not that widespread. However, it is just a matter of time before most people will be using this simple interface, even though the technology needed to support it is complex.

On his smart phone, Per can now see what time he should leave his apartment if he wants to catch a tram or bus, or use his electric car to get to work on time. If he decides to take his car to work, various artificial intelligence applications will have been utilized and actualized even before Per gets into the car. If Per sets the car's steering system to semi-automatic control, then the electric car will connect to a GPS system and the Internet to find the quickest and best route. In a future scenario, the car will be self-driving and Per will be able to use functions connected to his work while still sitting in the car. For instance, Per will be able to check his emails using voice recognition, and he can have the emails shown in text on the car's dashboard screen or be verbally read aloud by the car's loud-speakers. In a short-term future scenario, if a business associate who only speaks Chinese calls him, then this would not pose a problem, because the automatic translation program will be able to translate the Chinese voice into Norwegian, and vice versa. In other words, each of them would only have to speak in their own language and the other would understand in their own language. Today, this is only possible at a basic level, but in the near future, this will be more fully developed with the use of artificial intelligence. When Per arrives at his office and turns on his computer, there is a recommendation of a new book he should read, and a movie he should watch; the recommendation says this is a 99 per cent match to Per's likes. This is a function that is being continually developed with the use of machine learning that finds out what Per likes regarding various products.

This thought experiment shows that artificial intelligence is already in use today, and that by projecting what already exists, we have shown that in only a few years' time artificial intelligence will greatly affect people's everyday lives.

Some of the newspaper articles we read, the news we listen to and the book, movie and music recommendations we receive are created and produced using artificial intelligence, without us being aware of it (Avent, 2017: 1).

Many jobs have already been automated (Ford, 2016). First, many of the production jobs in the factories were automated, followed by jobs in distribution (Lima, 2017). When drones and self-driving trucks become a reality, millions of truck drivers will become unemployed. Of course, there will always be niches where drivers will be in demand, but these niches are becoming fewer and fewer (Avent, 2017). Today, we are already witnessing shops and department stores becoming more automated. These developments are being followed by the automation of management, information, communication and leadership functions (Johannessen, 2018). It is not only the fact that many jobs are disappearing that is frightening, but that many skills and competences are becoming redundant almost overnight (Ainley, 2016). Those who enter the job market today know that the skills they have learnt will in all probability have a short lifespan, because automation will result in their knowledge, skills and expertise becoming superfluous (Susskind & Susskind, 2015). Obviously, such developments affect people; people's psychological security is being eroded and the feeling of not being able to cope will increase.

Millions of new jobs will be created based on artificial intelligence, intelligent robots and new technology. The previous example of the Funen robotics industry cluster in Denmark is an indication of this tendency. However, in the near future, the labour market will be characterized by an increasing differentiation in wages. The future outlook for job seekers who possess specific and general competences is largely positive, while those with human and critical competences will often experience that available jobs have lower salaries, because their skills will be in less demand. This may be explained by the fact that organizations and businesses will prioritize those jobs and functions that are directly linked to value creation. Consequently, job seekers who only possess human and critical competences will experience that wage levels in available jobs will stagnate or possibly be reduced. OECD has predicted this possible future scenario (Avent, 2017: 243, note 4). It is worth noting here that in the near future, students and universities should focus on educational programmes that link specific-general competences with human-critical competences, as graduates will have greater opportunities when they enter the labour market. The rationale is that those who choose to study the human competences will also be able to include specific and general competences in their educational profile, which will increase the probability of a better salary, than if their profile only focused on human competences. This argument also applies to those with a main focus on critical competences.

There is great economic inequality today between the 1 per cent at the top of the economic hierarchy, the 9 per cent just below the top 1 per cent, and the remaining 90 per cent (Johannessen, 2020b). In the future, economic inequality will increase between the various subgroups within the 90 per cent group, because their wage levels will be related to which competences they possess, as we have attempted to show in Figure 1.3.

In other words, in the near future the contours of a two-sided trend will become evident. First, capital will be increasingly concentrated in the hands of a tiny minority and various large funds. Second, a person's competence will determine their wage level to an increasing extent; those with competences that are specifically in demand will be able to command a higher wage, while those without such competences will have a much lower income level.

A third trend that is already evident today is that an increasing proportion of the labour force is not included in the labour market. For instance, in the US, the participation of the labour force in the labour market has fallen from 76 per cent in 1990 to 69 per cent in 2015.[21] This may not sound like a large amount in terms of percentages, but it represents nine million unemployed workers (Avent, 2017: 3). We have also witnessed similar developments in the EU.[22] In addition, we know that about one-third of those attending upper secondary school (16–18/19 years) drop out, and do not complete their education; many of these will either be unable to enter the labour market or only be able to get poorly paid jobs in the service sector (Ainley, 2016; Johannessen, 2020b). Those who do not enter the labour market or who receive various forms of social welfare, possibly a future universal basic income, will clump geographically into areas where it is cheap to live. We can witness this trend already in European countries. For instance, in Denmark, many in this social group have moved to the islands in the south. In the US, this is evident in the country's richest state, California, which is characterized by a warm summer climate throughout the year; this state now has the largest growth in poverty of all the states in the US. About 16 per cent of the population of California lives below the official poverty line.[23]

Theoretical points

Throughout history, technology has changed our lives in many ways, from the very first tools used by humans, to the First Industrial Revolution that had its beginnings around 1750 in Britain. In the Fourth Industrial Revolution, the new technology, in the form of artificial intelligence and intelligent robots, is creating a new paradigm that is affecting our way of thinking (Schwab, 2016; Wilson, 2017). As the story about Per illustrates, much of our everyday lives already today, and even more so in the future, will be affected by the use of codes and algorithms about which we know little (Abd, 2017; Zhao et al., 2017). In other words, we are being manipulated by the use of various codes and algorithms, from the news we are presented with to the entertainment we 'choose' (Ford, 2016). It is the power behind these codes and algorithms that may threaten our customary way of life, our understanding of democracy and the way we relate to others (Mataric, 2007; Lima, 2017). As described previously, the emergence of the Funen robotics cluster in Denmark (and other similar clusters around the globe), and China's strategic plan for the future, Made in China 2025, which includes the aim of becoming the world leader in robotics, are both indicators that this new paradigm will affect us all, whether we like it or not (Gaskarth, 2015; Boutrup, 2018). We have witnessed how big data has been used to influence so-called democratic elections and also how data analytics can be used to influence people's perceptions. The new technology and the new technological paradigm that is underway are gaining strength, fuelled both by a desire for more profits and a desire for more power (Ford, 2016; Wilson, 2017). Profits and the quest for power may be said to constitute the two pillars of the new technological paradigm. Furthermore, the building blocks are artificial intelligence and intelligent robots (Frankish, 2014). To achieve this, the new technological paradigm is based on a global focus and a focus on expertise related to STEM competences (science, technology, engineering, and mathematics). The new technological paradigm is shown in Figure 1.1 below.

> Proposition: The new technological paradigm of the Fourth Industrial Revolution will reinforce the focus on specific competences, here referred to as STEM competences.

If the new technological paradigm becomes dominant, it will result in many social consequences. Jamie Bartlett (2018: 1) states that a *one-sided* focus on the new emerging technology could weaken democratic processes, our critical reflection and our ability to shape society. However, if the technology is used to tackle environmental problems, there is much evidence to suggest that this could reduce CO_2 emissions, promote greener production and contribute to meeting the challenges of the worsening environmental crisis. On the other hand, this may also lead to an increased focus on specific competences, at the expense of what we refer to here as general, human and critical competences (see Figure 1.2).

There is no doubt that the new technological paradigm is winning the battle for people's attention. Moreover, this paradigm may also shatter another paradigm, which we are promoting in this book. The paradigm we are talking about is a

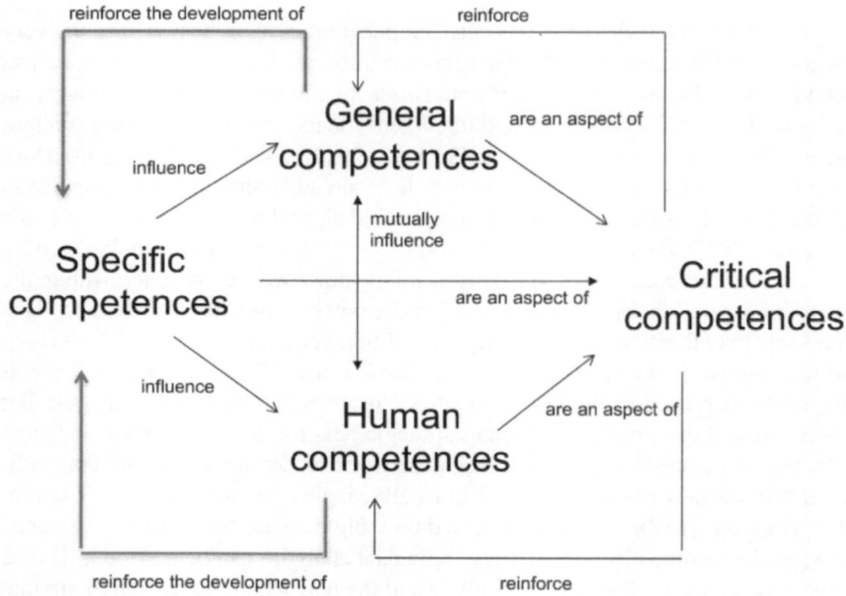

Figure 1.2 The balanced-competence paradigm of the Fourth Industrial Revolution

balanced-competence paradigm. In this paradigm, there is a balance between the specific, general, human and critical competences (see Figure 1.2).

> Proposition: The balanced-competence paradigm in the Fourth Industrial Revolution is based on an integration of the four competences: specific, general, human and critical competences.

We have shown the balanced-competence paradigm in Figure 1.2.

Artificial intelligence and intelligent robots are no longer something that are only written about in science-fiction literature (Lima, 2017; Wilson, 2017). Large companies, such as Google, Amazon, Alibaba, Apple, Netflix etc., invest very large sums in these technologies (Ford, 2016; Xie, 2017). Small and medium-sized companies around the world are also making considerable investments, as was described earlier in the case of the Danish robotics industry cluster. Moreover, as also previously mentioned, China plans to make very large investments in order to fulfil its aim of becoming the world leader in this field, as specified in their strategic plan, Made in China 2025 (Boutrup, 2018). When such a demand for competence reaches our universities, and when parents' dreams for their children's future education also include the opportunity for them to acquire such knowledge and skills, much of the new knowledge development at most educational levels will revolve around developing competences related to this field

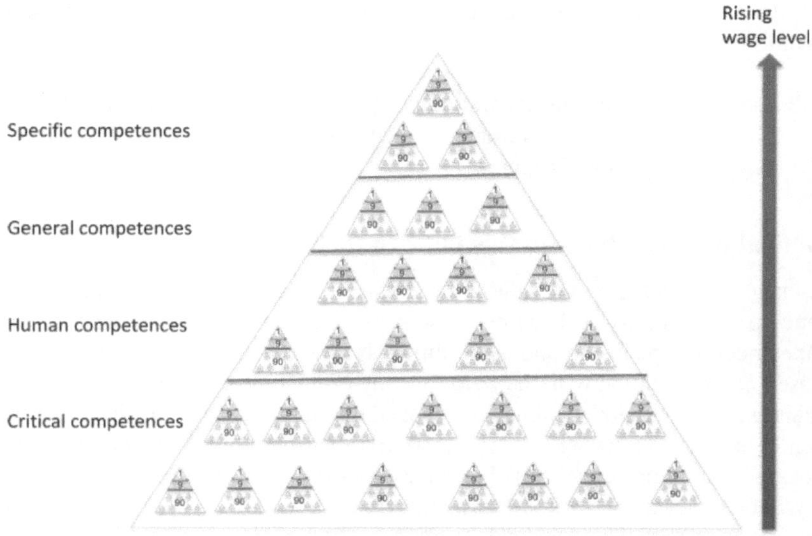

Figure 1.3 The future wages hierarchy

(Gershuny & Fisher, 2014; Susskind & Susskind, 2015). In other words, this is what we mean by the 'new technological paradigm' and the specific competences (STEM) that will be focused on. When high salaries and good working conditions are linked to STEM competences, most of those who have the opportunity will dance around this 'golden calf' (Ford, 2016). Against this background, it is relatively straightforward to project what the future wages hierarchy will look like. We have illustrated the future wages hierarchy in Figure 1.3.

The future wage levels shown in Figure 1.3 should only be understood as showing a general future trend and may differ both within the various individual competences and also between them. The point of illustrating the future wages' hierarchy is to show the general wage structure, not to suggest that there will exist any absolute and impenetrable walls between the various categories. The small hierarchies within the large pay group (90 per cent) are intended to illustrate that within the individual competence areas, there will be various social niches that have different wage structures, compared to others in the same competence area. The figures within the small hierarchies inside the large group are only intended to show that a small section will, regardless of their competence profile, be able to receive top wages within their social niche, while others will come further down the hierarchy. The figures 1, 9, 90 of Figure 1.3 are therefore a rough estimate that intends to show the trend that only a few will be at the top of the various social wage niches, possibly 1 per cent at the very top, 9 per cent in the top tier, and then 90 per cent who have a much lower salary than those in the top 10 per cent.

The main point, however, is that if the new technological paradigm prevails, then wage developments will, as a general rule, follow the overall wages hierarchy shown in Figure 1.3.

Proposition: If the new technological paradigm becomes dominant in the global knowledge and innovation economy, wage developments will follow what is shown in Figure 1.3.

Practical utility: what can this be used for?

The insights provided by the new technological paradigm and the balanced competence paradigm may be used by those people who wish to know what type of competences will be in demand in the future. It is recommended that these insights are used in combination with the field of study or the type of work which the individuals are most passionate about and especially interested in, and which they can become good at and master. It is these criteria that the individuals may use when choosing their future education. We have proposed four classes of competences that will be important (cf. Figure 1.2), and within each of the four classes, there are four different types. Thus, in total, there is a rough categorization of 16 different areas of competence that one can choose with relative safety (cf. Figure 1.4). To acquire a job with a good salary, we have suggested that students should aim at an educational profile that focuses on 'specific competences'. However, whether one will have a 'good life' if one uses salary level as the only criterion is another matter.

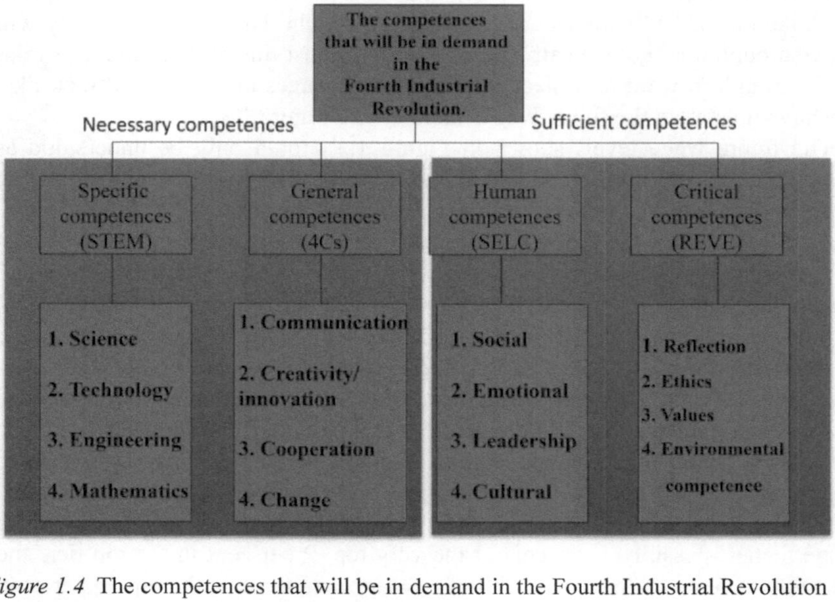

Figure 1.4 The competences that will be in demand in the Fourth Industrial Revolution

The benefits of this insight for universities is obvious. In one form or another, universities should be able to offer the four classes of competences, because these are competences that will be in demand in any democratic society. To recap on these four classes of competences – they include the specific competences (STEM), the general competences (the 4Cs), the human competences (SELC) and the critical competences (REVE).

Our main practical message in this book is that artificial intelligence and intelligent robots may turn out to be a godsend to us humans, on par with when Prometheus,[24] of Greek mythology, gave fire to humanity. However, in this context, we should remember that Prometheus was punished by Zeus for stealing fire and was sentenced to eternal torment. In other words, in our quest to develop scientific knowledge, if we develop intelligent robots and artificial intelligence by only focusing on specific and general competences, we could suffer the same fate as Prometheus, that is eternal torment. Thus, we may do well to remember one of Aristotle's principal ideas, the importance of maintaining the Golden Mean in life by finding balance. In a practical context, it is politicians and leaders in the educational sector, not least the universities, who should focus on the Golden Mean in terms of the competences, knowledge and skills they offer to students. Specifically, this book aims to point out the importance of balancing specific and general competences against human and critical competences, that is the importance of developing and maintaining a balanced-competence paradigm.

At the beginning of the Fourth Industrial Revolution, those people with a low-level of education or with skills no longer in demand will be those who struggle most. Moreover, those who have chosen to follow an education focusing only on human and critical competences will come off worse in terms of pay than those who focus on studying specific and general competences.

What we do know is that life has already become difficult for many people who do not have the necessary competences in a labour market that is being continuously automated; that is automation is increasing in strength and encompassing ever larger parts of the labour market.

Based on this, we can make the following assumptions:

- Those with little education will have difficulty finding employment.
- Without the right competences, job seekers can expect lower pay.
- An educational profile that ten to 15 years ago provided a secure job, such as a bachelor's degree, will, in the near future, not guarantee a job at all but only serve as a springboard for taking a master's degree and possibly a PhD.
- For an ever-increasing proportion of the population, finding a job that you can live off is becoming increasingly more difficult. Uncertainty has increased and will continue to increase at the beginning of the Fourth Industrial Revolution.
- The previously mentioned developments will also have political ramifications, resulting in major changes.

- People no longer believe that the established political parties have answers, as those parties are unable to address the problems they are facing.
- In many countries, the National Populist parties have become magnets for frustrated workers, for those who have not yet entered the labour market and those who feel their futures are uncertain.

The reasons for the previously mentioned developments may be largely linked to the new technological paradigm. Automation is a necessary consequence of the new technology and the digitalization that has spread to most industrialized countries since the late twentieth century. The development and use of intelligent robots and artificial intelligence will only reinforce this development. New technology will automate many more jobs, resulting in many workers losing their jobs. However, millions of new jobs will be created, but only for those people with the right competences. In addition to automation, the global knowledge economy has resulted in many unskilled and semi-skilled jobs being transferred to other regions of the globe with lower labour costs, such as China, India, Malaysia, Bangladesh, Myanmar and Pakistan. In these countries, economic development has created millions of new jobs (Gaskarth, 2015). This has also led to the strong growth of the Chinese middle class (Boutrup, 2018). However, this book will mainly focus on the OECD area and on the challenges and problems that will result from this new technological paradigm.

Conclusion

We have investigated the following question in this chapter: What competences will be in demand in the Fourth Industrial Revolution? The short answer is given in Figure 1.4. Figure 1.4 also shows how the rest of the book is organized.

Notes

1 In this book, we use the term artificial intelligence to refer to the ability of machines to perform human cognitive functions, e.g. learning, thinking, perceiving, reflecting, reasoning, creativity etc. (Terney, 2018: 13).
2 https://en.wikipedia.org/wiki/Xi_Jinping
3 STEM is an acronym for science, technology, engineering and mathematics.
4 In this book, we use the term 'case letter' to refer to a brief extract from a longer case study, focusing on a specific point we wish to emphasize in a description or analysis. The term case letter was originally coined by Henry Mintzberg (2012).
5 *Jyllandsposten* (a Danish newspaper) 20 February 2019, page 15 (global).
6 This case letter is based on reports in the Danish newspaper *Jyllandsposten*, 25 February 2019, page 5 (Business Section).
7 *Jyllandsposten* (Danish newspaper) 18 January 2019, page four (Business section).
8 Ibid., 1 February, page 12.
9 Ibid., 31 January, page 13.
10 Ibid., 29 January 2019, page nine.
11 Ibid.
12 www.information.dk/debat/2019/01/joseph-e-stiglitz-green-new-deal-tilbyder-sjaeldent-glimt-haab, Website of the Danish newspaper, *Information*.

13 *Jyllandsposten* (Danish newspaper) 8 February 2019, page two (Business section).
14 Ibid.
15 Ibid., 20 February 2019, page 15 (global).
16 Ibid., 30 January 2019, page 14.
17 'Political broiler' is an expression used in Scandinavia to refer to politicians who have been 'broiled' in parties, that is they have most likely never had any other profession.
18 Formulated by the Norwegian philosopher, Zapffe; refer to: https://en.wikipedia.org/wiki/Peter_Wessel_Zapffe
19 When intelligent robots are linked with other intelligent robots in a global cluster of competences, we use the term intelligent informats instead of intelligent robots.
20 Our thought experiment has used some ideas from a thought experiment in Thomas Terney's book: *Kampen om fremtiden* ('The struggle for the future'). Terney has a PhD in artificial intelligence. In addition, we have taken some ideas from Ryan Avent's book, *The Wealth of Humans: Work and its Absence in the Twenty-first Century* (2017). However, the main body of our thought experiment is our own work.
21 US Bureau of Labor Statistics current Population Survey (2017).
22 EUROSTAT labour force Survey, 2017.
23 *Jyllandsposten* (Danish newspaper), 24 February 2019.
24 https://en.wikipedia.org/wiki/Prometheus

References

Abd, K.K. (2017). *Intelligent scheduling of robotic flexible assembly cells*, Springer, London.

Ackoff, R. (1981). *Creating the corporate future, plan or be planned for*, John Wiley & Sons, New York.

Ainley, P. (2016). *Betraying a generation: How education is failing young people*, Policy Press, Bristol.

Arendt, H. (2006). *Eichmann in Jerusalem*, Penguin Classics, London.

Avent, B. (2017). *The wealth of humans*, Penguin, London.

Barrow, C.W. (2019). *The entrepreneurial intellectual in the corporate university*, Palgrave, London.

Bartlett, J. (2018). *The People vs. Tech: How the internet is killing democracy (and how we save it)*, Ebury Press, Penguin Random House, London.

Bleuler, H.; Bouri, M. & Mandada, F.C. (2017). *New trends in medical and service robots*, Springer, London.

Boutrup, C. (2018). *Den store tech revolution: Sådan former Kina vores fremtid*, People's Press, København.

Bruce, D. & Crook, G. (2015). *The Dream Café: Lessons in the art of radical innovation*, John Wiley Sons, New York.

Brynjolfsson, E. & McAfee, A. (2014). *The second machine age: Work, progress, and prosperity in a time of brilliant technologies*, W.W. Norton, New York.

Ford, M. (2016). *The rise of the robots: Technology and the threat of mass unemployment*, Oneworld, London.

Frankish, K. (2014). *The Cambridge handbook of artificial intelligence*, Cambridge University Press, Cambridge.

Gaskarth, J. (Ed.). (2015). *China, India and the future of international society*, Rowman & Littlefield, London.

Gershuny, J. & Fisher, K. (2014). *Post-industrious society: Why work time will not disappear for our grandchildren, Center for Time Use Research, Department of Sociology*, University of Oxford, Oxford.

Goleman, D. (2018). *HBR emotional intelligence boxed set*, Harvard Business Review Press, Boston.

Handy, C. (1995). *The age of unreason: New thinking for a new world*, Random House, New York.

Handy, C. (2002). *The elephant and the flea: Looking backwards to the future*, Random House, New York.

Johannessen, J.-A. (2018). *The workplace of the future: The Fourth Industrial Revolution, the precariat and the death of hierarchies*, Routledge, London.

Johannessen, J.-A. (2019a). *The emergence of the Fourth Industrial Revolution: An historical introduction to knowledge management and the innovation economy*, Emerald, London.

Johannessen, J.-A. (2019b). *Automation, capitalism and the end of the middle class*, Routledge, London.

Johannessen, J.-A. (2020a). *Singularity innovation*, Routledge, London.

Johannessen, J.-A. (2020b). *What is wrong with capitalism*? Emerald, London.

Johannessen, J.-A. (2020c). *Building the innovation economy*, Routledge, London.

Johannessen, J.-A. (2021). *Artificial intelligence, intelligent robots and ethics: An intelligent ethical robot communicating about morality with an un-ethical human being*, Routledge, London.

Klein, N. (2019). *On fire: The (burning) case for a green new deal*, Allen Lane, New York.

Kurzweil, R. (2005). *The singularity is near: When humans transcend biology*, Penguin, London.

Kurzweil, R. (2008). *The age of spiritual machines: When computers exceed human intelligence*, Penguin, London.

Lima, P.U. (2017). *Autonomous mobile robotics: A system perspective*, CRS Press, New York.

Mataric, M.J. (2007). *The robotics primer*, MIT Press, Boston.

Mintzberg, H. (2012). *Managers not MBAs: A hard look at the soft practice of managing and management development*, New York.

Ross, A. (2016). *The industries of the future*, Simon & Schuster, New York.

Schwab, K. (2016). *The Fourth Industrial Revolution: What it means, how to respond*, World Economic Forum, Geneva.

Stiglitz, J. (2019). *Information* (Danish newspaper). www.information.dk/debat/2019/01/joseph-stiglitz-green-new-deal-tilbyder-sjaeldent-glimt-haab (Access date: 1 March 2019).

Susskind, R. & Susskind, D. (2015). *The future of professions: How technology will transform the work of human experts*, Oxford University PressUP, Oxford.

Svarre, P. (2019). *Hvad skal vi med mennesker*, Gyldendal, København.

Terney, T. (2018). *Kampen om fremtiden: Forstå kunstig intelligens*, Gyldendal Business, København.

Wilson, M. (2017). *Implementation of robot systems: An introduction to robotics, automation, and successful systems integration in manufacturing*, Butterworth-Heinemann, New York.

Xie, S. (2017). *Advanced robotics for medical rehabilitation*, Springer, London.

Zhao, J.; Feng, Z.; Chu, F. & Ma, N. (2017). *Advanced theory of constraint and motion analysis for robot mechanisms*, Academic Press, London.

2 General and specific competences

Introduction

- In the future, competences will relate to communication, creativity, change and collaboration.
- All competences will have to include familiarity with coding, intelligent algorithms and artificial intelligence.
- A person's mastery of such competences will depend on their having a passion for their work and a desire to excel at it.
- Success in the Fourth Industrial Revolution will balance competition against collaboration, alongside adaptability, creativity and innovation.

The old industrial economy, which needed unskilled workers, skilled workers and university graduates, is now consigned to history. Previously there were enough jobs for everyone, but now there will only be jobs for people with special competences. Robots and artificial intelligence will take over most of the jobs from which unskilled workers could previously make their livings. The story of what has happened is well known, and Alec Ross (2016: 4) provides three keywords for this development: automation, technology and globalization. Regardless what competences are in demand in the Fourth Industrial Revolution, there are four areas of competence that will be decisive for success: communication, creativity, collaboration and change (Ross, 2016; Johannessen, 2021). The Fourth Industrial Revolution, with its use of intelligent robots and intelligent informats,[1] will dramatically change the economy resulting in new opportunities, and activities that were previously profitable will become vulnerable to global competition. Global competition, just as much as new technology, is destroying old methods and opening up new opportunities. No matter what old methods of production are destroyed, and what new methods emerge, there will be demand for people who can communicate and for people who are creative and can generate innovation. We will need to understand that collaboration is also beneficial for ourselves and that we can succeed in this new era as long as we are prepared to adapt continually (Johannessen, 2019b). Change has become the new stability.

While the middle class in the US and Europe, and throughout the OECD area, is being subject to pressure and falling in numbers, the middle class in China and India is growing exponentially (Johannessen, 2020a, 2020b, 2020c). This book, and this chapter, will discuss what expertise people will need to acquire in the US, Europe and the rest of the OECD area over the next 20 years. Indirectly, and possibly more directly than we may imagine, this will also affect countries such as China and India, as their economies are evolving to the current level of the OECD area. Consequently, what applies to the OECD area over the next 20 years will also apply to China and India over the next 30 years. This assumption is based on the fact that robotization, artificial intelligence, technology-driven innovation and globalization will have as much significance for economic developments in China and India as it will have for the US and Europe. Admittedly, there will be a time lag, but the assumption is that this time lag will be quickly reduced, because global competition and the rapid spread of innovations globally will contribute to reducing the time lag considerably. This assumption is based on innovation theory (Johannessen, 2019a, 2019b, 2020a, 2020b), which holds that innovations emerge where:

1 The real and relative costs are high
2 There is declining real and relative productivity
3 There is declining real and relative quality
4 The rate of dissemination of innovations is greatest
5 New knowledge has the potential to become new technology.

From an innovation theory standpoint, this explains why Europe, the US, China and India, to name a few key areas, will develop differently economically but will even out over time. This means that the challenges and problems that the US and Europe are facing today will be roughly the same challenges that China and India will encounter a little further into the future.

Robots, artificial intelligence, intelligent robots and intelligent informats will affect developments in the West, in both urban and rural areas such as businesses in Charleston in West Virginia; the coal belt in the US; Mehamn, a fishing village in Norway; and Holstebro, a trading town in West Jutland, Denmark. However, they will also affect the developing world, such as the cities of China, Shenzen and Shanghai, and the towns of Vietnam, India, Middle and South America, South Africa, as well as other parts of the world. Although the different areas and countries around the globe will be affected at different times, sooner or later they will all be affected by this development. Therefore, there will be a global demand for specific competences, but the locations of this demand geographically will involve a time lag.

'Here comes the robot, there goes the job?' That is the smart and intelligent robots will greatly affect all our lives in the not-so-distant future – not least in the labour market. Some researchers are even investigating whether or not intelligent robots in the future will have the ability to be creative and also possess consciousness (Reese, 2018; Johannessen, 2022). Is there such a thing as a robot-proof job? In principle, all jobs, regardless of the level of expertise, will be exposed to the impact of intelligent robots and artificial intelligence. Will the future be jobless? Are some areas of work more exposed to changes than others in the time to come? If robots can also be creative, what challenges will this represent for creative educational programs in our colleges and universities? If intelligent robots can understand and speak all the Earth's languages, how will communication between people be affected? If most jobs will be affected by intelligent robots, will this increase unemployment or can everyone live a good life in a jobless future?

It is true that some of the foremost people working closely with artificial intelligence fear for the future,[2] such as Elon Musk, Stephen Hawking and Bill Gates. However, it is also true that many other researchers in the field view artificial intelligence and intelligent robots as a social challenge, but a challenge that can be turned into something positive. This is the view of perhaps the most foremost in the field of artificial intelligence research, Andrew Ng. Mark Zuckerberg of Facebook is also positive about the future social developments related to artificial intelligence. Andrew Ng goes as far as to say that 'fearing a rise of killer robots is like worrying about overpopulation on Mars'.[3]

Not surprisingly, our position is somewhere between the two viewpoints mentioned earlier. The most interesting question should be how will technologies such as nuclear power, nanotechnology, genetic editing, artificial intelligence, intelligent robots and intelligent informats or any other technology be developed and used, and how will society benefit from their use? On the one hand, if we assume that technology can be used to benefit everyone in society, then the new technology will constitute a positive quantum leap for the lives of most people. If, on the other hand, we assume that the development and use of new technology will involve a struggle between people to acquire the necessary future competences and that only a few at the top will benefit financially from the new technology, then it is also probable that a modern Luddite movement[4] will emerge, something that would be destructive to society as a whole. Technology is always part of a social system. Therefore, the assumptions about technological development that do not consider the social systems in which the technology is developed and used are about as interesting as discussing whether pigs can fly or not.

Regarding competence, the fear is that intelligent robots will automate most functions in the workplace. If this becomes the future reality, then it will only be a negative development, if we do not have a social solution to this challenge. On the other hand, if no solution can be found, then most people will experience problems. Therefore, it is crucial that we find a solution to an automation of work functions, where intelligent robots can do most of the paid work. In this context, it may be of advantage to bear in mind Aristotle's views on paid work: *All paid work drains the soul and makes it wither;* the goal of work, according to Aristotle, is to make time for leisure.[5]

If we start from this perspective, then it is not paid work that will be the most essential, but having something meaningful to do, something one is passionate about and engaged in that will be important. Future society need not be characterized by a permanent economic crisis and unemployment for millions of people, but rather a society in which people can enjoy the fruits of a huge increase in productivity that will occur when intelligent robots and artificial intelligence are fully implemented in the economy. However, this is based on the assumption that societies will be developed for the benefit of the majority, and not just a minority, that is the few at the top of the social hierarchy. On the other hand, there will always be a need for someone who performs various functions in society. It is the competence that will be needed to carry out these functions that we will focus on in this book, not the leisure time that will provide well-being and a comfortable life. In this chapter, we will focus on the general and specific competences that will be in demand.

As we have noted earlier, many leading people in the field of artificial intelligence, such as Mark Zuckerberg and Stephen Hawking, have expressed great doubts about what the future development of artificial intelligence will lead to. However, we should also keep in mind that new technology, as a general rule, has led to increased productivity and higher wages in the past. Therefore, the development of the new technology will probably also result in increased productivity and higher wages. Those people who have the competences and skills that are in demand will also receive a significantly higher salary than at present. However, the problem is that there will not be a need for everyone in the jobs of the kind that exist today, because intelligent robots will take over many, if not all, of the jobs, i.e. through automation and informatization,[6] which will make most of the paid work superfluous.

The absence of work may well prove to be the norm in the Fourth Industrial Revolution. On the one hand, as mentioned previously, Aristotle believed that *all paid work drains the soul and makes it wither*. On the other hand, both Adam Smith and Karl Marx believed that man is constituted by work.[7]

One objection to those who view artificial intelligence and automation as a technology that will make all human work superfluous is 'the lump of labour' fallacy (Avent, 2017: 6); that is the view that there is only so much work to go around – 'the lump', so that when intelligent robots take over most of this 'lump', there will be fewer jobs for people. However, history shows us that this view is fallacious. New technology creates new needs, and consequently, new jobs are created and new skills are demanded. In this chapter, we will explore communication, creativity, collaboration and change competences related to the new technology.

We will investigate the following question in this chapter:

> What general and specific competences will be in demand in the Fourth Industrial Revolution?

To answer this main question, we will address the following sub-questions:

> Q1 In what ways will communication competence be in demand in the Fourth Industrial Revolution?
> Q2 In what ways will creative skills be in demand in the Fourth Industrial Revolution?
> Q3 In what ways will collaborative competence be in demand in the Fourth Industrial Revolution?
> Q4 In what ways will change competence be in demand in the Fourth Industrial Revolution?

We have summarized, abstracted and shown the introduction in Figure 2.1. Figure 2.1 also shows how the chapter is organized.

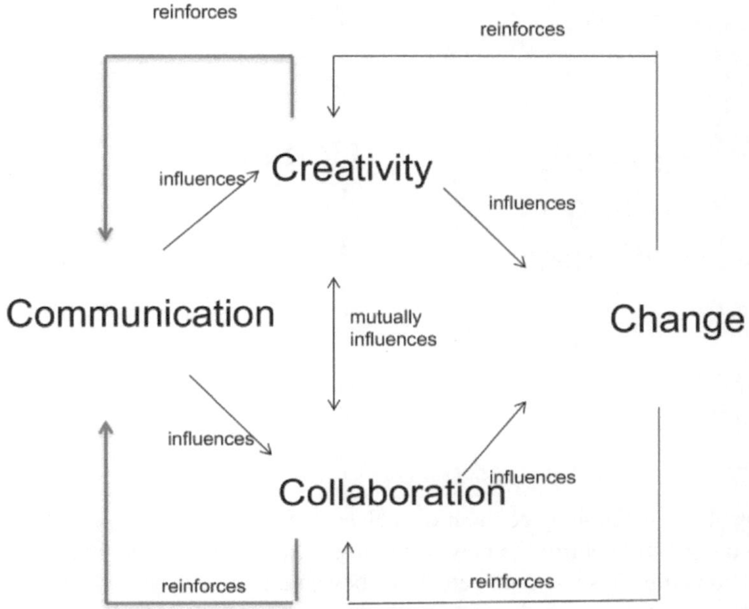

Figure 2.1 General and specific competences

Communication competence

In this section, we will address the following question: in what ways will communication competence be in demand in the Fourth Industrial Revolution? We will examine communication in relation to the new technology. In today's world, communication has largely become synonymous with the digitalization of communication upon which people have become completely dependent, at least in the industrialized world. We are increasingly being controlled and influenced by digitalization, that is the use of digital and communication technologies, which includes everything from intelligent robots, artificial intelligence to 'block-chain' technology (Johannessen, 2020c). The new digital technology affects the development of our institutions, our organizations and our lives. It is also affecting how we live together and how we communicate in society. In the past, those who controlled and owned capital were the ones who largely controlled societies, whereas, in the future, those who control our lives will be mainly those who understand and manage the new technology. Moreover, there is much evidence that indicates that there is a very close relationship between those who control the new technology and those who control cash flows. This is already evident in

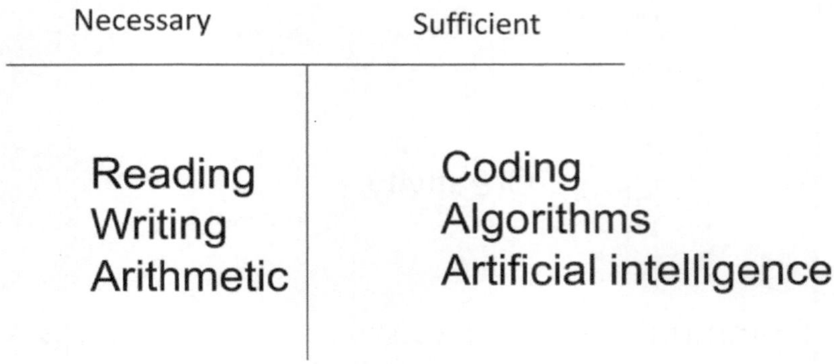

Figure 2.2 Basic competences in the Fourth Industrial Revolution

the ways large technology companies such as Amazon, Google, Apple, Microsoft and so on, greatly control the new technology and the flow of capital. Thus, it is what such companies communicate, how they communicate, and with what effect they communicate that will affect both the macro and micro levels in society (Susskind, 2018).

With Johannes Gutenberg's invention of the printing press in 1450, and the liberalization of thought associated with the Renaissance in the fifteenth and sixteenth centuries, reading and writing became important basic skills; if we add arithmetic to this set of skills (the three Rs), then these basic skills have been considered essential since the nineteenth century Industrial Age. Of course, these basic skills are still necessary today, but the focus is changing, and they will not be sufficient in the Fourth Industrial Revolution. To meet the challenges in the Fourth Industrial Revolution, it will be necessary to acquire new skills and competences based on the knowledge and application of coding, algorithms and artificial intelligence. We have illustrated this in Figure 2.2.

Narratives

Case letter 1

'Knowledge is power' is a well-known saying. Perhaps we should reformulate this to read 'coding is power'. Henning is having a discussion with Nils, an old friend from his student days, who is now professor of anthropology at their old university.

'You have to understand a culture in order to communicate', says Nils.

'I'm not so sure about that', says Henning, 'because algorithms and artificial intelligence will merge in the coming years, and then culture will become inherent to the codes'.

'I have to admit', says Nils, 'that I don't understand any of this stuff about algorithms, coding and artificial intelligence, but I have no faith in the idea that culture can be captured by these technological solutions'.

'No', says Henning, 'that's my point. It's not about faith, but about knowledge. Thus, from that point of view, we can continue to use the saying "knowledge is power". In a few years' time, intelligent robots will be communicating with other robots. A robot will be able to understand and interpret what another robot is saying, even though Robot 1 is in Kansas, US and Robot 2 is in Shanghai, China'.

'Yes, that's possible', says Nils, 'but of course those are intelligent robots. What about people?'

'I haven't explained myself well enough', says Henning. 'Intelligent robots will not look like humans or anything you might have seen or read about in sci-fi films and literature. The intelligent robots I'm talking about exist at a nano-level – like a tiny chip you or I could have in our ears. This chip would be packed with codes and algorithms that evolve through use. In other words, the algorithms that are used in these nano-robots or nano-computers are evolutionary, or if you like genetic, and they will change and learn according to what or whom they come into contact with. To give one example, it would be as though you, Nils, were communicating with a person from China. And that person could understand what you were saying, and even though you don't speak Chinese, you could understand what the other person was saying'.

'So isn't that actually just two people communicating with each other?' asks Nils.

'Well, I'm a little unsure how to respond', says Henning, 'but at a minimum we would have two people who are using extremely powerful technology to be in contact with each other. We could think of the intelligent robots they would be using as tools for bringing humanity closer together, but basically yes, they would be two people communicating with each other'.

Case letter 2

The technological companies that dominate the business world today, such as Facebook, Amazon, Google, Microsoft, Apple and others are built up around a technology that uses a simple binary code, that is a two-symbol system of '0' and '1' that is used in complex digital communication systems. The binary code is the basis for digital information and electronic communication that is used by the new technologies that are associated with the Fourth Industrial Revolution. Before the digital age, our original knowledge in the West was built around a 26-letter Latin alphabet (and its various adaptations that can comprise extra letters). Thus, it may be said the complexity of our basic communication model has been reduced from 26 characters to two characters. If we imagine that the human genetic code can be decoded to a represent string of binary 0s and 1s, then one can envision that those organizations and companies that will be able to exert global power will be those that develop such genetic-editing technology; this power will be facilitated by their knowledge, control and handling of people's genetic codes. Gene editing tools have already been developed that can reinforce people's strengths and attenuate their weaknesses (Johannessen, 2021, 2022). So, what might this be good for, one might wonder? Well, if the genetic code can be edited, then we may be able to greatly reduce or completely eradicate illnesses that have plagued humanity since the dawn of creation, such as cancer, immune deficiency diseases, malaria, cardiovascular disease etc. The large profits of new companies that control digital communications and human genetic coding will enable them to become world leaders in less time than it took the digital platform Instagram to accomplish their meteoric rise, and for Kodak to sink into bankruptcy after failing to embrace digital technology (Johannessen, 2020a, 2020c). The digital technology of the future, based on the binary system of '0' and '1', will be able to greatly expand into the field of emerging genomic technology. As mentioned, the expanding use of genomic technologies will have an enormous potential for treating and curing diseases. If we become free from sickness, then who knows what will appear from Pandora's box – which paradoxically may be "any source of great and unexpected troubles."[8] Of course, we will not free ourselves from all our troubles, but being able to get rid of life-threatening illnesses will be an enormous human good. Indirectly, this may be attributed to a complexity reduction from an alphabet of 26 characters to a binary system of two characters. Such a complexity reduction can greatly simplify our lives, although it is evident that a new complexity will arise through the use of codes, algorithms and artificial intelligence based on the 'simple' binary system.

Description

A letter sent from one end of the country to the other and delivered by the postal carrier may take any number of days. Today, the same letters, in digital form, such as an email, can be sent in a matter of seconds. With the introduction of intelligent robots and artificial intelligence, communication between continents can also take place in a matter of seconds. In the near future, with improvements in translation technology, we will be able to write in our own language and have the text translated into the language of the recipient almost simultaneously. This will also apply to spoken messages. The previously mentioned developments will of necessity revolutionize communication.

The postal carrier who was made redundant by the increase in digital communication and reduction in paper mail had to develop new skills. He or she may possibly find work in a telecommunications business, or another business that deals with digital mail delivery; alternatively, he or she may have, for example gotten a job in a transport company that delivers products that people have bought on the Internet.

When artificial intelligence is further developed – towards singularity (Kurzweil, 2005, 2008; Johannessen, 2020a, 2020c), the probability is that information and communication functions in the workplace will be more or less fully automated. This development will make it difficult for the postal carrier in the earlier example to find a job similar to the one he or she had before the job redundancy. In other words, productivity will increase, and automation will take over many jobs. Those who still have jobs, such as those with competence in the new technology, will most probably receive higher wages. Those who lose their jobs due to automation will most probably have to enter into temporary work contracts, with no security regarding employment or pensions. Just as human muscular power was outstripped by various kinds of tools and machines ranging from the invention of the wheel to the invention of the steam engine, artificial intelligence and intelligent robots will out-compete our ability for logical-rational thinking. Taking up this fight against artificial intelligence will be on the same level as a man trying to out-compete the power of a steam-powered engine at the beginning of the Industrial Age. It will be both absurd and irrational.

We are not constituted as human beings because we have a high logical and rational intelligence. Our strength is not necessarily rational intelligence but the fact that we have intelligence to adapt to a changing world. When new tools are invented and utilized, we are able to change our behaviour. This is our strength. Possibly, Ashby's Law of Requisite Variety (Ashby, 1956) more clearly explains our identity than the fact that we are the most intelligent beings on the planet. Even Aristotle, who lived roughly 2,500 years ago, believed that once humans had invented tools and machines that could perform work functions, we would no longer need 'slaves' (Aristotle, 2000). Tools and machines have always changed people's jobs and identities. Those who are unable to adapt to the continually changing world will always experience difficulties in their lives.

The fact is that information and communication have become more important than production and distribution in the value creation processes in the global economy. In the future, it will be how we adapt to changes in relation to these two elements that will determine whether we are able to adapt to the new technology in the Fourth Industrial Revolution.

The modern intelligent robots and the artificial intelligence they possess are neither some kind of Frankenstein monster nor modern-day trolls. They can be developed in ways in which we cannot possibly imagine. For instance, concerning Darwin's theory of evolution, it may be the case that humans are not yet finally 'evolved'. Possibly, the 'new' human may be a being with artificial intelligence and an intelligent nano-sized robot implanted in the ear, neck, foot or the like. In this way, our ability to handle challenges and problems will increase exponentially.

We have illustrated the previously mentioned description in Figure 2.3.

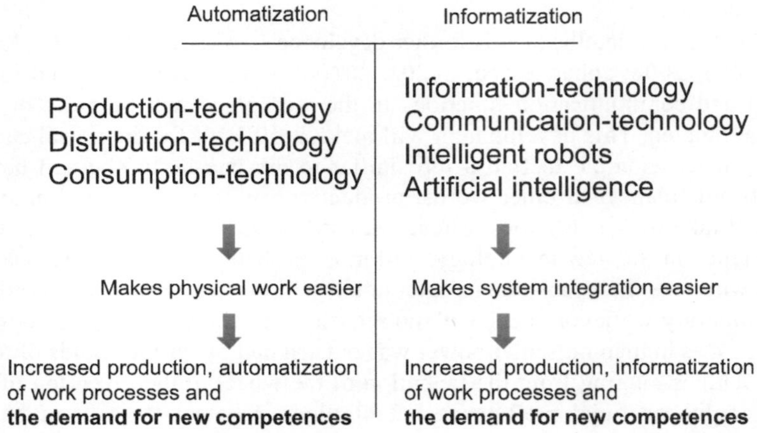

Figure 2.3 From the automation of production and distribution, to the informatization of communication

Analysis

Some people are better at communication than others; using various channels and means, everyone tries to the best of their ability to communicate, and they achieve a certain degree of success. This process is an inherent quality of communication. However, in the future, the new technology in the form of artificial intelligence and intelligent robots will transform the way we communicate and relate to each other.

We are aware that changes are taking place, but we do not know what challenges will meet us around the next corner. *Or do we actually know?*

1 We know that new technology is changing our working life, society and how we relate to others.
2 We know that artificial intelligence will change our everyday lives.
3 We know that increasingly more professional study programmes and courses at universities will need to include technological competence.
4 We know that the new technology will increase productivity in production and distribution chains.
5 We know that all the administrative processes in organizations and society will be informatized.[9]
6 We know that many traditional degree programmes are becoming outdated and will perhaps disappear from college and university prospectuses.
7 We know that algorithms, coding, simulation skills and artificial intelligence will be in demand in the future.
8 We know that the new technology will change the way we relate to each other.

9 We also know that people and societies are not yet ready to face the challenges that intelligent robots and artificial intelligence will pose.
10 We also know that we will have to deal with the social tensions that will arise, when some people are waged-employees, while others receive a so-called universal basic income from the government.
11 We know that in the future people's identities will be threatened.
12 We know that people's pride will be threatened by the new technology.
13 We know that with the use of autonomous vehicles, society will need to consider the ethical aspects of embedded forms of artificial intelligence regarding decisions that will have life and death consequences in the case of unavoidable accidents.
14 We know that linear thinking, that is cause-and-effect thinking, which has served us for hundreds of years, possibly thousands, will be challenged by new ways of thinking.
15 We know that profitability will no longer be the only criterion we will have to focus on if we are to survive in a world where the environment is severely threatened.
16 We know that old ideologies will have to be replaced.
17 We know that digital technology will create entirely new political alliances.
18 We know some of the future positive and negative consequences that will be caused by the global economy.
19 We know that the big cities will grow even bigger and populations will become older.

On the one hand, we know quite a lot already and can project future scenarios, although we cannot of course be specific. On the other hand, we know that the new technology today and in the near future only represents the beginning of a new industrial revolution that we must all relate to sooner or later.

Theoretical points

We often hear people say that the new technology is so complex that it is impossible to say anything sensible about what will emerge in the future. We should rather wait and see, they say. Of course, this is an erroneous idea, because we may wake up tomorrow and see what we didn't want to see; in this context, 'plan or be planned for' is a good piece of advice (Ackoff, 1981). We should 'create our own future', otherwise we will have to adapt to what others have created, which will not necessarily be in our best interests (Ackoff, 1981).

It would be a mistake to resign and say that changes are happening so quickly that we cannot know what will emerge in the future. The bottom line is that we very probably know what developments will emerge, from what we can extrapolate from established trends and statistical projections, and because we create changes as a society, even if we do not do them independently. Intelligent robots, artificial intelligence and intelligent algorithms will appear on the horizon in the Fourth Industrial Revolution. What we obviously cannot know yet are all the applications and consequences of these new tools for individuals, organizations, society and the global system. On the other hand, we can envision some of the consequences, so that we may be better prepared for possible eventualities. The upheavals we assume will emerge will be as great as those caused by the Agricultural Revolution, the First Industrial Revolution, and even the emergence of language in human societies, says Susskind (2018: 4). Therefore, it would be a grave error to just wait and see what happens without preparing to make changes and adapt to new developments.

Proposition: Using the new technology, we should create the future we want.

For thousands upon thousands of years, humanity did not experience many great changes. Before the development of agriculture, humans lived mainly in hunter-gatherer societies, in which people's lives followed the same rhythms year in and year out. Even with the development of agriculture, the changes were relatively slow. However, the Industrial Revolution that began in the 1750s in Britain led to dramatic changes. The more rapid rate of change after this period increased the complexity of most institutions, organizations and societies (Harari, 2015). With the low rate of change over thousands of years in the historical context, it is not surprising that we have a built-in aversion to the rapid changes that are occurring today, which are likely only to increase at the beginning of the Fourth Industrial Revolution. It is approximately 5,000 years since the first civilizations saw the light of day (Susskind, 2018: 4–5). Yet, the developments we have witnessed from the 1950s onwards with the emergence of the first computers, the last 30 years with the use of Internet and the last 10–15 years with the emergence of smartphones, reflect this increasing rate of change. With the rise of artificial intelligence, intelligent robots and intelligent informats, the rate of change will not only dramatically increase, it will become the only 'stable' factor in our lives. Therefore, it will not be enough merely to adapt to these changes. As individuals, organizations, societies and a global system, we must plot our future course and decide which direction we wish to take.

Proposition: We should co-create the society we want to live in.

Practical consequences

Of course, we do not have data or information about the future, so we cannot describe or analyze what we do not know. However, we can develop different scenarios based on extrapolations, projections, assumptions and expectations of what may come. Many of the scenarios we create are unlikely to actually happen – this, of course, is not the purpose of scenario development. The purpose is to prepare people, organizations and societies for the developments that may occur. The scenarios are intended as intelligent estimates of the main features that will develop in the future. The greatest risk is associated with not attempting to project what may happen but waiting to see what happens and then adapting to the changes.

It is often the case that we tend to either reject or diminish the importance of technology we do not understand, that is artificial intelligence, intelligent robots and intelligent informats.

The World Wide Web was originally developed by Tim Berners-Lee in 1989, as a means of sharing information among scientists at Cern. From these beginnings, the Internet was developed, which completely changed our information and communication world. However, few, if any, at the time understood the significance of Berners-Lee's invention.

Intelligent robots, intelligent informats, artificial intelligence and evolutionary and genetic algorithms will not only affect us as consumers, but also as citizens. The new technological paradigm, in which the previously mentioned elements will become a practical reality, will completely change our everyday lives. For instance, it will change our everyday jobs, diagnosis and medication treatment, our children's education, where we choose to live and so on. Indeed, our whole culture will be greatly affected by the new way of thinking. It does not take much insight into these processes to understand that the new technological paradigm will greatly affect the national and international political systems, and in this way, it will also affect our everyday lives. For instance, China's strategic plan, Made in China 2025, states that it aims to become a world leader in the new technology of intelligent robots and artificial intelligence (Boutrup, 2018; Gaskarth, 2015). Taking this and other factors into account, we can begin to realize the impact the new technological paradigm will have on global politics.

The practical consequences of the new technological paradigm can be expressed in one sentence: 'the people who are mad enough to believe they can change the world, are the ones who often do'. The theoretical basis for this statement is mentioned earlier by Ackoff (1981): 'plan or be planned for', and 'create the corporate future'. Throughout history, we have witnessed the practical impact of those people who have adopted such thinking, such as Martin Luther, Vladimir Lenin, Mahatma Gandhi, Mao Zedong, Martin Luther King and many others who have created the world they wanted to be a part of.

Those people who are satisfied with the status quo, those who only adapt to changes in the outside world, are the ones who will be left behind when the new technological paradigm becomes a reality. The rationale is that intelligent robots and artificial intelligence have the capability to change the world dramatically, just as electricity, the internal combustion engine and the Internet and computers have changed the world. All systems will be greatly affected, that is the economic, political, social and cultural systems and even the biological system. The future biological changes may perhaps be the most difficult to comprehend. When technology has already developed to the point where genetic editing has become almost as easy as text editing, then it is not difficult to envisage that the biological system will also change dramatically.

However, the point is not to understand what can be changed, but to be part of the driving forces in the change process. The point is not to interpret, but to create the future we want to be a part of. This can be done by being active at various levels – in our schools, in our entrepreneurial environments, in our universities, and so on, so we can forge a strong link between knowledge development and knowledge application.

Technology cannot be developed in a vacuum – neither can technology be the tail wagging the political system, because this would only serve the privileged and the powerful. Political communication is as important as the technological development of new products. Just as the philosophical system helps us to understand ourselves, and the world around us, the technological system should help us to change our lives for the better; in this context, the political system should function as a driving force to help people achieve a better life, regardless of their political stance and perspective.

Sub-conclusion

The question we have examined in this section is: in what ways will communication competence be in demand in the Fourth Industrial Revolution?

To sum up, we have argued for the following points:

1 Communication competence will emphasize knowledge and skills relating to coding, algorithms and artificial intelligence.
2 Information and communication technology will place an emphasis on infostructure at the expense of infrastructure
3 Communication technology will promote system integration, which in turn will lead to the informatization of administrative processes in social systems, while at the same time promoting automation of the production system.
4 The practical utility of communication as a discipline beyond information and communication technology will manifest itself in interpretation, participation and sharing. This will be done in the specific communication process by each individual selecting from his or her area of knowledge, experience and memory. He or she will select something from a problem area, and thus de-select something else. Finally, he or she will be left with an abstraction of the concrete starting point. To make sense of this abstraction, he or she will communicate with others to arrive at a mutual understanding.

Creativity

In this section, we will explore the following question: in what ways will creative skills be in demand in the Fourth Industrial Revolution?

In the future, it is most probable that we will need to develop new ideas and innovations in science, business and industry in order to sustain ourselves. In other words, creativity will play a crucial role; we will need creative people and teams to create genuine innovative ideas. At a time when computers will largely take over much of the archiving and memory functions, we will be relieved of these tasks. In this context, we might suggest that there are so-called good and bad memories. In a creative sense, on the one hand, a 'good' memory is not necessarily one we associate with a computer that can store vast amounts of information, and then extract exactly the same information at the touch of a key; in the creative sense, we might call this a 'bad' memory. A 'good' (creative) memory, on the other hand, does not remember everything that has been stored. The 'good' memory changes and creates 'new' memories from what has been stored. This type of memory associates and creates something completely new from what has been originally stored. It is therefore not reliable in the sense that we can extract exactly the same information that was originally stored as we can with a computer. The 'good' memory is creative and makes something new that has never been seen before in the world. At a time when we are searching for innovative ideas, it is the 'good' creative memory that will be crucial. Of course, we are also interested in storing and retrieving what we have stored safely – a memory that we can rely on – but we have computers that can do this. We do not need to burden the creative memory with this type of task.

Narratives

Case letter 1: from the future

The future research and development of intelligent robots and artificial intelligence will mainly be in the hands of nine large companies: Google, Microsoft, Amazon, Facebook, IBM and Apple (the 'G-MAFIA') in the US, and Baidu, Alibaba and Tencent (the 'BAT') in China.[10] The competition and collaboration between these nine companies that control the future development of the technology that will revolutionize artificial intelligence and intelligent robots will be able to create new emergents relatively quickly. When some scientists claim that the last major technological innovation that was launched was the smartphone in 2007 (Chace, 2016: 249), then they overlook the undercurrent of research activities that is necessary for the advanced artificial intelligence of the future to materialize. One such undercurrent that has already materialized is gene editing. To claim that such technology is not a technological innovation well above the level of innovation represented by the smartphone level is based on a lack of knowledge and ignorance of the findings that have already emerged.

In her report, Amy Webb has uncovered hundreds of such technological undercurrents, each of which will be just as important in the near future, as the smartphone has been.[11] Among these are collaborative robots (which we refer to here as informats), autonomous robot teams, molecular robotics, soft robotics, ethical robots, robotic 3-D printing, robot teams for the development of evolutionary algorithms, computational journalism, robotic language translation, simulation using synthetic datasets, robot journalism, algorithmic fact checking, holograms, the use of DNA hard drives, artificial cells, nano-robotic nurses, nano-robotic doctors, precision medicine using nano robotics ('submarines' in our veins), smart intelligent glasses, intelligent hearing aids, technological clothing, decentralized diagnosis and hospital and medical services (compact mobile hospitals).

The prerequisite for the development of each of the previously mentioned new technologies is *creativity*.

Case letter 2: from the past

There is an old Scandinavian saying, 'If you shout in the forest, you will get an answer'. However, if 1,000 people were to shout in the forest at the same time, they would certainly hear a response, but it would be impossible to interpret one single response, because it would be drowned out by the other 999 responses (echoes) coming back from the forest at the same time. As an amateur pilot, the Swedish inventor Hakan Lans was all too familiar with the problems of congested air traffic and the limitations of positioning technology which in the past was dependent on radar. Radar had limited accuracy, because of the 'collision' of signals – in other words, as illustrated in the analogy earlier concerning the 1,000 echoes in the forest. It was in 1981 when Lans was pondering over this problem of 'colliding echoes' that he read about the Global Positioning System (GPS). He realized that if this new technology could be utilized to establish the exact three-dimensional position of aircraft, then this would be of enormous advantage to both pilots and air traffic control. These thoughts led Lans to creatively develop what would eventually result in the STDMA data link – his ground-breaking invention (patented 1997). STDMA is far more accurate than radar. Using the GPS system, STDMA today manages both air traffic and maritime traffic security (Lagercrantz, 2000).

Creativity can be understood as a creative moment in which one's whole body receives signals from a knowledge repository of which one was previously unaware. This knowledge repository may be referred to as hidden knowledge (Johannessen, 2020a, 2020c). Creative people do not produce just one single idea, but countless ideas. This is what leaders need to be aware of. Organizations should be structured in such a way as to encourage individuals to have such moments of creative insight. Why is this important? A quotation from Johansson (2004: 91) might provide clarification: 'The strongest correlation for quality of ideas is, in fact, quantity of ideas.' We could rephrase this to read: let the thousand flowers bloom. In other words, the point is to organize the generation of ideas in both individuals and teams so that their ideas gush forth like spring water, as though they are flowing from an ideas pump or an ideas fountain.

Description

Creativity will be crucial to success in the Fourth Industrial Revolution, because innovations are the driving force that will count most in competition (Chace, 2016). In addition to this insight, it is important to understand that creativity can be learnt (Csikszentmihalyi, 2016). That is to achieve success, effort, hard work and perseverance are just as important as innate ability (Colvin, 2016: 1–17). If creativity is not innate, how can one develop this ability? To answer this question, it will be advantageous to use two categories: the necessary and the sufficient conditions for creative success. Two elements are important regarding the necessary conditions. First, one must clarify what one is passionate about, i.e. where one's passion lies within the field in which one operates. Second, one needs to be clear what one wants to be good at. Regarding the sufficient conditions, the following three elements are crucial. First, perseverance plays a very important role in achieving creative success. Second, one needs to work with one specific problem area over a long period of time (Duckworth, 2017). It is in this context that one often hears that it is necessary to work within a specific field for at least 10,000 hours. That is practical experience within the specific field over a long period of time is critical to achieve creative success. Third, all the practical experience of what you want to be extremely good at should be focused; there should be an intentional purpose behind every hour of the 10,000 hours of work (Johansson, 2004: 1–11).

In addition to the elements related to the necessary and sufficient conditions, we can include what is referred to here as operational conditions. We know that innovations often breakthrough at the intersection of established areas of knowledge (Johansson, 2004: 5). Consequently, it is always important for creative researchers to keep an eye on other areas of knowledge when developing innovative new ideas. For teams, it is important to organize various knowledge domains into one and the same group but to also ensure that the team is oriented towards complementary competences in the outside world. For organizations, it is important to develop teams that fulfil both the necessary and sufficient conditions but at the same time pay attention to what is happening within adjacent fields of knowledge in the outside world (Hansen, 2018). It is therefore up to individuals, teams and organizations to find out where this intersection lies, because innovations will break through in this area.

To exploit the innovations that can emerge in this intersection, it is important to keep an eye on the connections between all the levels crucial to operational success. Intersections and connections apply to both disciplines and culture (Johansson, 2004: 6–7).

We have illustrated the previous description in Figure 2.4.

Analysis

Searching for intersections, and then linking knowledge to facilitate idea generation, is an intentional strategic process. However, it is not necessarily a good strategy to just sit and wait for innovative ideas to emerge by themselves at the intersection between the various disciplines. If you want your ideas to flow like an ideas fountain, one has to stay focused on the intersection 'point'. Figuratively, this may be likened to mining for gold, although there may be no evidence of the mineral on the surface. To find the gold, one needs to excavate beneath the surface. One way to go about excavating to find the gold mine of good ideas is to use a collaborative team to link together various knowledge domains. Or to express this in the words of Jim Collins (2009), you have to get the right people on the bus, the right people in the right seats, and then make sure you drive off in the right direction (that is stay focused).

The point of the bus analogy is that you first have to have a goal, a purpose for what you are doing. Then you have to bring together the right people with expertise in different knowledge domains. Then you need to organize the collaboration so that the contact areas between the different knowledge domains become as fruitful as possible. This way of organizing to create ideas is quite different from organizing into individual disciplines, so that the knowledge domains are

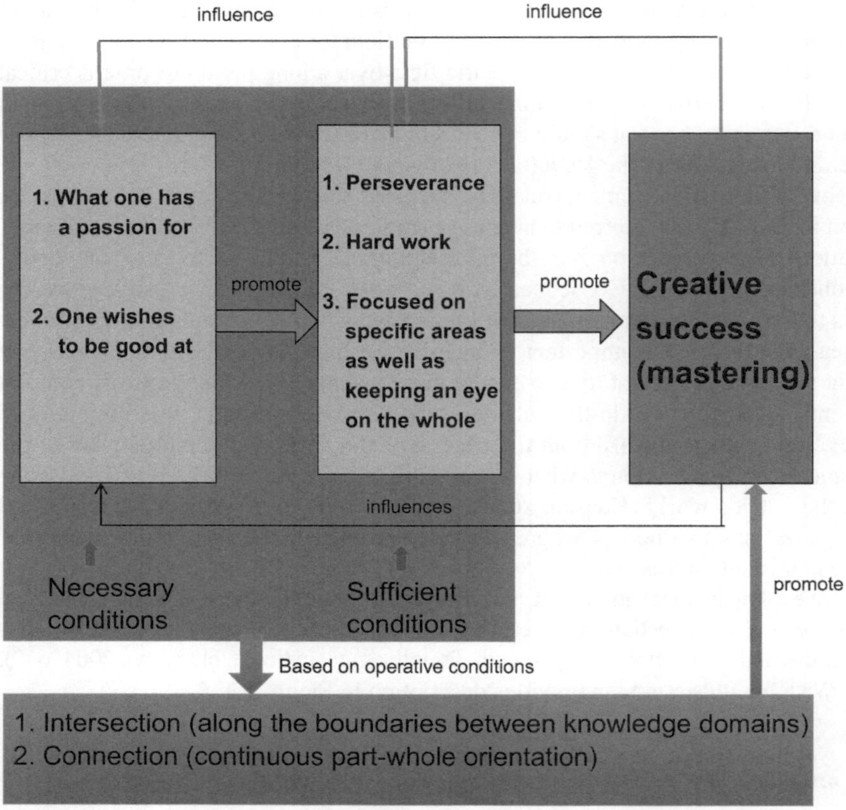

Figure 2.4 Creative success

distinctly separated. To facilitate the creation of innovations, many domains of knowledge as possible need to come into contact with each other; the aim is that these domains will then merge producing a surge of ideas. We can call this an *ideas-fountain organization*, because the intention is that as many ideas as possible emerge from such a way of organizing. For instance, six knowledge domains could be selected from an intersection, and then six teams composed of six people from the various domains could be formed. The six teams could then be organized as a cross-functional professional group. The purpose of this ideas-fountain organization is to organize the creation of as many ideas as possible in the areas that the system is supposed to be best at. What the system is designed to do is the starting point for the development of ideas. In other words, the ideas-fountain is aimed at very clear work tasks. When people are organized in relation to the intersection, then sooner or later this will trigger new and creative ideas, leading to creative success and mastery for individuals, teams and the organization

(Johansson, 2004: 11–20). This type of organization may be said to be successful when it produces new ideas that also are of value to the system. The utility value may be linked to value creation for some organizations, while other factors may be of more interest to other organizations, such as the reduction of CO2, or creating higher ethical awareness, and so on. The point here is that utility is not necessarily linked to a financial bottom line. The claim that creative ideas can be both innovative and useful (without necessarily producing value in economic terms) can be found in the work of creativity researchers such as Teresa Amabile (1996) and Mihaly Csikszentmihalyi (2016), as well as innovation researchers (Johannessen, 2018, 2019a). It is the practical usefulness to the person(s) using the idea that indicates whether an idea has become innovative or not (Johannessen et al., 2001: 20–31).

We have illustrated the ideas-fountain organization in Figure 2.5.

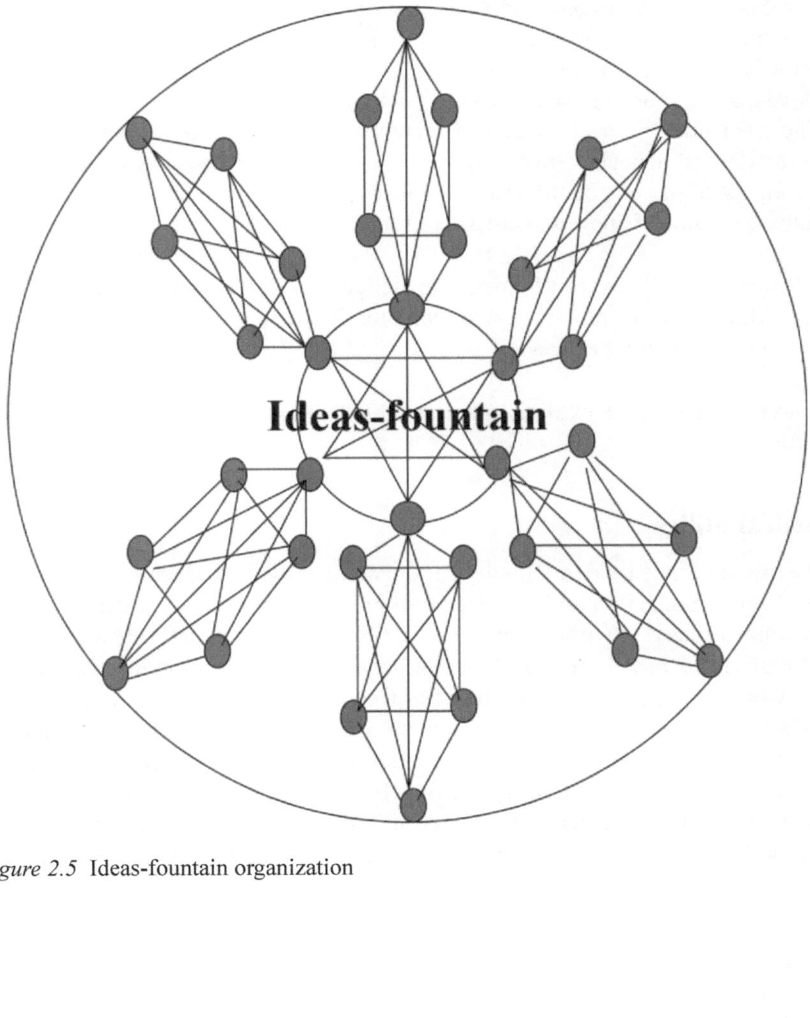

Figure 2.5 Ideas-fountain organization

Theoretical points

The points of connection are increasing in the global innovation economy. This means that complexity is increasing and more and more areas of knowledge are coming into contact with each other. From empirical observations, this development appears to lead to an ever-greater convergence of disciplines and themes that were previously far apart (Reese, 2018). However, there is also another trend, which reaches back several hundred years, and that is an ever-increasing specialization within the individual fields. The link between disciplines and fields should therefore be organized on the basis of this specialization trend, i.e. this is not something that will emerge by itself.

Hidden knowledge is the name of the domain of knowledge from which creative innovation derives its energy and ideas. We need to organize this knowledge domain if we are to exploit it for the creation of new ideas. The domain is as complex and theoretically weighty as explicit knowledge, tacit knowledge and implicit knowledge (Johannessen & Stokvik, 2018). The examples of new connections between disciplines are many: biology and technology, communication and technology, psychology and technology (artificial intelligence), information and technology etc. However, technology as a technical phenomenon is not of interest here, but *technology as a social phenomenon.* It is how technology can be developed and used in social systems that is in focus, not technology in itself.

The connecting points between different disciplines need to be coordinated, so the creative and new can emerge by means of creative bridges between the various areas. Without this coordination, no ideas will be able to cross the bridges to become that which is new and creative.

> Proposition: To exploit hidden knowledge, the domain of knowledge from which creative new ideas can emerge, the domain needs to be organized through explicit processes.

We have illustrated the explicit processes that exploit hidden knowledge in Figure 2.6.

Practical utility

The exploitation of hidden knowledge, the application of hidden knowledge, as well as the organization and management that foster creativity may be regarded as random processes without any certain result. This is exactly how it should be. Creativity is based on a random component. Therefore, it is imperative that those working with the exploitation of hidden knowledge continuously look for both intended and unintended consequences of the knowledge domains when they engage with each other. The new elements that emerge do not in any way have to be what you were necessarily looking for. Therefore, it is easy to overlook important results that emerge. However, it is the results that were not intended, which will often prove to be what is truly innovative and which creates value for

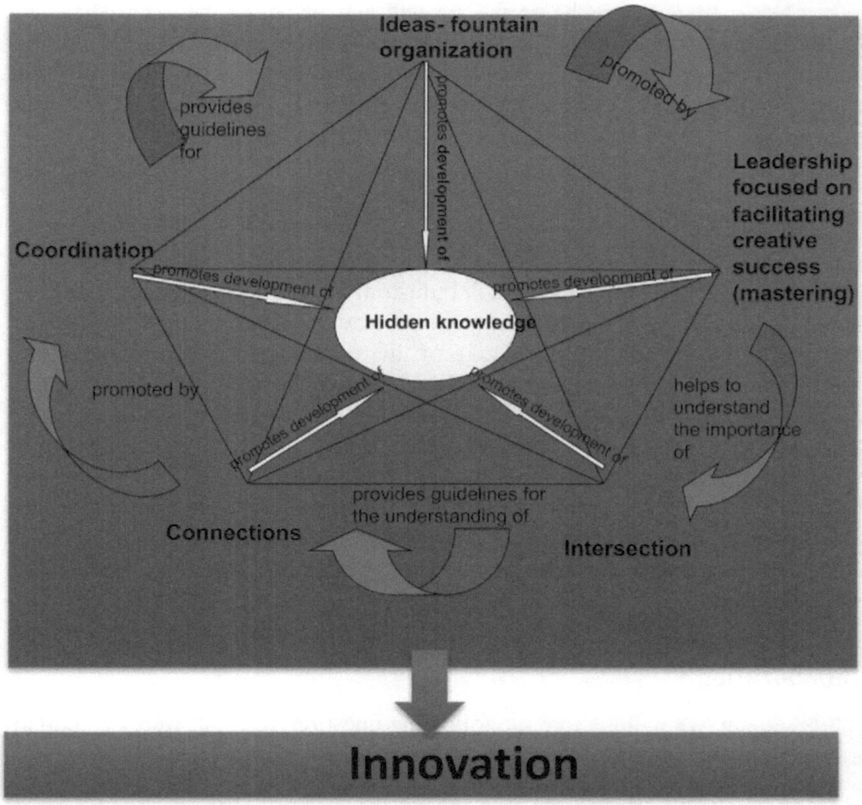

Figure 2.6 Organizing the exploitation of hidden knowledge

the individual and for the business or organization. This is a type of observation, or 'seeing', where you constantly keep watch out of the corner of your eye while moving forward. In other words, you are not only focused on the desired results but also aware of the results that were not expected, and which may only become important when viewed in the light of a completely different domain of knowledge. This is where hidden knowledge lies buried.

It is when organization is based on facilitating that different knowledge domains intersect, instead of organizing the knowledge domains in silos with waterproof seals between them, that the creative new has the opportunity to flourish. However, we have to keep in mind that the intersection of the knowledge domains needs to be organized and managed so that there are links between them; otherwise they tend to withdraw into themselves and return to the safe and secure life within their closed knowledge silos.

An indicator that the individual is close to exploiting hidden knowledge is when he or she experiences that he or she masters new areas. At the team level, hidden knowledge can be exploited when disciplines are organized so they intersect and coordinate with the aim of joint creative production. At the organizational level, an indication that one has successfully organized the exploitation of hidden knowledge is when innovations emerge where it was least expected.

Sub-conclusion

In this section, we have explored the following question: In what ways will creative skills be in demand in the Fourth Industrial Revolution? The short answer is that in the future, hidden knowledge will become the new domain of knowledge that will be exploited and knowledge of this domain will be in demand. The rationale is simple. It is in this domain of knowledge where the creative new that leads to innovation can be found. The more practical answer is that creativity is crucial if we are to produce value creation at all levels, and it should be organized and managed. To drive forward the creativity of the individual, we have developed a leadership model, where creative success and mastery are the intended results. We have shown this in Figure 2.5. To organize the creativity of teams, we have proposed an ideas-fountain organization, which we have shown in Figure 2.6.

Collaboration

In this section, we will explore the following question: in what ways will collaborative competence be in demand in the Fourth Industrial Revolution?

'Be competitive if you want to be successful' has been the mantra of the business world. However, at the beginning of the Fourth Industrial Revolution, it may be questioned whether being competitive is the only crucial social mechanism for success. In the present and past, it has generally been believed that being competitive is the prerequisite for financial success. Even within biology and evolutionary theory, competition or the struggle for survival has been emphasized as important. There has perhaps been too little focus on the fact that survival in Darwinian theory is rather linked to adaptation. When adapting to the environment, being competitive is not the most important factor, but rather collaborating with the others in the group. Trying to compete with the strongest can be a very foolish strategy and will often lead to failure.

'Don't hit those who are smaller than you' is something we often heard when we were growing up. If you are going to 'fight' (compete with) someone, it is of course the ones you have the possibility of winning against you are going to fight with; the opposite might suggest some kind of mental aberration.

In modern strategy literature, being competitive is usually viewed as the correct strategy (Porter, 1986). We do not intend to polemicize against Michael Porter here, but merely imply that most of the booming businesses in the global economy since 2000 have succeeded by changing strategy – not by competing, but by creating those products, production processes and distribution channels that are innovative, that is not by competing with what already exists. The examples of this new strategy may be found in the major companies of today, such as Google, Microsoft, Amazon, Facebook, IBM, Apple, Netflix, Baidu, Alibaba and Tencent.

Although 'Red Ocean' competition (competition within industries already in existence) may still be relevant, it has been supplemented by so-called 'Blue Ocean Strategy', that is industries not yet in existence – unknown markets (Kim & Mauborgne, 2015). This strategy does not focus on competition, but on creating products and services that are not offered by other businesses, but which the market needs. For instance, these products may be created by combining old products into something innovative and new.

The struggle to survive in both the evolutionary and economic spheres has been turned on its head and rephrased to mean that competition is the most important factor. However, it is nearer the truth that in both the evolutionary and economic spheres, it is the balance between competing and collaborating that is the most important necessary social mechanism for survival. In addition, the sufficient social mechanisms such as adapting, creativity and innovation are also important. Competition is just one element in the struggle for survival.

Stating that competition is the most important social mechanism for success is no more than a fixed idea, which does not agree with the theory of evolution, nor is it shown by empirical evidence with regard to the success of individuals, teams, businesses or nations.

The underlying element of success is the culture and ideology that dominates the spirit of the times. Culture and ideology may be understood as the constant interaction between part and whole which is needed to operate within a context. This says something about social systems that are constantly evolving. This may be understood in relation to the fact that it is sometimes competition that is dominant, while at other times it is collaboration. However, neither of the two factors has precedence simply because this is expressed in a fixed idea as mentioned earlier – a fixed idea that may have an ideological basis. It is rather the case that competition and collaboration are part of a creative symbiosis that aims to promote what the system is designed to do. Complex social systems both compete and work together to make the best out of situations. If one factor becomes dominant, then the system will collapse. It is the reciprocity of the symbiosis and the understanding that the two factors combine which result in some systems being successful, while others disappear into the oblivion of history. In other words, competition and collaboration are not two opposites, but rather mutually supportive of each other, in the way thesis and the antithesis depend on each other to create synthesis.

In plain text, the Fourth Industrial Revolution will have more need for collaborative systems than for systems that base their existence on competition. 'Greed is good, said Gordon Gekko in the film *Wall Street* (1987). However, too great an emphasis on competition at the expense of collaboration is directly harmful to any social system. Therefore, we need to identify how collaboration will be in demand in the Fourth Industrial Revolution.

The introduction in this section is shown in Figure 2.7.

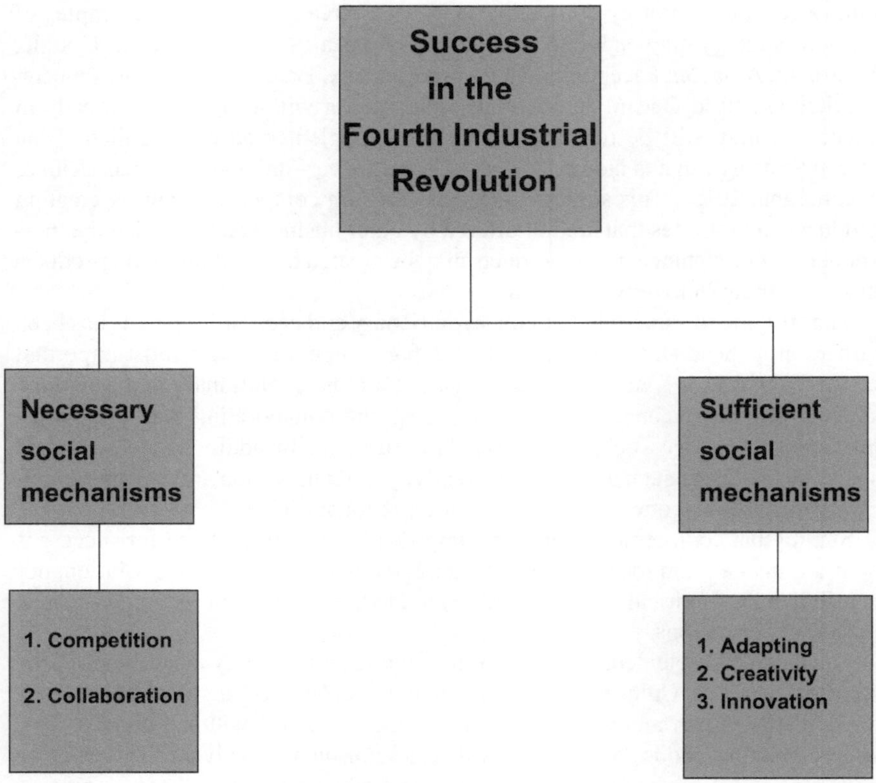

Figure 2.7 Collaboration and success

Narratives

Case letter 1: a theoretical reflection

Traditionally, aspects of morality and ethics have not been viewed as being a necessary part of the study of the natural and formal sciences. Newton did not consider the moral aspect when he saw an apple fall from a tree, which caused him to ponder the nature of gravitation. However, in modern times, morality and ethics have become increasingly incorporated as important aspects when researching the formal, natural and social sciences. One of the factors that contributed to this increased focus on morality and ethics in these branches of scientific study is the development of artificial intelligence and intelligent robots. Self-driving cars, emotional and social robots and many other applications of artificial intelligence have placed morality and ethics at the centre of most scientific projects within these fields. Why are we addressing the topic of morality and ethics in a study of collaboration as an important competence in the Fourth Industrial Revolution?

Moral sensibility and moral intelligence will be crucial for whether the new technology will be accepted by most people, so as to avoid the emergence of a modern Luddite movement.[12] To achieve this, collaboration is crucial at all levels. Collaboration is linked to mutual help to achieve something that we, as individuals, cannot manage alone. It isn't random connections that will enable collaboration in the Fourth Industrial Revolution, but systemic connections. This means that all connections influence and are influenced by all other connections. Further, of necessity, a type of learning will be essential to facilitate collaboration in the Fourth Industrial Revolution. This is evident in the development of evolutionary algorithms, genetic algorithms, learning algorithms etc. When algorithms are designed to learn and develop themselves, then the intelligent robots that use these algorithms will be something qualitatively new in the evolutionary process. It is at this point that one can talk of a link between the biological and technological evolutionary process. To avoid the complete derailment of society, moral sensibility and collaboration in this systemic evolutionary process will be crucial.

We have illustrated aspects of collaboration in the Fourth Industrial Revolution in Figure 2.8.

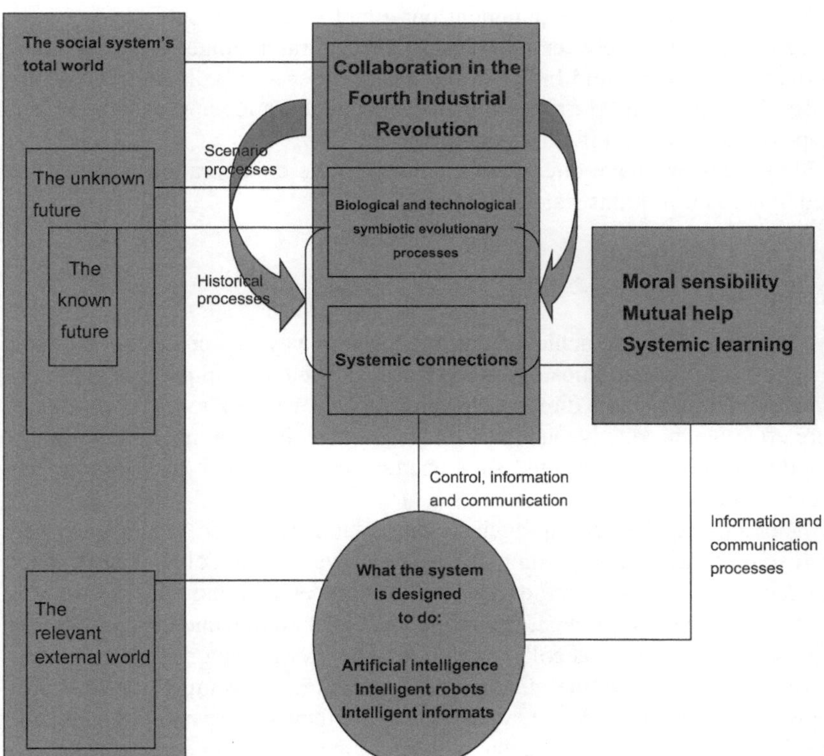

Figure 2.8 Aspects of collaboration in the Fourth Industrial Revolution

Case letter 2: a different theoretical reflection

Researchers in the field of artificial intelligence and intelligent robots are not only looking at collaboration between biological and technological systems; to learn about collaboration, and how collaborative functions perform, many scientists are focusing on the human brain to investigate how the functions of the brain work together in order to create true intelligence. In our brains, evolution has, over millions of years, added layers of functions to adapt to the world around us. The development of the human embryo strangely mimics aspects of the evolution of life on Earth, which has taken millions of years. For the future intelligent robot that has embedded evolutionary and genetic algorithms, the same development will take only a few units of time.[13] The evolution of fish to homo erectus ('upright man') has taken millions of years. The road from the homo erectus to homo sapien ('wise man'), that is a human with a well-developed moral intelligence is much shorter, although we might say that 'the fully moral human' has still not reached the end of this road. Possibly, reflections focused on the nature of 'the moral robot' may also result in 'the moral intelligent human being' finally emerging from a technological and biological symbiosis! Moral intelligence also seems to be linked to a form of social sensibility, a subtle intuition and awareness of social tensions. In this context, memory is an anchor that maintains our established behaviour.

There may be a link between moral sensibility, moral intelligence, the symbiosis between technology and biology, and the emergence of collaboration at the expense of competition. Moral intelligence and collaboration appear to be linked to a type of moral sensibility that is future oriented.

In Figure 2.9, we have attempted to illustrate the collaboration that will be needed in the Fourth Industrial Revolution.

Description

Collaboration is linked to achievement, in the same way that creativity is linked to innovation, and communication to trust, and that change competence is important in maintaining a stable direction towards a goal. We work together because it is more effective, productive and performance-enhancing than not collaborating. So, we do not collaborate because someone tells us to, but because we know that it will benefit us.

Collaboration is often set up against competition. However, this is a skewed view in some contexts for the simple reason that we have to collaborate in order to compete with those who are defined as our competitors, and who we want to win against in a specific context. Consequently, collaboration and competition are not necessarily opposites, as collaboration may be viewed as a necessary prerequisite for competition. On the one hand, collaboration and competition may also be viewed as two distinct ideas. On the other hand, they are systemically interconnected. It is therefore not the case that collaboration collapses into competition. To understand the simultaneous existence of collaboration and competition, it may be helpful to analyze the two concepts in a macro-meso-micro schema (Bunge,

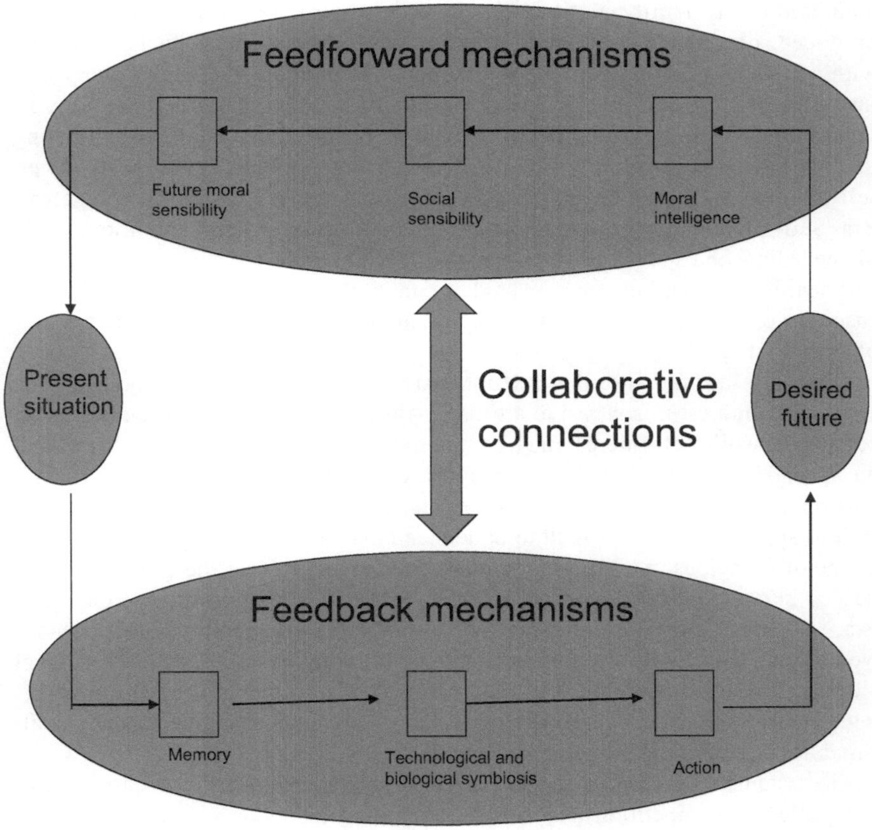

Figure 2.9 Collaboration as a function of feedforward and feedback processes

1990). At the macro level, a distinction may be made between collaboration and competition. However, this is at an overall macro level. At this level, one can of course reflect on the two concepts as opposites, leading to two different behavioural dispositions. If one collaborates at this level, it may be claimed that one triggers various actions that have specific consequences. On the one hand, competing will trigger completely different actions. Of course, this is correct at this level.

If, on the other hand, we take the analysis down to the meso level, which is at the organizational level, then, as we have suggested earlier, competition will lead to collaboration. Thus, at the meso level, there is no contradiction between collaboration and competition, as the one is a prerequisite for the other.

If we go one step further down to the micro-level, which is at the level of the individual, then competition can be perceived as resulting in benefits for the individual. At the micro level, researchers often claim that such self-interest promotes motivation and individual commitment.

There is much to suggest that most people will think first of themselves and their immediate family in situations in which scarce resources are exploited, produced, distributed or shared. However, self-interest must not be confused with selfishness and greed. On the one hand, throughout the evolutionary history of humanity, self-interest has been one of the strongest principles for survival (Johnson & Johnson, 1989). Altruism, on the other hand, is something that appears in extraordinary situations and contexts (Kohn, 1992: 3). However, self-interest should not be regarded as something that is 'less moral' than altruism. Self-interest may be said to constitute the 'normal' human condition, while disregarding one's own self-interest and, for example risking one's own life and health to help others may be said to constitute a special case. These special cases are of course admirable, but they do not constitute the 'normal' behaviour of the majority.

Thus, it is not the case that self-interest is something morally reprehensible. Nor is self-interest in contrast to altruism. Altruism is a special variant of human behaviour, while self-interest may be said to be the general rule. The general and the special belong to two different categories. Comparing two different categories will often lead to so-called category errors. This may be likened to comparing fruit to apples. It is not difficult to understand that such category errors represent a type of fallacious reasoning. Of course, no one can answer the question: What do you like most: fruit or apples? It is the same case with self-interest and altruism, although we may feel this represents something more complicated, because we are taught to think in either/or contexts. The opposite of self-interest is not altruism, but greed. The opposite of altruism is not self-interest, but egoism. Self-interest is not related to a specific political system, such as capitalism or socialism, but is an essential human characteristic.

The arguments presented earlier regarding self-interest and altruism may also be applied to competition and collaboration. In other words, competition and collaboration are not necessarily insoluble contradictions. On the contrary, collaboration at one level may function as a prerequisite for competition at another level. The point is that you have to be aware of what level you are operating on before you can say anything about the relationship between competition and collaboration.

In the case of collaboration, the success of one individual or organization will promote the success of the other. In competition, the success of one individual or organization will not necessarily promote the success of the other. This is the thinking that mainly lies behind the opposition between competition and collaboration. In Figure 2.10, we have shown a different representation from this way of thinking. It shows that when considering the relationship between collaboration and competition, it is the system-level that will determine the nature of the relationship.

We have illustrated the previously mentioned representation in a macro-meso-micro schema, which is a further development of Mario Bunge's Boudon-Coleman diagram (1990).

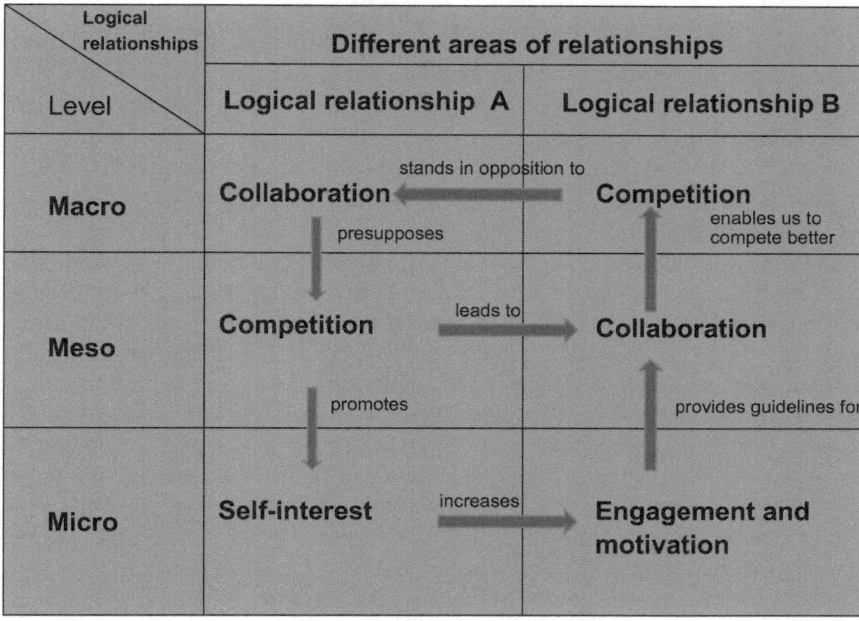

Figure 2.10 Macro-meso-micro schema

Analysis

In the twentieth century, performance was often related to the ability to compete, the role of national governments and the role of the market. As a general rule, collaboration was understood from a competitive context, that is one collaborated to perform better than a competitor. In the twenty-first century, however, this situation is completely different. Digital systems, and eventually artificial intelligence and intelligent robots, will constitute the framework of production and distribution systems. Those who control technology will also control social systems, say both Jamie Susskind (2018) and Shoshana Zuboff (2019). The large technology companies, in collaboration with the state (as an institutional necessity), will, through various forms of algorithms, set the boundaries for people.

The picture that emerges is that evolutionary, genetic, and intelligent and learning algorithms will change society as much as the First Industrial Revolution changed production, urban landscapes and people's living conditions. In such a world where technology and technology companies determine the dominant logic, the ability to collaborate will be crucial to individuals, organizations and nations.

Why will collaboration be more in demand in the Fourth Industrial Revolution than at any time before? The simple answer is the higher degree of complexity.

The most important reflection in Figure 2.10 is related to two aspects. First, there is no real contradiction between competition and collaboration. The contradiction is ideological and constructed. Second, self-interest is possibly the most normal of human characteristics throughout evolutionary history. However, it is the boundary between self-interest and greed that is of interest, because it is these two elements that are opposites.

Most of us look up to great religious leaders who attempt to show the way to a higher moral behaviour. We can find these leaders in all the major religions. We are also deeply impressed by admirable human beings who promote altruism and selfless behaviour. However, the question is really why we should look up to such admirable people who are implicitly saying through their behaviour that our behaviour related to self-interest is not good enough. What these admirable people do is make us believe that there is something wrong in our self-interest. That greed is wrong is self-evident from the very definition of the word. However, why should helping others who are strangers or enemies (as we have heard from many historical narratives, such as the story of the Good Samaritan), be better than helping your friends or family? We assume that there is a tension between the two behaviours. If this was not the case, then the parable of the Good Samaritan would not have held so much interest for people over the last two millennia. The story of the Good Samaritan begs the reader to admire the behaviour of the highly moral character, the Good Samaritan, and implicitly entreats the reader to mimic such behaviour. However, although this may be the intention of the story, such stories can sometimes result in the opposite of what was intended. The explanation is that if our own behaviour linked to self-interest is not considered good enough from a moral and ethical perspective, then such an attitude, even if not intended by religious leaders and their moral adherents, may lead to bringing out the worst in human beings. That is, it may lead to submitting to others, such as religious leaders, who claim they know how we should behave. This type of submissiveness may easily lead to a type of blind obedience and a lack of critical attitude towards governments and religious leaders. In its consequences, humans may be thus transformed into flocks of sheep that blindly follow orders and do what they are commanded to do. History shows us countless examples of the negative consequences of what such blind obedience and herd mentality can result in. What initially looks like a highly moral act by religious leaders and their moral adherents can, in its social consequences, lead to the opposite of what was intended. We know that the road to hell is paved with good intentions. However, good intentions are not enough. Collaboration competence will be required in the Fourth Industrial Revolution if we are to create a better society.

Collaboration does not require the absence of tension and conflict, but of competition. Collaboration really means working together to produce something. However, this does not mean that you need to be in physical contact with each other, or in face-to-face communication. Collaboration is linked to reciprocity, interdependence and trusting that others do what is expected, even though no control mechanisms are used.

Theoretical points

In general, collaboration, teamwork and basically helpful attitudes produce better results than selfish behaviour (Dahrendorf, 1973; Frank, 2012: 1). However, an obvious danger of engaging in collaborative projects is that others may take advantage of our contributions, while we get nothing in return. In other words, the person who gives may risk losing everything. If this kind of attitude sneaks into collaborative projects, we will all lose out (Pruit & Kimmel, 1977; Fiske, 2004). According to Martin Nowak and Roger Highfield (2011), the acts of being generous, giving, helping others who need assistance and forgiving those who fail to provide us with assistance are all founded on a basic understanding that we are all best served by working together. Accordingly, two apparently contradictory motives are co-existing: 1 self-interest and 2 the desire to collaborate and belong to a group.

In neoclassical economics, people are viewed as being basically selfish. Even when people are helping others, they are doing so covertly and in fact adopting a long-term perspective based on their own self-interest (Bowles & Gintis, 2003, 2011). The thinking is that people are basically selfish, unless there are incentives that encourage collaboration or giving and helping others. This is often described as incentive-based collaboration (Nowak & Sigmund, 1998: 573–577). However, if we build trust into a relationship, we avoid investing in control mechanisms to find out whether the other person is promoting his or her own interests when we are not around. What is happening in such relationships is that we give and collaborate right up to the point at which we find that we can no longer trust the other person (Axelrod & Hamilton, 1981: 1390–1396).

In neoclassical economics, all policy and analysis is founded on a basic assumption that people behave selfishly (Bowles & Gintis, 2011). There is another approach, however, which is based on cultural evolution (Richerson et al., 2016). This approach views human development primarily from a collaborative perspective in which individual self-interest is not the most important factor, although it is not overlooked (Caporael et al., 1989: 683–699). There are many examples of people valuing membership in a group more highly than their own self-interest (Baumeister & Leary, 1995: 487–527). This must not be understood to mean that those who have a need to belong to a group are necessarily motivated by altruistic factors. According to Roy Baumeister and Mark Leary, their reward lies in membership in the group (1995: 487–527). The risk for people who behave in this way is that they may be betrayed by someone in the group who values self-interest more highly than membership in the group. Experiments show, however, that the vast majority of people value belonging to a group above self-interest (Axelrod & Hamilton, 1981: 1390–1396; Diamond, 2013). This is particularly true when synergies arise through collaboration. One example of such a synergy would be the generation of new knowledge that results in innovation (Boone et al., 2008). For example innovation may arise when a person is dependent on the competence of the other people in the group in order to use his or her own competence: in other words, when complementarity is a prerequisite for innovation (Obstfeld, 2005).

There is not necessarily a contradiction between neoclassical self-interest and the views based on cultural evolution. What functions on one level does not necessarily function on a higher level and vice versa. Thus, competition and collaboration in relation to such an understanding need not be contradictory. In some contexts, A and B may compete, while in other contexts collaboration may be more advantageous. Why some people choose to compete while others choose to collaborate may also be linked to the business culture (Chiao & Cheon, 2010), individual differences among people and people's values (Declerck et al., 2013).

> Proposition: Group belongingness and collaboration will be more crucial to achieving success than self-interest in the Fourth Industrial Revolution.

The psychologists John Darley and Bibb Latané are credited with starting the scientific investigation of prosocial behavior (1968, 1970). Their main finding regarding where no one intervened to help victims in emergency situations was that although people care, they might not intervene for reasons that weigh heavier than choosing intervention. As a rule, emergency situations are often unfamiliar and complex, and most people do not have the necessary experience to tackle such situations. There are of course those whose professions have trained them to identify and understand such situations, for instance firefighters, police, doctors, nurses, relief workers and so on. However, no matter what training people may have, empathy also plays an important role in prosocial behaviour.

Empathy is the capacity to understand the feelings or experiences of another person by placing oneself in their situation. Showing people empathy shows that you respect them and their dignity and that you are taking responsibility for them (Benhabib, 2004, 2016). This helps not only the person who is the recipient of such respect but also the person showing empathy. Showing someone respect in this way also improves their mastering ability (Eden, 2003: 91–122). The effect of doing this may also prove to be a self-fulfilling prophecy, i.e. because you believe the other person is mastering a situation, then it is highly probable that they *will* master the situation (Eden, 1990: 394–398). This is called the Rosenthal Effect or the Pygmalion Effect, i.e. higher expectations lead to an increase in performance (McNatt, 2000: 314–322).

Prosocial practices represent a new perspective on how businesses can achieve success and promote innovation (Grant, 2014; Gladwell, 2009). In a single sentence, this may be expressed by saying that businesses perform and innovate better when people help each other (Cherry, 2010). Thus, prosocial practices are the key to success, because they help businesses to succeed by building a helping culture (Reis & Gable, 2003: 129). An apt slogan in this context is, 'give and you will get'. Although this may seem to be a worn-out cliché, empirical research shows us that it is also true (Grant, 2014; Cherry, 2010; Reis & Gable, 2003). Practice shows us that those who are generous achieve success. However, in our competitive world, the view that the individual who gives and is generous is also a winner seems counter-intuitive (Burt, 1995). Empirical research shows us that being competitive in every context is not necessarily productive, but being generous and giving can in many contexts be a social mechanism that leads to success (Grant, 2014). The same applies to alliance building. Mutual alliances open up opportunities to create success (Uzzi & Dunlap, 2005).

It is also possible to present yourself as a giver while actually positioning yourself to be the one who actually receives what the other gives. This behaviour is also found in employees who 'kiss up and kick down'; i.e. employees who are positive towards their superiors but behave negatively towards subordinates. However, it is often such negative behaviour towards others that ultimately causes them to fall (Vonk, 1998). This applies to both leaders and employees.

In the theory of 'give and take' that Adam Grant (2014) has developed, there is an interesting observation concerning management: narcissist leaders will most likely cause an organization to fail (Chatterjee & Hambrick, 2007: 351–386; Nevicka et al., 2011: 1259–1264). Narcissist leaders are takers and not givers, and everything is ultimately 'about them'. One way to identify narcissist leaders and takers is to study their verbal and written presentations. If they seem to overuse first person singular pronouns, such as 'I' and 'mine', then it may be the case they are takers with narcissist traits (Grant, 2014). Givers tend to use plural pronouns such as 'we', 'us', 'ours' etc. (Chatterjee & Hambrick, 2007: 351–386). Givers also use a style of communication that is inquiring and listening. They are also not afraid to show their own vulnerability and mistakes, something which takers and narcissist leaders rarely do (Nadler et al., 2003: 91–109).

Proposition: Showing others that they master what they are doing will improve their chances of success and their innovative capability.[14]

Practical utility

The entire human world consists of 'other' people, with the exception of oneself (of course!). This is something the 'exception', i.e. the individual, should reflect on. The individual is entirely dependent on other people seeing some kind of advantage or benefit in taking responsibility for them. Consequently, it is for this reason that the individual should always take responsibility for other(s). This small irony may serve as an introduction to the discussion later of how taking responsibility for others can promote success and increase the degree of innovation for both the individual and other(s).

This ironic situation also leads to the truism that 'practice makes perfect'. In other words, if the individual is to master something, then it's only a matter of practice. However, empirical research shows us that this is both true and false at the same time (Huckman & Pisano, 2006: 473–488). This can be explained by the fact that when you work in a team, for instance, as a leader, a teacher, a doctor, a financial analyst, a consultant, a knowledge worker, a staff member and so on, practising will result in you performing better within the team and organization you are working in, i.e. practice makes perfect. Yet the experience gained within one team or organization does not necessarily mean that you will completely retain your mastery if you switch to another team or organization. The experience gained when practising is both context-dependent and linked to the team or organization in which the experience was gained (Groysberg et al., 2008: 1213–1230). For instance, a surgeon who is part of a medical team will improve when he or she learns to work better together with the other team members. The surgeon will become familiar with the skills of the other team members – as well as their strengths, weaknesses and limitations. Furthermore, the others will become familiar with the skills, strengths and weaknesses of the surgeon. This experience cannot be fully transferred if the surgeon starts to work in another hospital. The same applies to other professionals such as teachers or various leader positions when switching jobs (Huckman & Pisano, 2006: 473–488). In other words, specialists will not always be able to fully transfer their expert knowledge to another organization. This probably applies to most experts in fields where people work in teams. This can be explained by the fact that it is the team's competence that is crucial to their success, and not necessarily the expert knowledge of a single individual (Groysberg et al., 2008: 1213–1230). This may be one of the reasons that knowledge workers, managers, and others who are considered highly skilled in one organization do not necessarily perform at the same high level in another organization. In other words, research shows us that it is very difficult to transfer expert knowledge from one organization to another. Research shows us rather that people who perform extremely well in one organization experience a significant drop in their performance when they move to a new organization (Groysberg et al., 2008: 1213–1230). Research also shows us that performance can be lower than in the previous organization measured for an average of five years. However, it must also be said that some of the experts maintained their level of performance. The condition was that when they transferred to a new organization, they took their team with them (Groysberg et al., 2008: 1213–1230). After this review of the relevant research, we may rewrite the expression 'practice makes perfect' with 'practice makes *the team* perfect'. In other words, you are always dependent on others when you operate in social systems. Being a so-called 'Robinson Crusoe on a desert island' is not possible in the business world (and even Robinson Crusoe had his Man Friday with him!). Thus, we depend on others for our own success. If we take this into account, then we should also take responsibility for others – if not for any other reason than the fact that it is a prerequisite for our own success.

Adam Grant calls building a helping culture in groups 'expedition behavior'. He cites Jeff Ashby, a NASA astronaut, who says the following about this type of behaviour: 'Expedition behavior – being selfless, generous, and putting the team ahead of yourself – (this) is what helps us succeed in space more than anything else' (Grant, 2014: 86).

Talented people who achieve success are often envied, and they often experience that others put stumbling blocks in their way (Eugene & Glomb, 2010:

889–901). However, there is one exception. If these talented individuals are givers, they will no longer be 'ambushed' by others. On the contrary, the talented givers are then rewarded for their achievements (Hardy & Van Vugt, 2006: 1402–1413). This may also partly explain why collective behaviour often leads to success to a greater degree than individual competitive behaviour (Willer, 2009: 23–43).

In other contexts where ideas that threaten the status quo are actualized, research shows that the ideas of 'takers' are faced with scepticism, because it is assumed their ideas are motivated by personal motives. However, the ideas of givers are received positively and discussed openly. This also applies when givers' ideas threaten the status quo (Grant et al., 2009: 31–55). This can also have major implications for the development of ideas related to innovation.

Leaders should be aware of the fact that all their colleagues need to 'be seen'. Everyone, without exception, wants to be credited for their contributions. These contributions may be in different areas: for instance, it may concern a product, a development story for the business, helping those who perform well and so on. Not giving credit to colleagues can result in major negative consequences for a leader. If leaders are to succeed in reaching their goals and the goals of the organization, it is crucial that they give credit to those individuals who have made it possible for the leader to show the results which he or she has been given credit for (Oshinsky, 2005: 205–206).

Empirical research shows that we tend to attribute our own contribution in a relationship more importance than is objectively true. However, it is mainly the takers and not the givers who commit this error (Ross & Sicoly, 1979). The motivation of takers in a collaborative relationship is to make sure they get more than they give (Caruso et al., 2006: 857–871). The givers are motivated by the collective end result. They also consciously develop a habit of saying that *we* did it, or they don't take personal credit for something but refer rather to the group. Empirical research shows that it is also relatively easy for matchers and takers to develop this habit (McCall, 1995: 49–64). Since language may be said to shape reality, this research can have consequences for behaviour in organizations.

One of the positive consequences of the givers' behaviour in an organization is that they have 'ambassadors' who constantly talk well of them. The takers, on the other hand, have people who constantly talk disparagingly about them. The givers also have a greater ability to forgive others for behaviour or actions that have had negative consequences. The givers thus try to create an environment of psychological safety, where failure is part of achieving success (Bowles & Gintis, 2003, 2011). Empirical research shows that it is more probable that innovations will be developed in a psychologically safe environment (Edmondson, 1996, 1999; Obstfeld, 2005). This is also an important reason why leaders should invest in givers and be careful about hiring takers.

It has also been shown that takers are less likely to adopt the perspective of others (Burton, 2011: 131–137), while givers have a greater ability to put themselves in the position of others and take their perspective (Nordgren et al., 2011).

Those who manage to step out of their own frame of reference and take the perspective of others also exhibit a higher degree of creativity and innovation (Grant & Berry, 2011).

In work situations, there are always some tasks and activities that an employee is not that keen on, or perhaps they feel they lack the expertise to perform the task well. On the other hand, there may be other employees who more than willingly are interested in doing the task. In such situations, employees can help each other by changing their tasks and activities with each other, something which is termed 'job-crafting'. Management can encourage and facilitate such collaborative behaviour in the organization. However, when job-crafting and customizing jobs, two things should be kept in mind. First, the employee should have interest in doing the job. Second, it should be relevant to the business. Job-crafting has been shown to improve both employee and organizational performance and may be understood as an innovative practice in relation to traditional work practices (Berg et al., 2008).

Sub-conclusion

In this section, we have explored the following question: in what ways will collaborative competence be in demand in the Fourth Industrial Revolution?

The tentative answer may be formulated as follows: if one develops hypotheses and models of reality, for example which say that most people are selfish and have little interest in others, then the hypotheses and models that are developed in light of this thinking are not only *models of* social systems but will have consequences that include them *becoming models for* social systems.

In other words, if we assume that people are selfish and if we act as though this is the objective truth, then this may become an objective truth if enough people believe in this hypothesis. Because economists have been assigned a dominant role in the social sciences over the last 50 years, this type of thinking not only permeates the social sciences, but also the social systems this thinking is applied to. It may be understood as an example of a self-fulfilling prophecy. It is even the case that when one has employed this type of thinking over a period, one will find support for the view that it applies in practice, because the models and concepts have become the dominant logic in practice.

Further research could employ a quantitative design, whereby one could conduct a larger empirical investigation to test the relationships between givers, matchers and takers in relation to innovation.

Change

In this section, we will explore the following question: in what ways will change competence be in demand in the Fourth Industrial Revolution?

Employee turnover often means that organizations have to replace lost expertise. In other words, in the present and past, because of the relative stability, the expertise demanded by organizations represents a relatively constant factor.

Thus, when one employee leaves, the organization needs to employ someone with similar expertise. However, in the not-so-distant future, at the beginning of the Fourth Industrial Revolution, the rate of change will increase exponentially (Chace, 2016). It might be said that the only stable factor in the future will be change (Johannessen, 2018, 2019b). This will put great pressure on employees and not least on management. For both management and employees, it will be important to attempt to create the workplace they wish to be part of, rather than wait until others create the framework conditions for their workplace. The Fourth Industrial Revolution will be mainly characterized by the introduction of new technology, especially artificial intelligence and intelligent robots. Therefore, both employees and leaders will need to adapt in step with changes in technology. Creativity and innovation will be competences will be especially in demand in the Fourth Industrial Revolution (Johannessen, 2020a, 2020c). Consequently, it will be important for employees, and especially leaders, to organize the business, and parts of the business, into cross-functional teams, because different knowledge domains will then come into closer contact, which will be an important prerequisite for creativity and innovation (Johansson, 2004). Furthermore, it will be important to envision and prepare for future changes. Therefore, there should always be several teams in the organization that perform this function through various types of future assessments, e.g. by using various scenario teams (Reese, 2018). Furthermore, both leaders and employees should possess change competence so that the whole organization will be able to adapt to constantly emerging changes. To achieve this, it will be important, both socially and psychologically, to become the change you want to see in the organization.

The brief introduction mentioned earlier has attempted to point out that organizations in the future will adopt a process-oriented rather than a functional-oriented organization. In process-oriented organization, the focus is always on the competence and expertise that customers consider to be important. In function-oriented organization, expertise is geared to solving particular tasks or carrying out various functions in the organization. In the case of employee turnover, function-oriented organizations replace the expertise they lose with a similar type of expertise. However, in process-oriented organization, the expertise and competence organizations need is constantly changing; consequently, in the case of employee turnover, it is not merely a case of replacing lost expertise with similar expertise when hiring new employees.

In Figure 2.11, we have illustrated the transition from a low rate of change to a high rate of change and how this affects the way organizations and companies will be organized.

In the following, we will examine what competences will be in demand when the rate of change is high, and where businesses and organizations tend towards adopting process organization. This also relates to the question we asked in the introduction: in what ways will change competence be in demand in the Fourth Industrial Revolution? In other words, it is change competence that deals with the transformation to process organization that will be in demand.

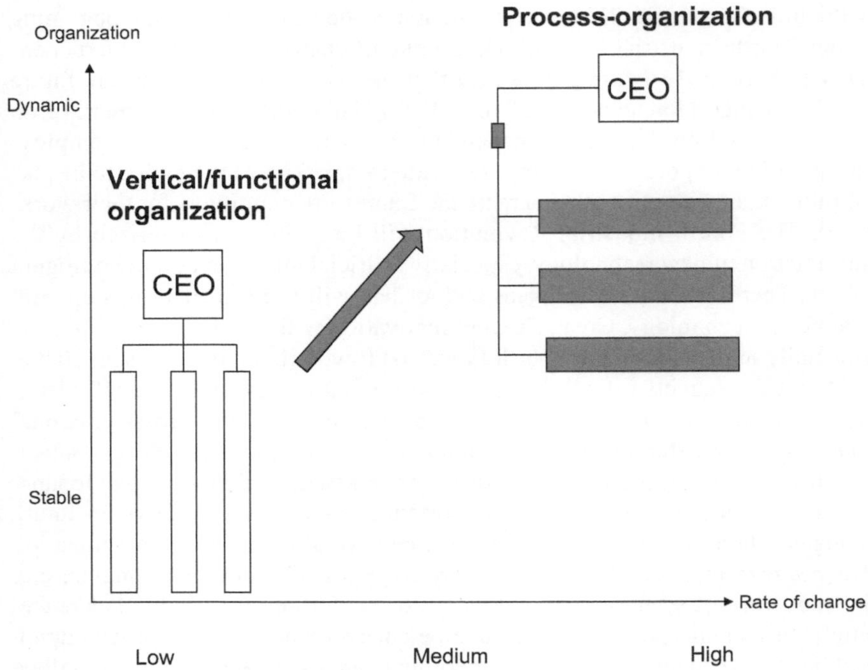

Figure 2.11 Different rates of change and how organizations and companies will be organized in the Fourth Industrial Revolution

Narratives

Case letter 1: job seekers may have higher education, yet they have little chance of getting a permanent job

Reidun had heard that higher education would guarantee her a good job with a good salary. Accordingly, she embarked on a university education. She had also heard that the rate of change would explode in the future, so that no one really knew what competences would be needed in seven or eight years' time, once she had completed her education. In fact, it took longer for Reidun to enter the labour market than she had originally planned. After taking time off to have children, she took nine years to complete her postgraduate humanities degree. When she went to her first interview, she got a surprise. Her educational qualifications were a pretty good fit with the competences the company had specified. There was just one slight problem. The first question they asked her was about her practical experience of using these competences. She could cite only summer jobs she had taken while she was studying and one or two days a week during the whole time she had been at university. She had no long-term consistent experience of using the competences she had learnt.

Reidun did not get the job. She was competing with people with less than half of her years of higher education, but who had relatively long practical experience with the kind of competence sought by the company.

Reidun is just one example of the many people now and in the future who will have university educations but struggle to find secure jobs. They will get short-term employment contracts lasting several months, but these will not be extended, because of the obligations this could impose on the employer. This is the workforce of the gig economy. The workers' jobs are insecure, even though they have completed many years of higher education. Their subject combinations are within a specific area of studies. For instance, few of those who have studied humanities for five to nine years (which would be to PhD level) have linked their studies to other areas such as coding, algorithms and artificial intelligence. Reidun's friend Kari, who took combined courses with history and anthropology alongside coding, artificial intelligence and intelligent algorithms was offered a permanent job before she had even finished studying.

Today, there have never been so many people worldwide who have completed a university education. Previously, a university education was a ticket to secure employment. That's no longer the case unless your studies include a technological subject such as coding, artificial intelligence or intelligent algorithms. If you include those subjects, you can also take subjects like history, art history and anthropology and get an extremely well-paid job.

Worldwide, there are approximately 170 million students. In China alone, there were approximately 8.3 million students in 2019.[15] There are at least five social mechanisms that have changed in relation to people's chances of getting permanent jobs after university.

1 First, who you are as a person has become much more important than the university certificates you send in with your CV.
2 Second, experience is important, although it may seem paradoxical that one needs experience to gain experience.
3 Third, everyone who applies for a job, regardless of their educational history, will have a great advantage if they also have competence in the areas of coding, artificial intelligence and intelligent algorithms.
4 Fourth, an academic education is no longer a minimum criterion for getting a secure job; it is just a necessary prerequisite for being considered. Large companies, such as Ernst & Young, for example have abolished their requirement for new recruits to have a university degree.[16]
5 Fifth, and this mechanism is a kind of synthesis of the other four social mechanisms, there will be an ever-increasing demand for change competence, i.e. the ability to adapt to a continually changing external environment.

Academic attainment is no longer the most important factor for getting a job. This means that if you have experience in e.g. software engineering, the Internet, systems analysis, multimedia development etc., and also have competence in the areas of coding, artificial intelligence and intelligent algorithms,

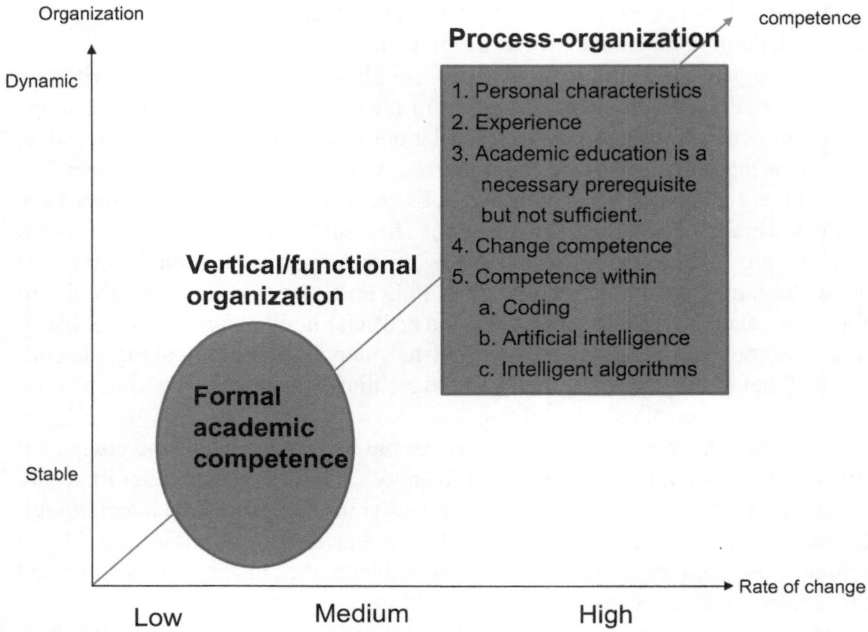

Figure 2.12 Competences that will be in demand in the future

then you have a greater chance of getting a job in the labour market of the future than if you have completed many years of education at a prestigious university.

When Reidun and many of her contemporaries produce their impressive certificates from well-known universities, all the certificates really show is what knowledge Reidun and her fellow students have acquired. The certificates say nothing about their personal qualities, their team-working skills, how they behave in groups, their skills or their ability to manage change.

Figure 2.12 shows what competences Reidun and her fellow students should aim to acquire in the relatively near future.

Case letter 2: when geographical location and offices will have no relevance anymore

In 2020, having an impressive job title and a large office gives employees the feeling of social status. However, in 2045 employees will gain status by being able to contribute something meaningful to others. The working environment was important in the twentieth century and was still of importance in the first two decades of the twenty-first century. However, by the middle of the twenty-first century, people's place of work will not necessarily be at a fixed geographical location; to a great extent, the individual workers will decide where they want to work; this could be at home, in a cafe, on the train, in a holiday cottage etc. The workplace was previously at a fixed location such as a factory or an office. In 2045, people's working environments will be completely different. To a great extent, employees will be able to choose the working hours that are most convenient, sleep in as long as they like, agree on a meeting with the management at a specific location when needed, and so on. In short, employees will largely determine their own working environment. However, work performance requirements will not be less than before. Individual employees will decide how much they want to produce though, and consequently decide what their own income will be. If they choose to produce X units of something, instead of the usual average of X + n, then the business they work for will probably agree. In other words, they produce a certain amount of work and are paid accordingly. Offices will have become a thing of the past for both employees and management. Employees and managers can arrange meetings when necessary and find a location where to have the meeting. There will be no need for many businesses to own work premises anymore. The business will consist of a network of people and organizations carrying out the business's activities. Recruitment will be global because the use of different languages will not pose a problem. This will be possible because one will have something like an advanced Google translate program implanted in one's earlobe, so one will be able to receive simultaneous translation of what people who speak different languages are saying, and vice versa. Ninety per cent of the employees will find themselves located in countries other than where the business has its head office, although 'head office' will be nothing like the head offices of today in terms of architectural dimensions. Businesses will have no need to own buildings when employees do not need offices. Offices may be rented temporarily at various locations when needed. Banks will have become the new technology companies. The CFO of any business may be sourced from the banking services the business uses. Similarly, HR departments will be outsourced to companies that specifically offer such services. HR graduates will be able to find work in companies that specialize in HR services, insurance companies that deal with HR-related questions or HR departments within consulting companies.

Today, software engineers may be found at various locations around the globe, such as in Bangalore, India; north of Beijing; and south of Hanoi. In the twentieth century, companies were often located in a specific building at a specific location, which housed all the company's expertise. By 2045, businesses will be synonymous with an 'idea', which materializes into production and/or services around the world, as the whole world will represent the business's field of operation. The core of the business, which will be an 'idea', will say something about what the business is designed to do.

In these future businesses, you work when you want to work, take holidays when it suits you, and enrol on further education courses when you feel the need.

You are always your own boss, even if you are part of a network where an idea-owner sits at the top of the hierarchy. Your salary will depend on how much time you spend working and your level of productivity.

In the twentieth century and well into the twenty-first century, the motto of companies was to 'hire the best', but only if they lived within a radius of approximately 60 miles from the place of work,[17] or if they were able to move house to satisfy this requirement. However, during the course of the 2000s, people will become more aware of the fact that it is possible to hire the best in the world without considering the '60-mile requirement', because new technology will make it possible for employees to fulfil their tasks despite being in another location. When you have the whole world as your recruiting base, and those who are hired can live wherever they want, you will be able to hire the best in the world, and not just the best within a 60-mile radius. Another significant factor is that the cost of hiring a person in Bangalore and Vietnam is lower than hiring someone with the same expertise who is located in the West, such as New York, London, Paris or Berlin. This will greatly affect the wage levels of employees in the Fourth Industrial Revolution.

Description

The lifespan of organizations has been greatly reduced. For instance, research shows that between 2000 and 2015, 52 per cent of the companies in the Fortune 500 have gone bankrupt, been acquired, merged with others or ceased to exist in one way or another (Ross, 2016). This indicates that change competence will become even more crucial at all levels in the future. The businesses that not only survive but also achieve great success will be the ones that are able to integrate change and learning systems into their operations, with leaders who continuously adapt the business to the outside world (Meister & Mulcahy, 2017: xiii).

Furthermore, it is important that both leaders and employees adopt the following strategies:[18]

1 Creating the workplace you want to be part of
2 Changing in step with technology (sufficient variation of competences)
3 Organizing into cross-functional teams
4 Supporting and participating in scenario teams
5 Becoming the change you want to see in the organization.

Most organizations have become global, either by participating directly in the global economy or by being subcontractors to others in the global economy. Consumers have also become global. They buy their goods in a global network and have goods delivered to the door by global logistics companies. The point of this is not that everything has become global, but what it means for people's workplaces, and the expertise demanded in such a market. Let's take an example. The workers located in Cambodia, Siberia, Pakistan, Uganda or Colombia all have access to participate in the production of parts for a larger product via telecommuting. Workers in the rich industrialized countries are unable to compete with the workers in the low-cost countries. The only possibility is if businesses increase productivity through new technology, i.e. intelligent robots, intelligent algorithms and artificial intelligence. However, the consequence of adopting such new technology is, regrettably, that automation renders millions of production workers in the rich industrialized countries unemployed. Those employees who remain in employment must, in addition to having a formal education, also have the competences shown in Figure 2.12. The change competence shown in Figure 2.12 is crucial for both employees and organizations. We have concretized this change competence in the five points previously mentioned, which we will examine in the further analysis.

In the Fourth Industrial Revolution, face-to-face interaction between employees, leaders, users and others will no longer be necessary due to the various technological solutions that will be available. For instance, interaction in a meeting, a teaching situation, a surgical procedure etc., will be possible via holographic representations linked to intelligent robots and artificial intelligence.

Assuming that such artificial intelligence is fairly evenly distributed throughout the world, the new technology will result in wage earners in the West having to compete with $10-an-hour workers in the low-cost countries. If no income distribution policies are implemented to counter the logic of profit, then it will be highly probable that earnings in the industrialized countries will fall significantly. On the other hand, wage levels in many telecommuting countries may rise considerably. What remains of the competence advantage of the wage earners in the industrialized world is shown in Figure 2.12. However, it will probably take a long time before low-cost labour in countries such as Cambodia will possess the necessary and sufficient competence to replace the Western competence elite. The exceptions are China and India. In these countries, around 2030, there will be enough expertise within both the specific and general competencies to compete and replace highly skilled workers in the West; in addition, these countries will also have large low-cost labour resources in the $10-an-hour category. Those in the West who plan to have children in the future will undoubtedly be unnerved by this insight regarding future job prospects.

We are witnessing a mass automation of blue-collar production workplaces. The so-called blue-overalled workers are increasingly being replaced by white-overalled engineers; namely manual work is being replaced by automation, and now only requires to be supervised by engineers. Moreover, between roughly 2025 and 2035, administrative functions and management processes will gradually be automated. To make a distinction between this type of automation and the automation of production processes, we will term this type of automation process, informatization, because it is the information processes in organizations that are being automated (Johannessen, 2019a, 2019b, 2020a, 2020c).

Internationalization, globalization and change have now become old news. What is new and different today, however, is the emergence of new technology. This technology is resulting in millions of people in the production and distribution processes being made redundant; fortunately for them, however, they are still needed as consumers. If there is no one to consume goods, capitalism and virtually all economic systems would quickly collapse, although they would collapse in different ways. Therefore, the capitalist system will always ensure that there is some form of demand that exists. Unfortunately, for wage earners in the West, there are billions of other consumers out there in the global economy. Consequently, the global labour market that pays $10-an-hour for unskilled and semi-skilled workers will be more than sufficient in the foreseeable future for capitalism to maintain consumption levels.

The extremely high rate of replacement of competences in the West is creating a completely new situation. The most important competition that will challenge workers in the West will not be from the $10-an-hour low-cost labour in developing countries, but from intelligent robots that are interconnected, which we term here intelligent informats (Johannessen, 2020a). However, there is one hopeful prospect for wage earners in the West, which is something of a paradox. When the new technology makes a great impact around 2035–2045, there will be a veritable explosion in competence development throughout the global economy. If this explosion is powerful enough, then the paradox that may occur is that this explosion will turn into an implosion;[19] that is local areas will come to play a greater role, rather than the global, and these 'implosions' will probably occur all over the world, where the new technology is put into use. In other words, if this occurs, and the explosion becomes so strong that it turns into an implosion, then local competence will become the most important competence; local competence is naturally protected by its context and natural boundaries.

Unfortunately for the Western middle class, we can already see that this implosion is occurring. This may be likened to watching a film of an implosion in slow motion. The reason is two-sided. First, the typical work functions performed by middle class employees will be informatized. Second, they will feel the brunt of intensified global competitive pressures. In the future, both of these trends will grow in quantity and quality.

Analysis

In this analysis, we will address the five change competencies mentioned earlier in the description.

Creating the workplace you want to be part of

Change competence is directly linked to the employees' identity and the meaning of their work. If the employees do not feel that the organization provides scope for personal development, then they will feel that they are excluded from the organization, and not be able to contribute what is needed, namely to create the workplace they want to be a part of. Engagement, participation, accessibility, but not necessarily being physically present at the workplace will form the basis for the employees who want to participate in creating their own future workplace.

If engagement falls, the organization will respond with management and control systems, which will then again result in a greater need for controlling procedures. If we look at Figure 2.11, then we can see that the organization will be transformed back to the past, where silo organization was common. If this happens, it is probable that the organization will not have the ability to face competition from others that have adopted dynamic change processes, resulting possibly in bankruptcy, or at best, being bought up by competitors. The commitment and engagement of employees is directly related to an organization's productivity. Organizations that fail to engender commitment in their employees will cease to be sustainable. The lack of commitment and engagement is also costly for organizations.

Possessing a variety of competences: employees need to change their competences as technology evolves (sufficient variety of competences)

It is not necessarily the most 'intelligent' individuals who achieve success in the global market, but those who are the most agile and adaptable. These individuals will be able to produce the required results faster and of a higher quality than others. It is results that will be most in demand at a time when everything is changing, from technologies to markets. Adaptability also means looking for opportunities that were not in the market before, and then trying to fill in these gaps in the market.

Technology covers two phenomena. One is technology as a tool, where problems are concentrated around the scientific study of artefacts. This is the domain of engineers and technologists. The second is technology as a social phenomenon. This belongs to the social sciences and the study of philosophy. The first phenomenon is linked to specific competences, while the second phenomenon is linked to general competences; both competencies were examined in Chapter 1. This is where adaptability to technology development is interesting. Those who are both adaptable and have the ability to motivate and engage others are more likely to succeed in the Fourth Industrial Revolution because they will be result-oriented.

To a greater extent than before, technology will become both a creative and a destructive factor at the beginning of the Fourth Industrial Revolution. Technology will create the new, but also destroy the old, resulting in economic and social crises. For the individual who wants to succeed, it will therefore be important to develop what we term here a 'variety of competences'. Figure 2.13 illustrates this variety of competences, which will be crucial to the success of the individual in the Fourth Industrial Revolution.

Organizing into cross-functional teams

Creativity and innovation are best 'nourished' within those areas where the boundaries of established knowledge and ideas intersect, which is termed 'the Medici Effect'. Therefore, a business that takes this into account when organizing

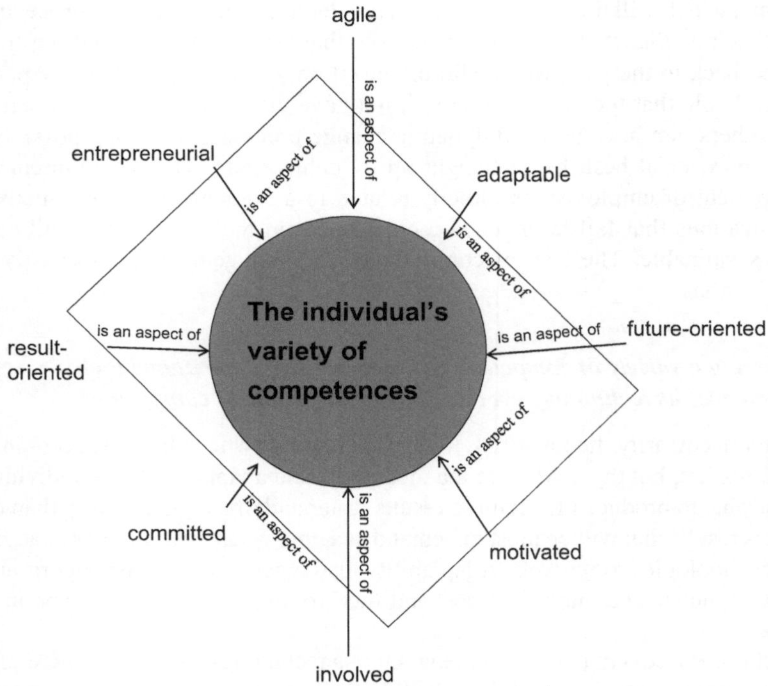

Figure 2.13 Variety of competences

will be the most likely to succeed. The creation of cross-functional teams is one way of implementing 'the Medici effect'. It is at the intersection of knowledge and ideas that new ideas and innovations will develop, resulting in an 'ideas-fountain' throwing new ideas up into the air, testing them, and then selecting some of these, and trying them out in the market. The ideas that have the right of life in this market will become the innovations that one can live off in the future. The ideas that are developed will be related to the goals of the organization. Therefore, it is crucial to develop those ideas which can become part of the organization's future. How can we make sure this happens in an organization? The answer lies in the knowledge we have that people will always reach for those goals that they are being measured against. Therefore, it is crucial to communicate to individual employees why they are being measured, how they are measured, what is measured and the consequences this process will have for the employee. For example one consequence could be that a team that produces an innovation that the market demands will receive a share of the profits the innovation creates for the business or organization.

We have illustrated the input and output of cross-functional teams in Figure 2.14.

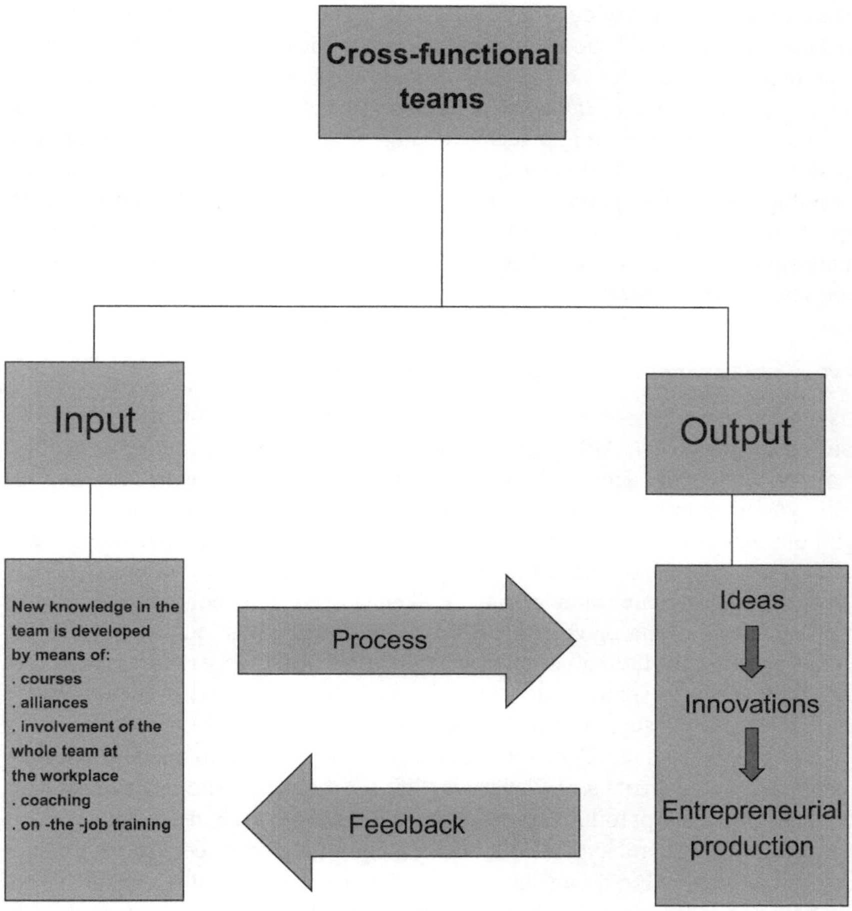

Figure 2.14 Cross-functional teams

Supporting and participating in scenario teams

Scenario thinking is a planning method used by organizations when preparing for the future. Of course, the various envisioned scenarios do not intend to precisely predict the future – this is not their purpose. The point is to prepare the organization for possible future situations, whatever these may happen to be. Scenario teams should be composed according to a diversity principle that takes age, gender, culture, ethnicity, knowledge background, methodological perspective, and so on, into account. In terms of age composition, the following generations should be included in these teams: Z-generation (20–25 +), Millennials (26–37), Gen X (38–56 +) and Boomers (55–75 +) (Meister & Mulcahy, 2017: 140).[20]

Change is not only something that these scenario teams need to focus on; it is a decisive factor for surviving as an organization. Those who are not on board with this basic premise should not be part of the team or the organization. Byron Reese, in the first sentence of his book, *The Fourth Age: Smart Robots, Conscious Computers, and the Future of Humanity*, states that 'The most distinctive characteristic of the last century or so might seem to be the enormous amount of change that has occurred' (2018: 1). However, human emotions have not changed, but new technology will affect people's emotions in different ways with regard to their expectations, hopes, dreams and fears of what is to come in the future. Scenario teams should seek to reduce fears and increase hopes of something better for everyone in the organization.

Becoming the change you want to see in the organization

It is not the strongest or the most intelligent that survives but the most adaptable, states Darwin's theory. Although Darwin's theory focuses on adapting to change, it says nothing about actually bringing about changes, to be precise, creating the future you want to be part of. Both Karl Weick (1979) and Russell Ackoff (1981) point out that those who want to achieve success should 'create the change they want to see', or in the words of Ackoff, 'plan or be planned for'. The one who only adapts to his or her environment may be likened to a chameleon that adapts to its environment by changing colour. This may be an admirable quality in a reptile, but not in a human. It is rather the case that we admire others who use their creative skills to change reality into something new. In this context, it should be said that few people will support change, if they do not know which consequences this will have for themselves. Therefore, it is only those people who manage to implement changes and create a new everyday life for the many who achieve success, not those who attempt to implement changes but fail to reach their goal.

The companies that have been in business for a long time seem to have something in common.[21] First, they are able to adapt to changes in the outside world, which we can term one of the Darwinian postulates. Second, they focus especially on creating innovations, i.e. they are actively part of the world in which they operate. Third, they are founded on and follow key values for which they stand and to which they are committed. Fourth, they give employees the opportunity to create the business they want to work in, i.e. they give the employees the opportunity to be job-activists. Fifth, they create the future that others will have to adapt to. Sixth, employees are given the opportunity to work on what they are passionate about and are good at, and that will make a difference.

We have illustrated how to become the change you want to see in the organization in Figure 2.15.

Theoretical points

Japan is the first country in the world where as many as one-third of the population around 2020 are over the age of 65. In the near future, it is highly probable

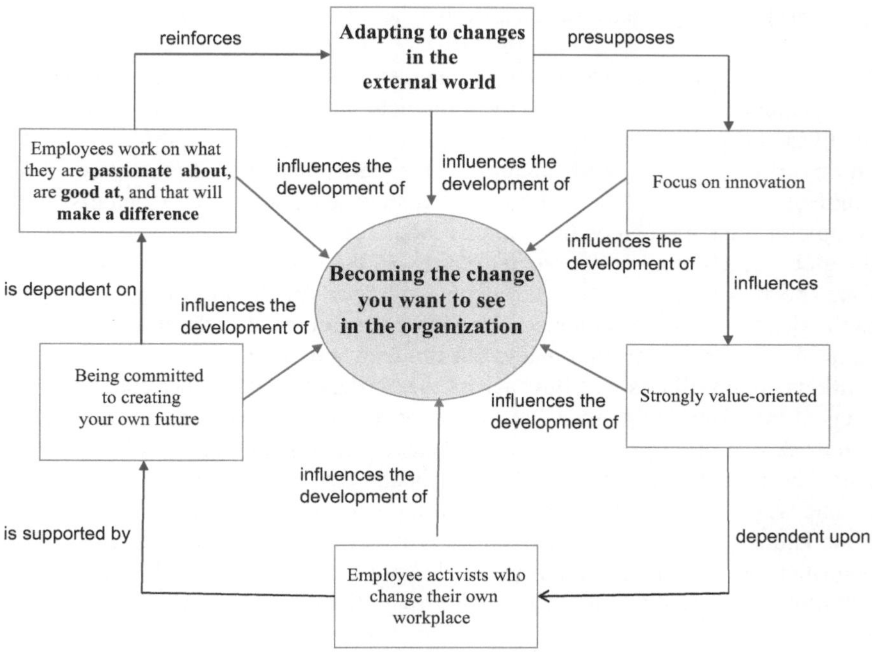

Figure 2.15 Becoming the change you want to see in the organization

that the whole of the Western world will follow this trend. To cling to a mid-twentieth century mindset, while this development is unfolding is, to put it mildly, like sticking your head in the sand. In the not-too-distant future, when the average lifespan will probably increase to around 90 years in the developed world, society's cohesive force will be threatened if one clings to the thinking associated with a twentieth century industrial logic. In the present, and more so in the future, not everyone is tired and worn out simply because they have passed the age of 70. Some 70-year-olds are perhaps even more creative and productive than those around 30–40 years. Of course, there are also 70-year-olds who are 'worn out' and no longer productive, but this is also the case among some 30–40-year-olds. Around 2050, it is estimated that approximately 40 per cent of the population in Japan will be over 65 (Ross, 2016: 15). The rest of the OECD area will quickly follow suit. In the future, there will not be enough people of caregiving age to take care of an aging population. To tackle these developments, the industrial logic of the twentieth century will no longer be adequate. New technology, such as artificial intelligence and intelligent robots will make a difference, but this will not be enough. Societies in the OECD area need to be organized in a different way than during the Industrial Age to meet the challenges of aging populations and falling birth rates.

Proposition: People should not be deprived of work because they have reached a specific age, because this prevents them from contributing to society.

New technological innovations have changed the lives of many people. However, the bottom line is that most technological innovations may have improved the lives of the rich, while the poor have had limited access, and thus the expectations of a good life. With increasing inequality and the current huge environmental challenge, this will have to change, or else social 'tsunamis' will completely change society. Innovations should be accessible to everyone around the globe, and not only to the richer regions of the world. This is a social necessity. The alternative is millions of people trying to find happiness by migrating to the richer, developed countries. It may be possible to stop the migration with some form of gunboat diplomacy, but the dam will sooner or later burst, and millions upon millions will flow across the borders into the richer countries. To prevent this from happening, the implementation of innovations in the poorer countries will provide self-help. For instance, the implementation of 'Marshall plans' in the poorer regions of Africa, Asia and Central and South America will be one way of furthering economic development in these regions. In addition, establishing technology and economics universities in these regions could also contribute to furthering economic development. Those who enrol in these universities would receive tuition funded through the various Marshall plans.

Proposition: Implement '100 Marshall plans' in Africa, Asia and Central and South America, because this will kick-start the economy in these areas and prevent economic migration.

A crucial change competence will be to have a purpose with what one is doing, as well as a passion about doing it. An important purpose in all change transformations is to mean something to others, that is be the difference that really makes a difference to others. Developing one's competence so that it is linked to one's passion and commitment will ensure the success of the individual and the business. However, this is only half of what is required in a change process. Commitment and passion may be hampered when societies and organizations go through great changes. The first reaction is often to oppose changes. This is where it is important to understand the purpose of the necessity of changes, and the purpose and importance of what one is doing. If one understands why change is needed, it is also possible to live with having less passion and dedication. However, if one is able to relate the two elements, passion and purpose, to each other, then one will ensure success (Hansen, 2018: 87–112).

Proposition: The greater the passion, commitment and purpose of what you are doing, the greater the probability a change project will be successful.

The leader who wants to implement changes and at the same time get results after the change has become a reality should have knowledge of the simple strategies that can motivate employees, such as the fact that employees appreciate being 'seen'. In other words, if the leader is able to positively influence employees during the change process, then this will be what the employees remember long after the change process has been completed.

> Proposition: If employees are left with a positive experience after a completed change process, it will be more probable that the organization and its employees will be successful.

In addition to the importance of commitment and passion, and positively experiencing change processes, to steer the change project safely into harbour, it is crucial that both the leader and employees possess perseverance (Duckworth, 2017).

As organizations become less silo-organized and more cross-functional in their work processes, the more this will affect the change competence of leaders and employees. As mentioned previously, creativity and innovation increase when businesses organize so that more areas of expertise come into contact with each other (Johansson, 2004). However, we know less about the change competence this requires of leaders and employees. What we do know though is that the leaders and employees who can work across competence areas in relation to making decisions, also achieve the greatest success for themselves and the business (Hansen, 2018: 119). Those who have the greatest influence to bring about change are also the people who can engage others emotionally (Berger, 2016).

> Proposition: The likelihood of a change process being successful is great if, in addition to dedication and perseverance, the importance of emotional engagement regarding the positive outcome of the change project is also considered.

Practical utility

The working environment will affect the performance of any business or organization. Based on this statement, the organization will need the necessary competence to improve the working environment (Model I). However, if one believes that the model should be more complex, that is that the performance also affects the working environment, then one will need to work according to an interactive or circular model (Model II). If the organization uses this model, then it will not only be competence on how to improve the working environment that will be needed, but competence related to how performance can be improved regardless of the working environment. It is conceivable that new technology, e.g. artificial intelligence and intelligent robots, will positively affect organizational performance. If one uses Model II as a starting point for one's thinking, then other types of competences will also be required than if one uses Model I as a starting point.

The point of this brief reflection is to point out that in all change projects, it is important to clarify which models are used as the starting point for one's thinking.

If you do not clarify the thinking that underlies change projects, they will very probably not succeed, because one will not have the necessary competence to complete the change project.

The practical implication of this reflection is that the models and thinking a project uses should be explicit, as this will make the project transparent, improving the chances of success. When the rate of change is high, such as it will be during the transition from the Third to the Fourth Industrial Revolution, it may not be appropriate to use either Model I or Model II as the basis for one's thinking in the change project; or a Model III, which integrates Model I and Model II. In this context, the leadership will need to reflect on what will be the most appropriate model to use, as the basis for their thinking in relation to the change project.

The changes that occur in the transition to the Fourth Industrial Revolution will determine these action dispositions. As we have described in the beginning of this chapter, all communication will be digitized. This concerns the transition from analogue thinking to digital thinking. As we have discussed earlier, in practice this will concern a transition from basic competences related to reading, writing and arithmetic, to competences based on coding, algorithms and artificial intelligence. It is also important during the process of organizational change that employees do not feel that the change model is being forced on them. This may sound like a paradox, and perhaps it is – the fact that the management imposes a change model on the employees, but that the employees do not perceive the change model as being forced upon them. Let us digress a little, before we address this paradox. If a decision is viewed as being the right decision, that is a rational and logical decision that people should follow, will such a decision be perceived as something that is forced on them from above? In such a context, it is highly probable that the decision will only be perceived as common sense. In other words, in such a situation, a decision that one is obliged to follow will be accepted as something that is necessary – a social mechanism that promotes one's own interests and which is also aimed at achieving a common goal.

In the transition to the Fourth Industrial Revolution, what will one be obliged to follow, but which will not be perceived as such? In short, the internalization of new technology will be perceived as a necessity. If, as many believe, technology and knowledge of technology can help individuals, organizations and societies to achieve a better life, then the frameworks related to technology will be perceived as necessary preconditions for increasing the well-being for most people. This constitutes a type of internalization of the necessity of new technology. Those who have this positive perception of technology will not perceive change projects related to technology as something that is forced upon them or as an abuse of power, but as a rational and appropriate course of action. This phenomenon is similar to the way people positively and subjectively perceive various philosophical systems, economic ideologies, religious beliefs and so on, without considering them objectively. If one perceives something as right, then it becomes right in its practical consequences, regardless of whether it is enforced on them as part of the implementation of an ideology.

When, not if, we have developed intelligent robots that can diagnose, medicate and perform surgical procedures, then we will have accepted this technology as a beneficial technology, because we know it is better than any alternative. We accept technology because it is rational and in our own interests, not because we are more attracted to technology than to human relationships. We adapt to new situations because it serves our best interests.

Thus, the transition from analogue thinking to digital thinking has in it an element of compulsion, the obligation of implementing new technology that most people will perceive as necessary and beneficial. However, it is crucial that we not only understand codes that govern this new technology, but that we are able to develop and apply them if we are going to achieve success in the Fourth Industrial Revolution.

The most important change in terms of competence at the beginning of the Fourth Industrial Revolution is that competence will be transferred from humans to the technological systems that humans have developed, i.e. intelligent robots, intelligent algorithms and artificial intelligence. For instance, today, it is no longer a bank employee who decides whether a loan applicant should be granted a loan, but an algorithm that assesses the application and reaches a decision in a nanosecond. There is much to object to regarding such a decision-making process. However, to make intelligent objections, one needs to have some expertise in algorithms. Although one may have such expertise, the probability that such decision processes will be criticized is small, because algorithms are viewed as necessary technological mechanisms that are to everybody's benefit. The circle is thus closed: if you are going to criticize, you should have competence, and if you have the competence, it is improbable that you will criticize the process.

Sub-conclusion

In this section, we have examined the following question: in what ways will change competence be in demand in the Fourth Industrial Revolution?

The short answer can be formulated in the following six points related to competence:

1 Process organization. The individual and the system should be aware that the old way of organizing knowledge, positions and power is now outdated. Competence should be organized so that it continuously responds to customers' demands, which results in the greatest productivity for the organization.
2 To manage such an organization, three areas of competence will be crucial: knowledge and the practical application of coding, artificial intelligence and intelligent algorithms.
3 Process organization and the new areas of competence require insight into what we term here 'hidden knowledge'. This is the domain of knowledge from which creativity and innovation emerge.

4 To cope with the new requirements, both in terms of a new way of organizing companies, organizations and other social systems, as well as the specific competence related to coding, artificial intelligence and intelligent algorithms, it will be important that the individual and the system have sufficient variation of competences. In other words, the system must at all times be able to change in step with the changes in the external world. This is based on the 'Law of Requisite Variety'.
5 The practical organization that will satisfy the four points previously mentioned will be cross-functional teams. These teams will be able to develop creativity and innovation better than other ways of organizing at the micro-level, because, as a general rule, creativity and innovation emerge where areas of knowledge overlap and collide with each other.
6 In the five points mentioned, we have oriented ourselves at the organizational and team level. In this last point, the focus is on the individuals in the organization. Every individual in the organization should seek to become the change he or she wants to see in the organization.

The six points related to the change competence that will be in demand in the Fourth Industrial Revolution are illustrated in Figure 2.16.

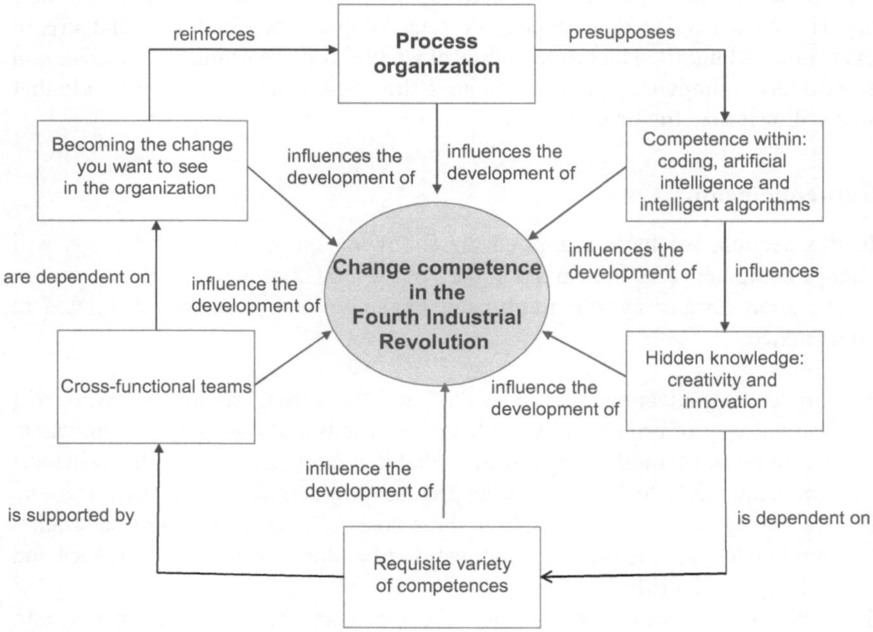

Figure 2.16 The change competence that will be in demand in the Fourth Industrial Revolution

Main conclusion

The question we have investigated in this chapter is as follows: what specific and general competences will be in demand in the Fourth Industrial Revolution? We have discussed four areas in relation to this question. These areas are:

1 Communication
2 Creativity
3 Collaboration
4 Change

The impact that those areas will have concerns everyone who is interested in questions relating to future competences. Of course, we cannot say precisely what impact these four areas will have, either individually or in combination. On the one hand, we can say that the Fourth Industrial Revolution will eradicate many of the ideas engrained in us by industrial logic. On the other hand, there is a time lag from the time one realizes that the new logic is relevant, until one lets go of the old logic. We have seen this throughout history, and there is nothing to suggest that things will be different this time. We will see this time lag in the educational sector, in democracy, in how we organize ourselves, how we exercise leadership etc. On the other hand, as a general rule, people who act according to this new logic will have an advantage over people who hold onto the old logic for too long. What happened between Kodak and Instagram is a good example of this. In the same way, the emergence of Amazon, Google and Facebook and so on offers clear evidence that businesses that base their business models on the new logic will be successful. This will also apply at a societal level, at a team level, and right down to the individual level. Becoming the change that one wishes to see in an organization is intended as an action imperative, not as a philosophical reflection or a theoretical hypothesis. If one makes this into an action imperative, then it will change how one relates to other people. It will have consequences both for organization and for leadership, and also for the competences that are required at a time when nothing is stable and it is difficult to find solid ground beneath one's own reflections. Such an action imperative will also influence our moral choices.

The old way of thinking, in which industrial logic has been a sustaining force, has served us well economically, technologically, politically, socially and even individually. Accordingly, we won't be able to adapt to a new way of thinking overnight. We will give ourselves some security by keeping a little of the old ways of thinking when the new ways are introduced. This will conserve the old system but will also bring a necessary element of stability into the change processes. In the Fourth Industrial Revolution, we will put question marks against what it means to produce, distribute and consume, and what are reasonable ways for nations and systems to cooperate. There are two key underlying questions. One relates to the consequences of the environmental threat. The other relates to the consequences of the economic inequality that is simply increasing at the threshold of the Fourth Industrial Revolution. In the future, production and distribution, as well as consumption, will be completely different from the industrial era. This does not mean that industrial production will fall, however. Quite the opposite. It simply means that things will be produced and organized in different ways than was the case previously. Competence profiles will not change only at an individual level. Competences will change both in terms of focus and locality. While industrial production took place in Western countries, there is much to suggest that these new technological competences will be focused in Asia, more specifically China and India.

Through the whole era of industrial logic, a key question has been how much the state should get involved in production, competence development, the individual's welfare and so on. Under the new logic, this question will become less important, even though it is precisely this phenomenon that we are now seeing in China. The key question in the Fourth Industrial Revolution will not be about

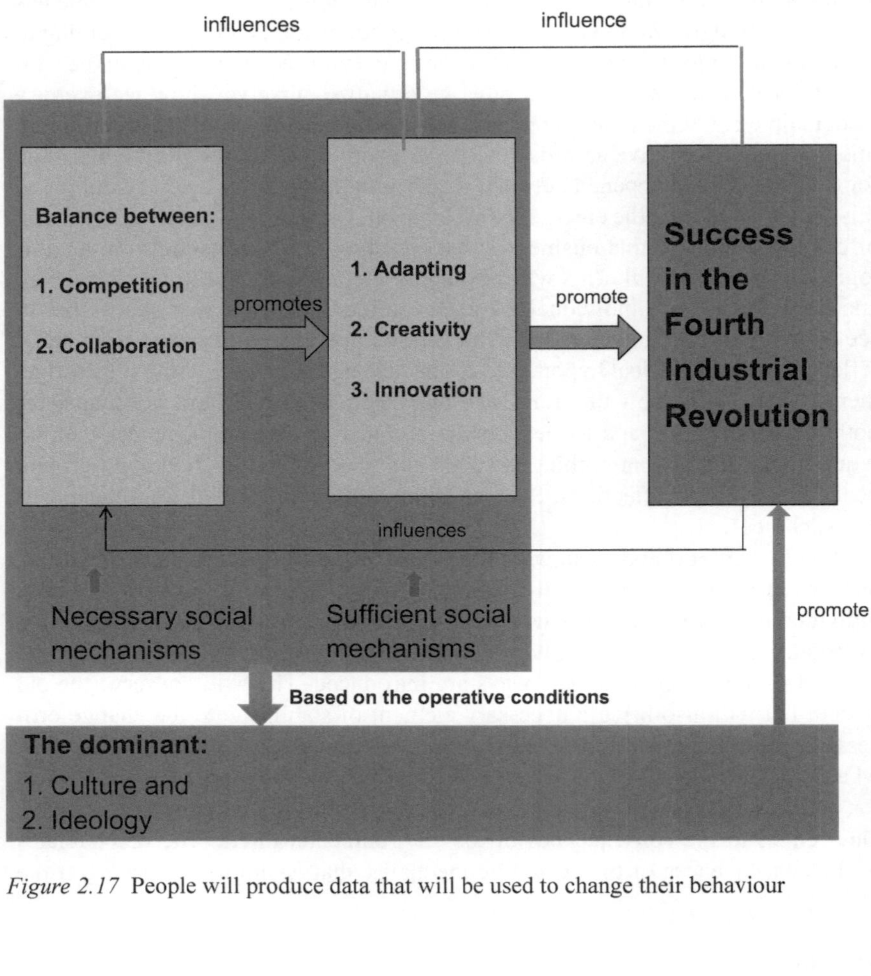

Figure 2.17 People will produce data that will be used to change their behaviour

the role of the state, but how much we should allow ourselves to be controlled by the digitization processes that are already underway and that will dominate all systems in the Fourth Industrial Revolution.

The specific and general competences that will be in focus in the future can be illustrated through people's transactions in the digital marketplace. Everyone's transactions will be extracted, analyzed, categorized, typologized and made into saleable data. We have outlined this trend in Figure 2.17. Figure 2.17 also illustrates how each one of us will become a producer of the data that will be used to influence our behaviour.

Notes

1 Informats are robots that are linked via global networks.
2 See for example Reese (2018: ix), regarding optimistic and pessimistic views of how artificial intelligence may affect people's lives in the future.
3 www.theregister.co.uk/2015/03/19/andrew_ng_baidu_ai/
4 https://en.wikipedia.org/wiki/Luddite
5 This is not an independent citation, but a paraphrase of comments in the Danish newspaper *Politikken*.
6 While automation will be implemented in the production aspect of businesses, informatization will be implemented in the administrative aspect of businesses.
7 Adam Smith in *The Wealth of Nations* (1776). Karl Marx in *The Communist Manifesto* (1988).
8 https://en.wikipedia.org/wiki/Pandora%27s_box
9 By informatization we mean the automation of information processes. We distinguish here between automatization and informatization in order to differentiate between infrastructure, which relates to the thinking of the industrial society, and infostructure, which relates to the thinking of the knowledge and innovation economy.
10 These acronyms are used by the future researcher Amy Webb in her 2019 report, page 11 (https://futuretodayinstitute.com/2019-tech-trends/).
11 (https://futuretodayinstitute.com/2019-tech-trends/)
12 https://en.wikipedia.org/wiki/Luddite
13 We use the expression 'units of time' because of the difficulty in predicting exactly how long this will take – as it could be seconds, minutes or days.
14 This is not linked to Kant's categorical imperative or to the teachings of the Sermon on the Mount.
15 *Jyllandsposten* (a Danish newspaper) 26 March 2019, page 28 (Employment Section).
16 Ibid.
17 This is just a rough estimate; the point is, though, that companies and organizations often required that employees live within travelling distance of their place of work.
18 Reese (2018), Susskind (2015), Zuboff (2019), Johannessen (2020, 2020a), Chace (2016), Avent (2017).
19 An implosion is something that collapses violently inward, as contrasted with an explosion that has a violent outward force. Implosions are often associated with black holes – the implosions of massive stars into black holes. Black holes have extreme gravitational force sucking material into their core, becoming very small by cosmic standards.
20 Calculated from 2019.
21 This insight is drawn from many different sources, both empirical and theoretical. The most important are Weick (1979), Ackoff (1981), Meister and Mulcahy (2017), Bateson (1972), Amabile (1996), Avent (2017), Johansson (2004), Reese (2018) et al.

References

Ackoff, R.L. (1981). *Creating the corporate future: Plan or be planned for*, John Wiley & Sons, New York.

Amabile, T. (1996). *The social psychology of creativity*, Westview Press, New York.

Aristotle. (2000). *Politics*, Penguin, London.

Ashby, W.R. (1956). *An introduction to cybernetics*, Chapman & Hall LTD, New York.

Avent, R. (2017). *The wealth of humans: Work and its absence in the twenty-first century*, Penguin, London.

Axelrod, R. & Hamilton, W.D. (1981). The evolution of cooperation, *Science*, 211: 1390–1396.

Bateson, G. (1972). *Steps to an ecology of mind*, Ballantine Books, New York.

Baumeister, R.F. & Leary, M.R. (1995). The need to belong: Desire for interpersonal attachments as a fundamental human motivation, *Psychological Bulletin*, 117:487–527.

Benhabib, S. (2004). *The rights of others: Aliens, residents and citizens*, Cambridge University Press, Cambridge.

Benhabib, S. (2016). *The claims of culture: Equality and diversity in the global era*, Princeton University Press, Princeton.

Berg, J.M.; Dutton, J.E. & Wrzesniewski, A. (2008). *What is job crafting and why does it matter*? Michigan University. http://positiveorgs.bus.umich.edu/wp-content/uploads/What-is-Job-Crafting-and-Why-Does-it-Matter1.pdf

Berger, J. (2016). *Contagious: Why things catch on*, Simon & Schuster, New York.

Boone, C.; Declerck, C.H. & Suetens, S. (2008). Subtle social cues, explicit incentives and cooperation in social dilemmas, *Evolution and Human Behavior*, 29:179–188.

Boutrup, C. (2018). *Den store tech revolution: Sådan former Kina vores fremtid*, People's Press, København.

Bowles, S. & Gintis, H. (2003). Origins of human cooperation, in Hammerstein, P. (Ed.). *Genetic and cultural evolution of cooperation*, MIT Press, Cambridge, MA. Pp. 429–443.

Bowles, S. & Gintis, H. (2011). *A cooperative species: Human reciprocity and its evolution*, Princeton University Press, Princeton, NJ.

Bunge, M. (1990). Boudon on anti-realism in social studies, in Weingartner, P. & Dorn, G.J.W. (Eds.). *Studies on Mario Bunge's treatise*, Rodopi, Amsterdam. Pp. 613–616.

Burt, R. (1995). *Structural Holes: The social structure of competition*, Harvard University Press, Cambridge, MA.

Burton, R. (2011). Pathological certitude, in Oakley, B. (Ed.). *Pathological altruism*, Oxford University Press, Oxford. Pp. 131–137.

Caporael, L.R.; Dawes, R.M.; Orbell, J.M. & Vandekragt, A.J.C. (1989). Selfishness examined – cooperation in the absence of egoistic incentives, *Behavioral and Brain Sciences*, 12:683–699.

Caruso, E.M.; Epley, N. & Bazerman, M.H. (2006). The costs and benefits of undoing egocentric responsibility assessments in groups, *Journal of Personality and Social Psychology*, 91:857–871.

Chace, C. (2016). *The economic singularity: Artificial intelligence and the death of capitalism*, Three CS Publishing, New York.

Chatterjee, A. & Hambrick, D.C. (2007). It's all about me: Narcissistic chief executive officers and their effect on company strategy and performance, *Administrative Science Quarterly*, 52:351–386.

Cherry, S. (2010). *Transforming behaviour*, Routledge, London.

Chiao, J.Y. & Cheon, B.K. (2010). The weirdest brains in the world, *Behavioral and Brain Sciences*, 33:88–90.

Collins, J. (2009). *Good to great: Why some companies make the leap . . . and others don't*, Random House Business, New York.

Colvin, G. (2016). *Talents are overrated: What really separates world class performers from everybody else*, Nicolas Brealey Publishing, New York.

Csikszentmihalyi, M. (2016). *The psychology of discovery and invention*, Harper Perennial, New York.

Dahrendorf, R. (1973). *Homo sociologicus*, Routledge and Kegan Paul, London.

Darley, J.M. & Latané, B. (1968). Bystander intervention in emergencies: Diffusion of responsibility, *Journal of Personality Social Psychology*, 8:377–383.

Declerck, C.; Boone, C. & Emonds, G. (2013). When do people cooperate in social dilemmas? A review on the neuroeconomics of prosocial decision-making, *Brain & Cognition*, 81:95–117.

Diamond, J. (2013). *The world until yesterday: What can we learn from traditional societies?*, Allen Lane, London.

Duckworth, A. (2017). *Grit: Why passion and resilience are the secrets to success*, Vermilion, New York.

Eden, D. (1990). Pygmalion without interpersonal contrast effects: Whole group gain from raising manager expectations, *Journal of Applied Psychology*, 75:394–398.

Eden, D. (2003). Self-fulfilling prophecies in organizations, in Greenberg, J. (Ed.). *Organizational behavior: State of the science*, Erlbaum, NJ. Pp. 91–122.

Edmondson, A. (1996). Learning from mistakes is easier said than done: Group and organizational influences on the detection and correction of human error, *Journal of Applied Behavioral Science*, 32:5–28.

Edmondson, A. (1999). Psychological safety and learning behavior in work teams, *Administrative Science Quarterly*, 44:350–383.

Eugene, K. & Glomb, T.M. (2010). Get smarty pants: Cognitive ability, personality and victimization, *Journal of Applied Psychology*, 95:889–901.

Fiske, T. (2004). *Social beings: A core motives in social psychology*, Wiley, Hoboken, NJ.

Frank, R.H. (2012). *The Darwin economy: Liberty, competition, and the common good*, Princeton University Press, Princeton.

Gaskarth, J. (Ed.). (2015). *China, India and the future of international society*, Rowman & Littlefield, London.

Gladwell, M. (2009). *Outliers: The story of success*, Penguin, London.

Grant, A.M. (2014). *Give and take: Why helping others drives our success*, W&N, New York.

Grant, A.M. & Berry, J. (2011). The necessity of others is the mother of invention: Intrinsic and prosocial motivation, perspective-taking and creativity, *Academy of Management Journal*, 54:73–96.

Grant, A.M.; Parker, S. & Collins, C. (2009). Getting credit for proactive behavior: Supervisor reactions depend on what you value and how you feel, *Personnel Psychology*, 62:31–55

Groysberg, B.; Lee, L.E. & Nanda, A. (2008). Can they take it with them? The portability of star knowledge workers performance, *Management Science*, 54:1213–1230.

Hansen, M.T. (2018). *Great at work: How top performers do less, work better and achieve more*, Simon & Schuster, New York.

Harari, Y.N. (2015). *Sapiens: A brief history of humankind*, Vintage, New York.

Hardy, C.L. & Van Vugt, M. (2006). Nice guys finish first: The competitive altruism hypothesis, *Personality and Social Psychology Bulletin*, 32:1402–1413.

Huckman, R. & Pisano, G. (2006). The firm specificity of individual performance: Evidence from cardiac surgery, *Management Science*, 52:473–488.

Johannessen, J.-A. (2018). *Innovations leads to economic crises: Explaining the bubble economy*, Palgrave, London.

Johannessen, J.-A. (2019a). *The emergence of the Fourth Industrial Revolution: An historical introduction to knowledge management and the innovation economy*, Emerald, London.

Johannessen, J.-A. (2019b). *Automation, capitalism and the end of the middle class*, Routledge, London.

Johannessen, J.-A. (2020a). *Singularity innovation*, Routledge, London.

Johannessen, J.-A. (2020b). *What is wrong with capitalism*? Verso, London.

Johannessen, J.-A. (2020c). *Building the innovation economy*, Routledge, London.

Johannessen, J.-A. (2021). *Artificial intelligence, intelligent robots and ethics: An intelligent ethical robot communicating about morals with an unethical human being*, Routledge, London.

Johannessen, J.-A. (2022). *Intelligent robots: Consciousness and creativity*, Routledge, London.

Johannessen, J.-A.; Olsen, B. & Lumpkin, G.T. (2001). Innovation as newness: What is new, how new, and new to whom, *European Journal of Innovation Management*, 4(1):20–31.

Johannessen, J.-A. & Stokvik, H. (2018). *Evidence-based innovation management: Creating entrepreneurship and innovation in organizations*, Emerald, London.

Johansson, F. (2004). *The Medici effect: Breakthrough insights at the intersection of ideas, concepts & cultures*, Harvard Business School Press, Boston.

Johnson, D.W. & Johnson, R.T. (1989). *Cooperation and competition: Theory and research*, Interaction Book, Edina, MN.

Kim, W.C. & Mauborgne, R. (2015). *Blue ocean strategy: How to create uncontested market space and make the competition irrelevant*, Harvard Business Review, Boston.

Kohn, A. (1992). Cooperation: What it means and doesn't mean, in Combs, A. (Ed.). *Cooperation*, Gordon and Breach, New York. Pp. 3–11.

Kurzweil, R. (2005). *The singularity is near: When humans transcend biology*, Penguin, London.

Kurzweil, R. (2008). *The age of spiritual machines: When computers exceed human intelligence*, Penguin, London.

Lagercrantz, D. (2000). *Håkan Lens: Ett svensk geni*, Bokførlaget DN, Stockholm.

Latané, B. & Darley, J.M. (1970). *The unresponsive bystander: Why doesn't he help*? Appleton, New York.

Marx, K. (1988). *The Communist Manifesto*, W.W. Norton, London.

McCall, M. (1995). Orientation, outcome, and other-serving attributions, *Basic and Applied Social Psychology*, 17:49–64.

McNatt, D.B. (2000). Ancient Pygmalion joins contemporary management: A meta-analysis of the result, *Journal of Applied Psychology*, 85:314–322.

Meister, J.C. & Mulcahy, K.J. (2017). *The future workplace experience: 10 rules for mastering disruption in recruiting and engaging employees*, McGraw Hill, New York.

Nadler, A.; Ellis, A. & Bar, I. (2003). To seek or not to seek: The relationship between help seeking and job performance evaluations as moderated by task-relevant expertise, *Journal of Applied Social Psychology*, 33:91–109.

Nevicka, B.; Femke, S.; Velden, T.; de Hoogh, A.H.B. & Van Vianen, E.M. (2011). Reality at odds with perception: Narcissistic leaders and group performance, *Psychological Science*, 22:1259–1264.

Nordgren, L.F.; McDonnell, M.-H.M. & Loewenstein, L.F. (2011). What constitutes torture? Psychological impediments to an objective evaluation of enhanced interrogation tactics, *Psychological Science*, 22:689–694.

Nowak, M.A. & Highfield, R. (2011). *SuperCooperators: Altruism, evolution and why we need each other to succeed*, Free Press, New York.

Nowak, M.A. & Sigmund, K. (1998). Evolution and indirect reciprocity by image scoring, *Nature*, 393:573–577.

Obstfeld, D. (2005). Social networks, the tertius iungens orientation, and involvement in innovation, *Administrative Science Quarterly*, 50:100–130.

Oshinsky, D. (2005). *Polio: An American story*, Oxford University Press, New York.

Porter, M.E. (1986). *Competition in global industries*, Harvard Business Review Press, Boston.

Pruit, D.G. & Kimmel, M.J. (1977). Twenty years of experimental gaming: Critique, synthesis and suggestions for the future, *Annual Review of Psychology*, 28:363–392.

Reese, B. (2018). *The fourth age, smart robots, conscious computers, and the future of humanity*, Artria Books, London.

Reis, H.T. & Gable, S.L. (2003). Toward a positive psychology of relationships, in Keys, C.L.M. & Haidt, J. (Eds.). *Flourishing: Positive Psychology and the life well-lived*, American Psychological Association, Washington, DC. Pp. 129–159.

Richerson, P.; Baldini, R.; Bell, A.; Demps, K.; Frost, K.; Hillis, V. & Zefferman, M. (2016). Cultural group selection plays an essential role in explaining human cooperation: A sketch of the evidence, *Behavioral and Brain Sciences*, 39. www.cambridge.org/core/journals/behavioral-and-brainsciences/article/div-classtitlecultural-group-selection-plays-an-essential-role-in-explaining-human-cooperation-a-sketch-of-the-evidencediv/638ED0187A9727D9D327661A91DE0759

Ross, A. (2016). *The industries of the future*, Simon & Schuster, New York.

Ross, M. & Sicoly, F. (1979). Egocentric biases in availability and attribution, *Journal of Personality and Social Psychology*, 37:322–336.

Smith, A. (1776). *An inquiry into the nature and causes of the wealth of nations*, W. Strahan and Cadell, London.

Susskind, J. (2018). *Future politics: Living together in a world transformed by tech*, Oxford University Press, Oxford.

Uzzi, B. & Dunlap, S. (2005). How to build your network, *Harvard Business Review*, December: 53–60.

Vonk, R. (1998). The slime effect: Suspicion and dislike of likable behavior towards superiors, *Journal of Personality and Social Psychology*, 74:849–864.

Weick, K. (1979). *The social psychology of organizing*, McGraw Hill, New York.

Willer, R. (2009). Groups reward individual sacrifice: The status solution to the collective action problem, *American Sociological Review*, 74:23–43.

Zuboff, S. (2019). *The age of surveillance capitalism*, Profile Books, New York.

3 Human competences

Key points in the chapter

- *Democracy and knowledge*: Artificial intelligence will lead to the democratization of knowledge.
- *The productivity paradox*: The greater the growth of productivity in the health-care sector, the more we can use the social and emotional competences of health-care workers.
- *Double competence*: At the threshold of the Fourth Industrial Revolution, creativity and innovation will be dependent on contextual familiarity and double competence.[1]
- *Avoiding perspectival blindness*: Having the ability to adopt another person's perspective is a social and emotional competence that will be in demand in the Fourth Industrial Revolution.
- *Transfer of decision-making*: We are on the threshold of a new cultural dividing line: until singularity occurs, the most important decisions will be taken by humans. After singularity, the most important decisions will be taken by intelligent robots.
- *Algorithmic capitalism*: A new kind of capitalism is being developed, which will profit from knowledge about our future behaviour.
- *Emotional incompetence*: An 'averted face' expresses a lack of empathy. As leaders of organizations, 'social eunuchs' are on a par with psychopaths: they smile at their superiors, while behaving destructively towards their subordinates ('sucking up and kicking down').
- *Creativity*: To trigger creativity and commitment, a leader should possess well-developed social and emotional competences that encourage people to engage with and participate in processes.
- *Leader syndrome*: This refers to situations in which leaders and leadership teams exist in an informational vacuum, such that they do not receive necessary information about what is happening in their organizations.
- *The intelligent robot as a mythological being*: Intelligent robots are emerging as the new heroes because they are fulfilling a desire for empathy and social intimacy. We might think of intelligent robots as representing a reincarnation of the opportunities we gained through the discovery of fire: a discovery that we have taken care of poorly, progressing from fire to the atomic bombs detonated

over Nagasaki and Hiroshima. The intelligent robot is the new superhero of contemporary mythology. It is more intelligent than humans and can help us, just as fire helped people survive darkness and cold in the past. Humans need help, and so the gods send help in the strangest forms: as ravens (Greek mythology), as whales (Christian religion), as fire, as hope, as love, and now as a 'superhero' – the intelligent robot – that is more intelligent than humans. When humans first discovered fire, they had to learn to control it, harness and fear it, so as to avoid injury. Intelligent robots may be said to have similarities to fire: they are beneficial but may also prove to be harmful. We could also interpret the climate crisis as a mythological narrative, something that the gods have thrown at humans to get us to understand that we must learn to work together as a community in order to overcome a trial imposed by the gods. The intelligent robot may be viewed as a superhero sent by the gods to help us understand that we are here to solve problems together, by acting as a community that does not categorize people as *insiders* and *outsiders*. If we are to see the intelligent robot as the superhero of our times, then we also need to understand that the gods are simultaneously vengeful and loving. They gave us fire, but also punished Prometheus for all eternity because he brought fire to humanity. The gods are giving us the intelligent robot, but they may punish us with the full force of their wrath in various ways such as mass unemployment, and even worse by taking away all control from humans. Heroes in the history of mythology come in various forms, as is happening now, with the intelligent robot.

- *Personal cultural competence*: Cultural competence is a general abstract concept that is linked to norms and values. The concept of personal cultural competence is intended to make concrete the ways in which these norms and values are inherent in people who do something to be at one with these abstract principles. Personal cultural competence exists in bystander-antagonist situations. Personal cultural competence is influenced by the signals transmitted by cultural competence in general. These signals are received within a historical period and within a specific context. Our point in this context is simply that these signals are received by all of us, but only a few of us react to them. Clearly, the people who do react have a more highly developed personal cultural competence than the rest of us. They are more sensitive to these signals and they are more disposed to act in light of these signals. In other words, they are more willing to embody the precise nature of the change that they and many others wish to see in the world.
- *Cultural psychology*: Our early cultural influence is like an anchor that holds us to a fixed point in our upbringing; no matter how much we may drift away from the anchorage point, we are still held by the anchor chain. We can understand this anchor and anchor chain as the social mechanism that creates our identity.
- *Human competences*: The more technology fills our social spaces, the more important human competences will be. The reason is that the meaning and purpose of what we do is created in social relationships, where tools are at best a help to achieve this.

Introduction

Technology is a tool that facilitates work. However, we should also be aware that work:

- Gives meaning to people's lives.
- Creates social relationships, both in the workplace and in other spheres.
- Has created social and economic hierarchies throughout history (Harari, 2015).

In the past, technology has strengthened social and economic hierarchies (Avent, 2017). However, now that we are approaching the Fourth Industrial Revolution, where the new technology is characterized by the use of intelligent robots, artificial intelligence and intelligent algorithms, it is probable that changes are underway. These changes will appear in the areas we least expect. The trades and professions we thought were 'safe' will also be affected by this new technology. For instance, in trades and professions such as:

- Clerks, consultants and others in the banking and financial sector
- Drivers in the transport sector
- Cleaning personnel in the service sector
- Doctors, nurses and care workers in the health-care sector
- Teachers in the education sector
- Journalists in the media sector.

Changes in employment structure will occur not because the demand in those sectors will decrease. On the contrary, demand for jobs that require social competence, emotional competence, leadership skills and cultural competence in these sectors will increase, but so will the use of technology. Intelligent robots with special competence to care for the sick and elderly are already being rapidly developed, because of increased demand for care workers and technical aids due to aging populations (Reese, 2018). Robots are already being used to support cleaning personnel in large hotels and hospitals, as well as other places. Self-driving cars will soon become a reality, which will affect the demand for drivers in the transport sector.

A survey conducted in the US shows that approximately 47 per cent of all jobs will be subject to automation around the time singularity occurs, i.e. around 2045 (Avent, 2017; Johannessen, 2021b, 2022). However, this does not mean that unemployment will increase. Millions of new jobs will be also be created. This will occur within the technical professions needed to develop and maintain the intelligent robots and the technology that surrounds them. In addition, millions of jobs will be created that require social and emotional competence, as well as leadership and cultural competence.[2]

A situation in which technology replaces established work functions but also creates new employment opportunities within new and old areas of work is of course nothing new. This has been the main trend within the last 2,000 years when technological improvements have been introduced.[3]

Consequently, will there be anything to fear when technology will only streamline and increase production, and increase the need for human competences? In the same way that the low-cost countries took the jobs away from the industrial workers of the high-cost countries, such as in the case of Detroit's auto factories, turning the city into a ghost town, cheap labour in global capitalism may also threaten income levels in the West. Millions of new jobs will be created, but millions of jobs will also be automated. The bottom line is that the millions of new jobs will have lower salaries than Western workers are accustomed to. For capitalists, it doesn't matter if the demand that keeps their profits up is driven by the labour of workers from the US, Europe, China, India (or the rest of Asia), or from Africa. However, it is the Western workers who will be the losers in the Fourth Industrial Revolution, not the workers of, for example China.

Moreover, global capitalism will function in such a way that the new jobs within the area of human competence will face strong competition from areas of the world where wages and welfare benefits are far lower than in most Western countries.

Can the cultural competence of professionals really be undermined by intelligent robots? To answer this question, it is perhaps of interest to consider new developments within the profession of journalism. Many articles we read in the newspapers today are now being written using intelligent algorithms, so-called algorithmic journalism (Avent, 2017: 1–5). Intelligent algorithms have learnt journalism and can compete with the best within the profession. They can even, in a more subtle way than many journalists, influence the thoughts of the readers without the readers realizing that they are being influenced. In a few years' time, the cultural worker in a newspaper or other media may be an intelligent algorithm that is in contact with other intelligent algorithms around the world. This cluster of intelligent 'algorithmic journalists' will be able to extract the necessary data from our own data transactions, so that they will be able to predict our behaviour better than we can ourselves (Zuboff, 2019). This algorithmic capitalism does not benefit from our work as such, but rather from the knowledge of our future behaviour (Johannessen, 2021a). This suggests that cultural competence will also be subjected to major changes at the beginning of the Fourth Industrial Revolution. Moreover, the younger generation (18–25 years) today consume news differently than previous generations, reading much less print newspapers. They choose rather to consume news using news websites or social networks, often on mobile devices, accessing channels such as Facebook, Instagram, Twitter etc. The point in our context is that it is not only journalism that will be transferred to intelligent robots, but the entire production of news will be largely automated. This ongoing automation of parts of the cultural industry indicates that it is not only the jobs of workers in the transport sector, and the printing and newspaper industries that will be automated. Workers in the cultural sector will also discover that their jobs are being threatened more and more by the new automation and information technology.

In the future, most professions will be affected by the new technology, both in the training and in the exercise of the profession (Susskind & Susskind, 2015).

The most important transition will occur when artificial intelligence is used more widely in the professions. This will result in the competence that was previously only available to a few people will now become available to the majority. It might be said that artificial intelligence will come to democratize knowledge. However, this democratization will require that people have knowledge of how to apply knowledge. If people do not have the opportunity to gain knowledge of how AI works, how it can be developed, coded, applied, developed for use in various professions and implemented in practical contexts, then democracy may be severely hampered in the Fourth Industrial Revolution.

According to Daniel Susskind and Richard Susskind (2015: 1), the professions that will be affected by the new technology are 'doctors, lawyers, teachers, accountants, tax advisers, management consultants, architects, journalists, and the clergy (amongst others)'. We will go one step further and ask the question: what professions will not be affected by the new technology? The answer is simple. In the future, none of the professions will remain unaffected by artificial intelligence and intelligent robots; however, few people need to fear this technology, given that the governing authorities show a willingness to make sure the technology benefits most people. It is an erroneous assumption to believe that the professions will disappear, or that the people in these professions will become redundant. Instead, we will witness a transformation of the professions and an application of artificial intelligence in work functions. Human competences will be crucial if the new technology is to be fully utilized. The new technology will reinforce, not reduce, the need for human social competence, emotional competence, leadership skills and, not least, the many aspects and facets of cultural competence.

Everyone will be affected by the new technology. The elderly will be able to work longer if they have the desire, energy and ability to do so. Those who are disabled will have the opportunity to be included in working life, because technology will be able to reduce the threshold that previously prevented them from participating. However, we will have to get used to the fact that nothing will be stable anymore – everything will change. Those who do not succeed in the new age will be those who must have stability to do their work. In the Fourth Industrial Revolution, change will be the only thing that is stable and complexity will become the normal state of affairs. It should be said, and cannot be emphasized enough, that if the technological developments are not controlled so that they benefit most people, then many will feel that they are superfluous and that their personal identity is threatened. As a consequence, their lives will seem devoid of meaning, and society's cohesive strength will be diminished. Previously in our history, we have not had the same need for control of technological development that we have now on the threshold of the Fourth Industrial Revolution. The rationale is simple. In the near future, new technology will permeate the whole of society, affecting every aspect of our lives. This was not really the case during the first, second and third industrial revolutions, when the steam engine and the internal combustion engine significantly transformed society; in the near future, artificial intelligence, intelligent robots and intelligent algorithms will enable rapid progress but will also result in fundamental changes that will affect everyone, from the cradle to the grave. It is how this new situation will require human competences that we will examine in this chapter. By human competences, we mean here: social competence, emotional competence, leadership competence and cultural competence.

Human competences may of course be categorized in other ways, but this is how we choose to examine these important and crucial competences in the Fourth Industrial Revolution.

The principal question we will explore in this chapter is: *what human competences will be in demand in the Fourth Industrial Revolution?*

To address this principal question, we have formulated the following four sub-questions:

Q1 What social competences will be in demand in the Fourth Industrial Revolution?
Q2 What emotional competences will be in demand in the Fourth Industrial Revolution?
Q3 What leadership competences will be in demand in the Fourth Industrial Revolution?
Q4 What cultural competences will be in demand in the Fourth Industrial Revolution?

Figure 3.1 shows a visual representation of the introduction and also shows how the chapter is organized.

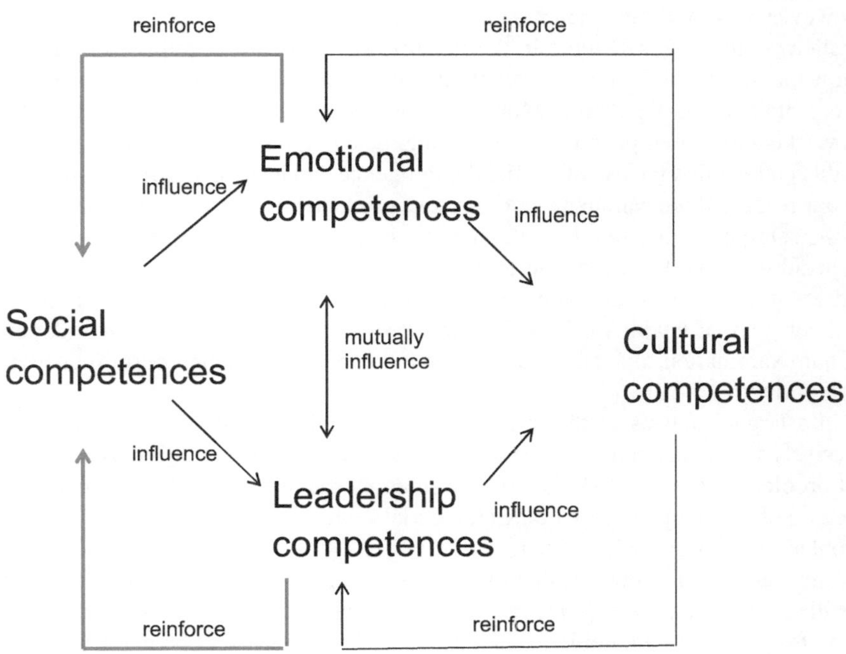

Figure 3.1 A model of the necessary human competences that will be needed in the Fourth Industrial Revolution

Social and emotional competences

In this section, we will examine the following question: what social and emotional competences will be in demand in the Fourth Industrial Revolution?

We are relatively optimistic that artificial intelligence and intelligent robots will complement human social competences. As a starting point, we can consider this assertion in relation to the health industry, namely hospitals, nursing homes, hospitals and other health-care institutions and facilities. Although developments in the Fourth Industrial Revolution will lead to new technology and economic efficiency being important in this industry, it is also highly probable that there will also be a need for skilled personnel who possess social and emotional competences. Health is an essential part of our well-being (Britnell, 2019). Within this sector, it is especially nurses who need to possess social and emotional competences. By using artificial intelligence and intelligent robots, this professional group will be able to fully use the knowledge and skills that they master particularly well, i.e. care and nursing, which constitutes the core of their training, and which is inherently linked to social and emotional competences.

Many, if not all, analysts are discussing what they view as a looming health-care crisis, because of an aging population, and the probable shortage of nurses and other health-care personnel in the future. An important point in this regard is that we often set our goals too low, so that they can more easily be reached. It is more this lack of ambition in setting low goals that is a danger also in the health-care sector because we are satisfied when we reach such low and mediocre goals. However, it is precisely such mediocre goals that are too low for us to solve the challenges that we will meet in the health-care sector in the future. Prognoses show that there will be too few health-care professionals in the future to meet the needs of an aging population. Moreover, the old-age dependency ratio – the ratio of workers to retired people – is increasing, posing considerable challenges. It is in this context that the use of artificial intelligence and intelligent robots can come to our rescue. If we can manage to increase productivity in the health-care sector at the same or higher rate than the number of elderly in need of care in relation to health-care workers, then the challenge will be solved. The more productivity increases in this sector, the more we will be able to use the social and emotional competences of health workers. It is this proposition that forms the foundation of our examination of social and emotional competences in the Fourth Industrial Revolution.

In a larger analysis of the challenges in the global health-care industry, it is precisely the inadequate number of health workers that is emerging as the largest problem (Britnell, 2019: ix). If we can apply the new technology that will be continually developed in the Fourth Industrial Revolution to this industry, then the problem will probably be solved.

The alarming prognosis is that by 2030, we will need roughly 40 million more health-care workers worldwide than we have today.[4] It is not difficult to comprehend that without being able to utilize new technology, it will be almost impossible to address this new challenge socially, economically and politically.

Narratives

Case letter 1: 2020

We enter the doctor's waiting room, take a numbered queue ticket and sit down to wait our turn. When we finally get to see the doctor, the experience is chilly. The doctor's communications seem mechanical, laced with an artificial kind of friendliness. It is as though the doctor in front of us lacks social and emotional competence and is able to apply only rational and logical competence.

This kind of coldly rational logic is what we would expect from an intelligent robot. But in 2020, it's not the robot but the doctor who adopts this manner. It's like bearing witness to Michelangelo's image of God extending his hand to humanity.[5] But in this case, the hand belongs to the doctor, rather than to God. Both the doctor and the patient share this understanding. We are like patients in the grasp of God's extended hand here on Earth, and that is also the feeling we are left with, once the diagnosis is made.

We sit in a chair positioned so it is difficult to maintain eye contact with the doctor. It is clear that the doctor doesn't want to have eye contact with us either. The doctor stares at the computer screen, asks a few questions and then carries on typing in silence. We await God's judgement expectantly, head slightly bowed. This is an encounter where one party sits and stares down at the floor, while the other sits and stares at a computer screen. The encounter is impersonal, cold, rational and non-inclusive. Patients feel as though they are interrupting the doctor simply by existing.

In such encounters, communications between doctor and patient take place in lowered voices. The situation feels more like a criminal interrogation, with no interest in anything except the obvious facts. This kind of encounter almost always results in a medical error because genuine communication is absent. What happens in the encounter between doctor and patient is an information-extracting process, not a communications process. The caring role of the nurse has been rationalized out of existence, as has the role of the secretary. What is left is the doctor, sitting at the computer in front of a nervous patient, who is awaiting judgement.

Doctors are overworked, have too many patients, and are forced to dissociate from their social and emotional instincts when dealing with patients, or at least to ignore them to a large extent. Misdiagnoses and medical errors are often the result of these 'mechanical' encounters (Topol, 2019: 1–23).

Case letter 2: 2045

Many fear that the use of AI, intelligent robots and intelligent algorithms in the health-care industry will turn health care into a more mechanical and cold experience for users. However, we take the opposite view. What turns health care into a mechanical and impersonal system is not so much the technology, but when doctors and nurses stare at computer screens avoiding contact with patients. We believe that the new technology will facilitate conditions for creating a more humane and caring health-care system based on human values. One might ask:

how can a cold machine based on artificial intelligence transform health care into a more humane and caring system rather than what was described in Case Letter 1? The answer is twofold.

First, doctors, nurses and other health-care personnel will have more time for patients when intelligent robots can take care of administrative and secretarial functions. Of course, this 'extra time' may pose a problem, if it is left up to the economists to calculate this as a productivity gain, instead of using the extra time gained for other functions. If this happens, then we will not have made any progress in terms of making the meeting between health-care professionals and patients more caring and humane. It will therefore be necessary for health-care professionals and politicians to seize the opportunity provided by the new technology to create the communication needed to facilitate a more holistic meeting between patients and health-care personnel.

Second, intelligent robots will be able to more effectively predict the various side effects and possible treatments of these, than any surgeon is able to (Topol, 2019). The reason is that surgical procedures can cause various side effects. An intelligent robot will be able to more quickly and accurately monitor a patient regarding central parameters than any doctor or surgeon, for example during and after a knee operation. One such case, when a surgeon failed to help a patient after a knee operation, is shown by Eric Topol (2019: 44–56). If the patient described by Topol, who is actually Topol himself, had access to an intelligent robot, the discomfort and pain inflicted on the patient by sheer ignorance on the part of the physician would most probably have been avoided. There are countless examples in hospitals where the knowledge exists, but where the doctors do not have the opportunity to apply the knowledge because it is very specialized. The consequences are often that patients have to suffer unnecessarily from the effects of various illnesses; in the worst cases, such incompetence can even lead to death. By using intelligent robots, this lack of knowledge can be transformed into practical knowledge, which doctors will be able to use.

We are fully aware of the fact that all the shortcomings in the health-care industry cannot be solved by using advanced technology, but it is certainly a beginning to gain knowledge about possible unexpected developments, so that we can intervene at an early stage. It has already been shown that artificial intelligence in the health-care industry has led to considerable medical advances. Regarding the future use of AI, Topol (2019), who is himself a doctor, says that it will be qualitatively better than the assessments made by doctors in all medical procedures. AI will be used to diagnose where doctors say it is not possible to make a diagnosis. With the help of AI, it will be possible to treat diseases doctors do not know how to treat. AI will be able to identify patterns in data where doctors can only see data. Intelligent robots will be able to predict a patient's development, where no physician is able to.

Case letter 3: emotional competence

We are all able to observe the emotions of people in our lives, while some of us are more emotionally competent than others. To perceive the emotions of others, we observe body language, faces, expressions, grimaces and the social dynamics around us. However, if we do not know what we are looking for, then we will 'see' very little. This may be compared to watching two chess players in action without knowing a single rule of the game. The whole game will seem incomprehensible and we will quickly get bored. We must have knowledge of emotions to understand what they mean; otherwise we can observe without seeing what is actually happening. Knowledge of emotions allows us to recognize how an action contributes to a larger pattern of behaviour; in other words, individual actions will not provide us with much information. The more you narrow down the field of observation, the less you will know about what is really happening.

Case letter 4: the legal profession between 2020 and 2045

Already today, several law firms are using artificial intelligence and intelligent robots to resolve disputes and advise their clients (Susskind, 2017). It is not difficult to envision how this tendency will increase in the future, and that new technology will greatly affect the practices of law firms by around 2045 compared to 2020. There are already a number of businesses starting to emerge in the border area between technology and legal work, which goes under the name of legal-tech. These businesses specialize in using artificial intelligence to provide legal services. When artificial intelligence becomes more advanced, it is not difficult to foresee how more legal issues of varying complexity will be solved using artificial intelligence.

Clients will be better served when it will be possible to access and interpret all the rules, laws, past court cases and legal practices in a much better and fail-safe way. In the future, intelligent robots that are connected to international practices in the field will be able to do this more efficiently than lawyers are able to do today. However, there may be one exception to this general rule, and that is when situations arise in which a strong degree of legal discretion is required.

Of course, no one knows precisely what the legal profession will look like in 2045. However, we know that the legal system and methods are designed in such a way that artificial intelligence will easily be able to adapt to the system. We also know that being a leader in an industry is no guarantee of survival, as was demonstrated by the bankruptcy of Kodak that had held a dominant position in the photographic industry during most of the twentieth century. In a short period, Instagram took over by embracing the new digital technology, something which Kodak failed to do. In the telecommunications industry, there are many similar examples. Nokia was outcompeted with the introduction of smartphones; they lost their leading position in the industry when they were unable to adapt to technological changes. The same development may occur in the legal industry. If the new technology is developed further and linked to new forms of organization that ensure quality at a fraction of the cost, then it is not difficult to foresee that the entire legal profession will go through radical changes. The following scenario may occur around 2040: all documentation related to legal methodology will be automated. At the same time, there will be a complete interconnection of all laws, rules and jurisprudence so that intelligent robots will have the necessary overview and also be able to use a certain degree of discretion when making assessments. If this occurs, and there is much that indicates it will (Susskind, 2017: 45), then electronic legal practices will most probably be established that can guide clients in many ways. Most probably, artificial intelligence will also be used in conflict negotiations that can take place in closed online communication systems, because the parties will be able to see the possible consequences of various solutions through analysis of available material. Costs for clients will fall, and we will therefore be able to see an increase in demand for these services. Moreover, it is highly probable we will witness the emergence of virtual courtrooms with virtual judges and virtual juries.

So how will it be possible to use social and emotional competences in the light of such a development? The immediate answer is that we will see a situation in which people who can operate and understand artificial intelligence will be able to help clients with low-level legal questions, and possibly even bring their cases via intelligent robots to a solution. These people in the new functions will not necessarily be qualified lawyers but may have a bachelor's degree combining various subjects, such as jurisprudence, communication competence and artificial intelligence. The emergence of businesses with such new competences will be able to offer a kind of 'legal first aid' to clients as an alternative to the costly services of lawyers and legal firms. Just as Kodak was replaced by Instagram, one can imagine a development where law firms will be replaced by 'Insta-law' businesses. These businesses will go from scope to scale, i.e. they will grow and make money by means of mass production rather than specializing in one specific legal area.

Description

We have shown in case letters 1 and 2 that social competence will be crucial for both effective and qualitative treatment of patients. In both case letters, we have tried to show that artificial intelligence and intelligent robots will promote social competence. Contrary to what many believe, namely that the new technology will lead to a colder society, we are of the opposite opinion: artificial intelligence will lead to a more caring and inclusive society. Of course, there are some prerequisites that must be met for this assumption to be realized. One of these assumptions is not to give economists with their spreadsheets easy access to businesses where social competence is crucial to value creation, no matter how one defines value creation. One thing that will be common to all definitions of value creation is that decisions that are often made in a split second can have major consequences for social systems. This occurs in hospitals (Topol, 2019); in the military (Goleman, 2006: 3); and in many other systems, industries and businesses. Social competence is crucial so that the decisions we make are the right decisions, which will promote the system's goal achievement. Social competence and emotional competence go hand in glove. Social competence is closely linked to being able to sense and then respond to a situation, often a situation that was not expected (Goleman, 2006). Emotional competence is linked to understanding and being able to understand the other's perspective (Goleman, 1996).

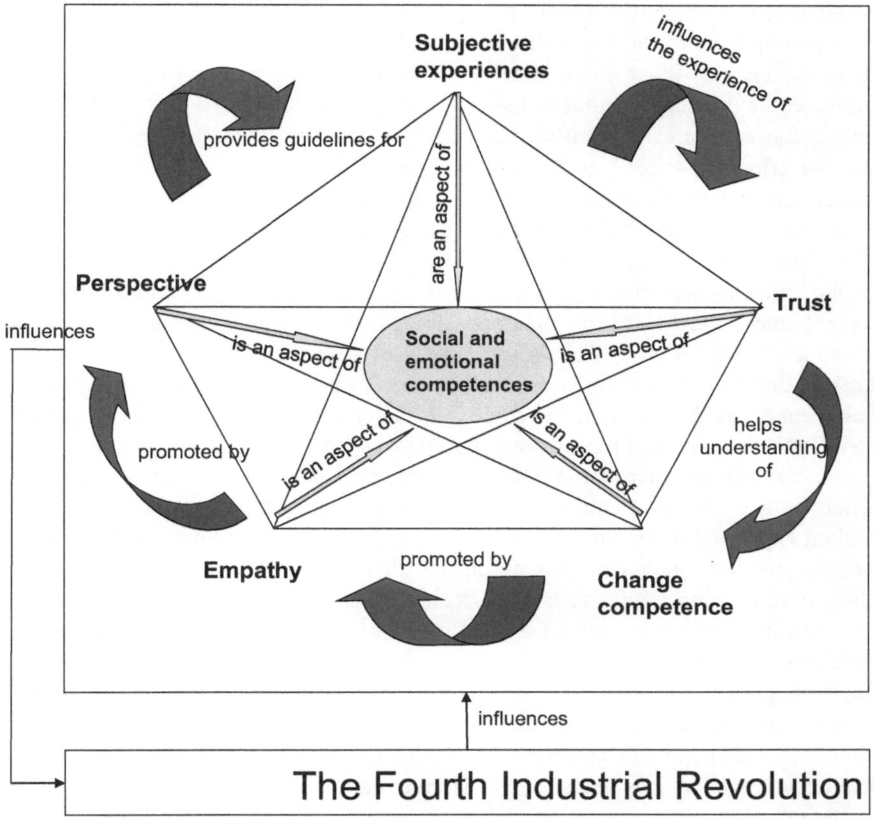

Figure 3.2 Aspects of social and emotional competences that will be in demand in the Fourth Industrial Revolution

In the following, we will describe the five elements linked to the question: what social and emotional competences will be in demand in the Fourth Industrial Revolution? We have shown these five elements in Figure 3.2.

Subjective experiences in relation to social and emotional competences

We are all in touch with our feelings at some level. However, there is a difference between our feelings and how they are expressed, i.e. our emotions (De Waal, 2019: 4). Feelings are internal subjective experiences, emotions are physical or mental states, which are objective. If you do not make a distinction between feelings and emotions, you risk confusing subjective experiences with objective states. In this way, the subjective feelings may be understood by the individual and the person one is communicating with as if they were objective realities. If something is perceived as objective, then it may quickly be understood as something that is true, an objective truth. The reality is that a feeling may thus become objective in its consequences. What is perceived as a subjective feeling, if communicated in a public context, becomes a formulation that may be an objective truth in its social consequences. For example if we say: 'I feel that you are being aggressive' – how do you affect the other person with such an utterance? First, few, if any, have perfect understanding of their inner psychological states, so that one can state that such and such is the full and complete state of my feelings at this moment in time (De Waal, 2019: 5). In making a specific utterance as the one previously mentioned, one chooses some aspect while disregarding other aspects of one's psychological inner state. Moreover, it is impossible to convey the whole picture, so one's utterance is only a part of one's psychological state that one is communicating, i.e. that one has chosen. However, when you say that you 'feel the other person is being aggressive', you frame the context in such a way that it affects the other person. One's personal feelings are thus placed in a specific context to which the other needs to relate. By uttering the statement, one places the other person in a situation whereby he or she has to defend himself or herself against the so-called subjective feeling expressed in the utterance of 'being aggressive'. Consequently, one places one's subjective feeling on a pedestal and then assesses the other's defence as something inferior: 'Winning is good, losing is bad'. In other words, the utterance of a personal feeling in such a way may be viewed as a strategy in which one has taken the first step in an attempt to win a position. But what does the individual in question gain? He or she has attempted to gain a position by framing a context, and thus taking a higher position, so that the other person needs a defence. By speaking about the other person in such a way, one has damaged the relationship; the subjective experience has thus become an objective reality in the relationship. Further, it is often the one who is framed in such a negative way, i.e. 'I feel that you are being aggressive', who has to take the first step in restoring the relationship. The 'victim' (of the utterance) is thus made into a scapegoat, and the scapegoat has to make the first concession in an attempt at reconciliation. The circle is thus closed and self-fulfilling: the subjective feeling has become real in its consequences.

What do so subjective experiences and feelings have to do with the social and emotional competence we will need when new technology becomes more ubiquitous in our lives? The simplest answer is that some are 'the makers and others are the takers' in social settings. It is therefore important to understand every context and how situations may develop when someone uses the rhetorical strategy of imposing their subjective experiences and feelings on others. This is important, because all, absolutely all the functions in working life, and in one's personal life, will sooner or later be exposed to the *power of the subjective experiences and feelings of others*. Therefore, we should have a reflected awareness of such situations in which some individuals attempt to take control of a situation by telling you, and maybe others, what they feel and express about a situation. What they are really doing is to frame the context in a new way, thus taking control of the signals the context sends out.

Objectification of subjective states is a conscious or unconscious abuse of power. The individual attempts to take control of a situation by showing what he or she feels, and feelings are real – or aren't they? Every profession will face this so-called 'real' experience, as if it is the truthful representation of a situation. In reality, it is nothing but a reaction to a situation one does not completely master or understand. The point is that no one, absolutely no one, has sufficient knowledge to state what is happening in a situation, including the one who assumes the role of mediating a personal experience about the situation. When lack of knowledge in this way tries to frame a situation, the context is objectified and becomes real in its consequences, while in reality it is nothing but a falsified and distorted contextual framing. This is where one can say that a subjectively expressed experience becomes objective in its consequences. If we are to cope with all the challenges life throws at us, then we should first and foremost have a clear idea about how knowledge of social and emotional relationships can be turned into real competence. We all have limited understanding of situations. Therefore, we should not force a context into a specific frame. However, if we do, then we make the context into a win-lose situation. One literally forces the other to take the first step in a reconciliation process. First, the other is subjected to a distorted perception, no matter how subjective and personal the perception may be. Then one forces the other to defend himself or herself in a context he or she does not recognize. In such a context, where the framing is done by another, the individual is exposed to a situation in which they will often lose out. It is the 'victim' of the 'abuse' who feels the need for reconciliation. The circle is thus closed: the subjective experience or feeling has become real and objective in its consequences. In Figure 3.3, we have shown the basic model of how subjective experiences can become objective in their consequences.

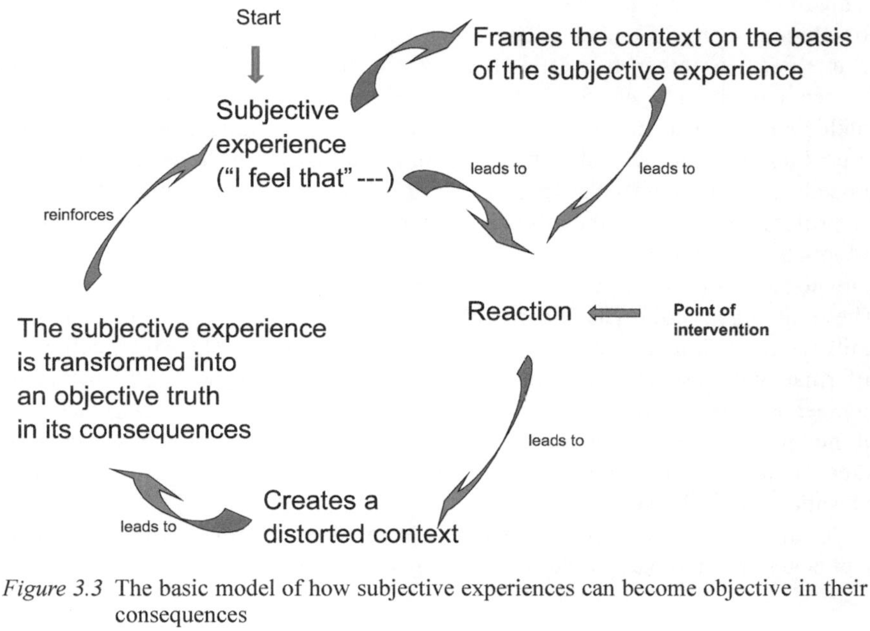

Figure 3.3 The basic model of how subjective experiences can become objective in their consequences

Trust as an aspect of social and emotional competence

Trust, or more precisely lack of trust, is a serious problem if social cohesion is broken down in any social system. We all have limited competences, which is why we turn to those who have the necessary specialized expertise. However, if these people do not meet expected standards but put their own welfare ahead of those seeking help, then trust will be eroded. It is in this situation that artificial intelligence and intelligent robots can restore the necessary trust. If a patient does not have confidence in the doctor's competence, this can be solved by developing intelligent robots that have both a general medical competence and special expertise in the area of medicine for which the patient is being examined. The intelligent robot will not be biased in the same way a doctor may be.

The same applies to lawyers, architects, nurses, teachers, and the vast majority of professions, where special expertise and discretion are important factors in the practice of the profession. In other words, it will be possible to use artificial intelligence, intelligent robots and intelligent algorithms in combination with a professional's expertise, or separately, to strengthen and restore confidence in the professions and professionals. If competence consists of knowledge, skills and attitudes, then artificial intelligence can help restore trust between the user and the professional or profession. In this way, the Fourth Industrial Revolution may be understood as a competence revolution in which the trust between professionals who possess expertise and those who use this expertise will be strengthened and restored. If this assumption is correct, then the Fourth Industrial Revolution will not only be a revolution of competence but also a revolution that will considerably affect most professions.

In the future, we will need institutions that are trustworthy and that will replace many of the functions that the professions perform today. In the Fourth Industrial Revolution, many of the functions of the various institutions will be entrusted to intelligent robots, artificial intelligence and intelligent algorithms. One can foresee a situation in which a surgeon or general practitioner is replaced by an intelligent informat. In a transitional period, this will be associated with a trust issue. Should we allow a robot, no matter how intelligent it is, to perform surgical procedures? No expert is an expert at everything. This is also the case in the medical profession. However, there is one possible exception. These are the intelligent informats of the future. The rationale is that they will be connected to all available knowledge within their functional area, which in this case is medical surgery. These intelligent informats will be able to globally scan millions of information units within their area of expertise in a fraction of a second. Thus, the intelligent informats will possess more expertise than the human expert we are accustomed to meeting in the profession, who most likely has acquired his or her knowledge of the profession by completing a medical degree many years previous, and who later has updated the knowledge and skills by enrolling in various continuous education medical courses.

Up until the present day, professionals have taken care of our problems and challenges. In the Fourth Industrial Revolution, intelligent robots and informats will be better equipped to solve these problems than the human professional expert. However, this is where the question of trust becomes essential. Today, we rely heavily on doctors, lawyers, nurses etc. We trust them because they have knowledge, they have a professional ethic, they practice the profession according to a standard and many have a service attitude we are satisfied with. If institutions are not established in the future that create the same trust in relation to intelligent robots and informats, we will have a trust problem related to the new technology.

Change competence as a social and emotional resource: change is the new stability

If the professions are to keep up with the developments described earlier, they will all have to change significantly. The teaching of the various professions at universities and institutions of higher education will need to adapt their degree programmes to include competences, knowledge and skills in coding, artificial intelligence and intelligent algorithms. Similar to the previous three industrial revolutions, the Fourth Industrial Revolution will not happen quickly. It may be more likened to an explosion in slow motion, where many changes only become evident after the explosion is over and the dust has settled. According to innovation theory, it takes approximately 40 years before a new ground-breaking and innovative technology, such as the steam engine, the internal combustion engine and the computer, result in fundamental changes throughout the whole of society (Johannessen, 2018, 2019a, 2019c). Therefore, the professions have about 20–30 years in which to adjust to upcoming changes.

However, those businesses that are able to link competence in the new technology to their specific professional competence will have a great advantage in relation to their competitors. For instance, a psychologist who can encode and develop intelligent algorithms to structure and systematize large amounts of patient data will be able to use this processed information to develop more accurate analyses and complete reports about patients. If this knowledge is also linked to the best forms of treatment for the patient, then the psychologist will have structured a diagnosis and treatment system that can offer a qualitatively better service.

The change competence in the example previously mentioned regarding the psychologist concerns not so much a desire to make completely radical changes, but rather to primarily develop competence in psychology and use technology to supplement and refine this competence. It is this approach that will constitute change competence in the Fourth Industrial Revolution – the capacity to develop professional competence in tandem with technological competence. It is the connections between these two competencies that will constitute the new innovative approaches and the new value creation in the Fourth Industrial Revolution.

Figure 3.4 shows a schematic representation of the example of the psychologist mentioned earlier and illustrates how an intelligent robot may be used by the psychologist in the analysis and treatment of a patient.

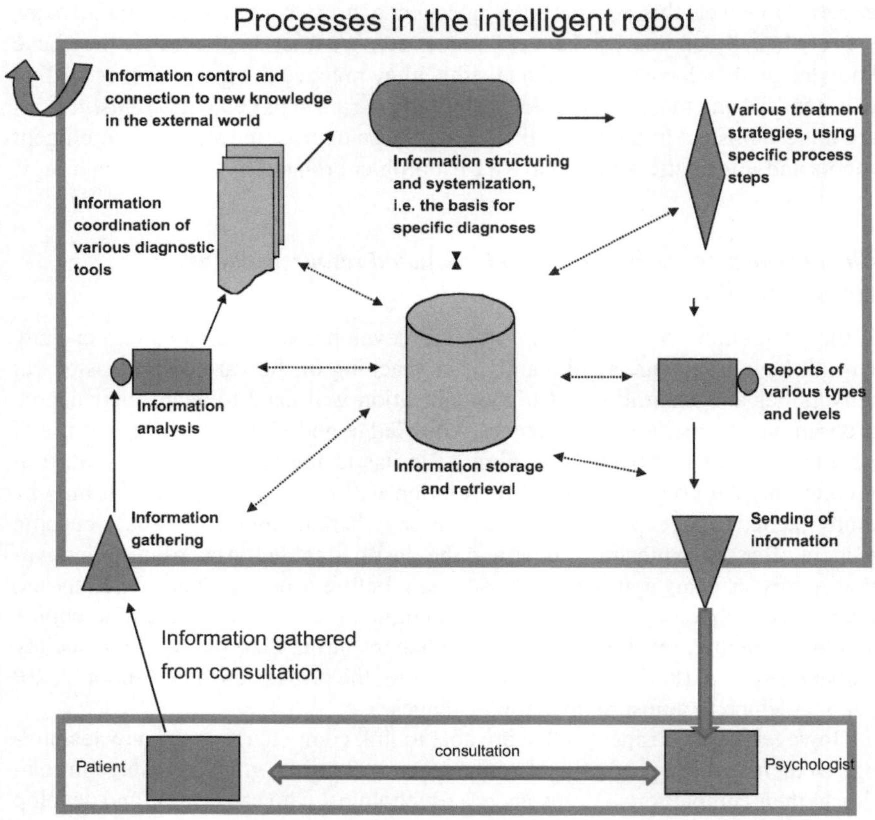

Figure 3.4 Artificial intelligence as supplementary competence in the Fourth Industrial Revolution

Empathy as a social and emotional resource

Empathy is perceived as the ability to understand and share the feelings of another. Professionals, such as doctors and nurses, often have face-to-face interaction with patients and users. A patient will soon notice if a doctor or nurse does not have an empathic approach; for instance, if the professional does not attempt to show a caring approach, and only stares at his or her computer screen, asking questions intermittently. It is not uncommon that patients are irritated by a doctor's lack of emotional competence, or by a nurse who averts his or her face avoiding eye contact. An intelligent robot or informat can be programmed to be as emotionally involved as required by a situation. When the use of intelligent robots becomes more widespread in the health-care sector, it will not necessarily be the case that the 'human touch' will disappear. Regardless of whether it is an intelligent robot or a human being performing a service, it is imperative that both the health-care professional and the intelligent robot possess social and emotional competence that meets the needs of the individual patient and situation. In other words, they must both have the capacity to show empathy, not so much possess the so-called 'human touch'. Thus, we are not of the opinion that new technology, that is intelligent robots and informats will reduce professional empathy. Of course, this may occur, but it also occurs in 2020, as we have attempted to describe in 'Case letter 1: 2020' mentioned previously, when a doctor was unable to adopt an empathic approach. The probability that the intelligent robot will not show empathy will be small because it will be programmed to show empathy. It may also be said that so-called face-to-face interactions are not the only way of showing empathy. Accessibility can in many ways replace face-to-face interaction. For instance, if a college professor informs his or her students that he or she is available 24/7 electronically (that is not physically present), then in many cases the students will feel this is good enough, and the level of perceived empathy will be considered adequate. Moreover, the students, patients and so on, may prefer online communication, as they will be able to use their time more efficiently.

It is therefore conceivable that 'informat professionals' can satisfy the experience and requirement of empathy much better than a human professional is able to do. It is quite clear that human interaction and human empathy will be diminished when the new technology takes over many of the functions of the traditional professions. However, this does not mean that empathy will be reduced; rather the opposite may happen.

Perspective as a social and emotional resource

Trust, empathy and the expression of subjective experiences often depend on which perspective one takes. Changing perspective requires that one has the necessary competence. One can choose to take one's own perspective, but one can also choose to take the other person's perspective. Taking the other person's perspective requires social and emotional competence, which will also promote goal achievement in a very effective way.

When tackling a problem or challenge that is felt to be difficult, five perspectives can be used to investigate different aspects of the problem. This strategy involves shifting our perspective in an ongoing situation. One approach here is to categorize our shift in perspective systematically, considering it from five different angles. First, we look at the problem or challenge from our own perspective. Here the question is: how does this benefit me? Second, we consider the other party's perspective. How does this benefit the other party? The third perspective is to attempt to see the whole problem from the perspective of a neutral observer. How would a neutral observer consider this problem or challenge? The fourth perspective is to try to see how the problem or challenge will affect the larger system of which the problem is a part. How does the problem or challenge affect the larger system? The fifth perspective is to attempt to view the problem in a part-whole perspective (systemic perspective). How is the problem affected if we alternate between part and whole?

We have shown the five perspectives in Figure 3.5.

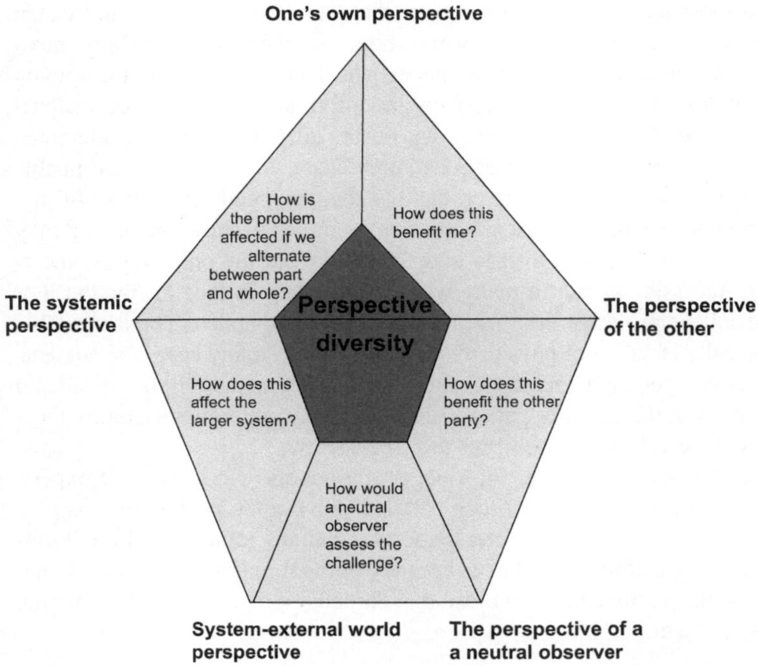

Figure 3.5 The five perspectives

Analysis

Let's take the example of the psychologist shown in Figure 3.4. This professional has a dual competence. First and foremost, he or she is a trained psychologist. Second, he or she has competence in coding. It is when working as a psychologist that he or she benefits from applying coding skills. By coding the various elements of a consultation, the psychologist formulates an AI process that can generate a patient report. Productivity thus increases, mainly regarding the improved quality of the patient report. The report includes more features than would have been the case if the AI process had not been applied. One of the points of this example is that without the psychologist's familiarity with the context and dual competence, it is unlikely that this innovative product could have been created. Creativity and innovation at the beginning of the Fourth Industrial Revolution will require contextual understanding and dual competence. The automation in this example does not lead to anybody becoming redundant, but to a better quality product. Of course, in another scenario, one can imagine that the patient consults an intelligent informat and not a psychologist. In such a case, automation would probably lead to many psychologists becoming redundant, as well as improving the quality of the patient interaction and thereby improving the product. The latter, however, describes a possible scenario in the distant future after singularity has long since occurred (Johannessen, 2020a). Another scenario is that no psychologists will be made redundant by the automation of the psychologist's competence, but that more people will be helped to treat their mental health ailments.

The previous description suggests that in the future, educational institutions will need to design new degree programmes to link the various professions to the technology expertise that will be required by the introduction of new technology. Moreover, there will always be a need for someone to maintain and improve the intelligent informats.

The utilization of the new technology in the Fourth Industrial Revolution, as described in the previous example concerning the psychologist, will not be something that is obviously visible, such as the steam engine or the internal combustion engine in the previous industrial revolutions. It will rather be a type of technology that will be integrated into already existing technology. Consequently, it will be invisible to most people, such as the patient and the colleagues of the psychologist, unless they have been made aware of the fact that it is there. If they don't know about it, they will not be able to 'see' it either. What they can see, however, is that the psychologist in the example is able to produce reports that are better than theirs and that will become the 'norm' in the profession. To recap, the new technology using intelligent robots, and later intelligent informats, will not be as visible as the technology of the three previous industrial revolutions.

The mass production of internal combustion engine vehicles not only completely changed transportation technology, but also radically changed and defined the modern urban landscape. However, the future new technology comprising intelligent algorithms, intelligent robots and the application of AI, such as in the case of the psychologist mentioned earlier, will not necessarily change the urban landscape, but it will increase the quality of urban life, if we think in a larger context than only the field of psychology. The future use of AI, intelligent robots and informats in hospitals will dramatically improve the quality of life in that diagnoses, medication, treatment and operations will all be improved. The automobiles in the twentieth and early twenty-first century were also related to social identity and social class; that is ownership of exclusive automobiles such as Mercedes Benz, BMW and Porsche is often associated with personal success. The use of the new technology, however, will probably not be associated with personal success, except in cases such as we have seen with the recent introduction of the new electric vehicle brand, Tesla. If we return to the example of the psychologist, he or she will be able to expand his or her psychology consultation practice by being the first to develop and use the technology. However, this advantage will quickly disappear the day other psychologists start to use the technology. It is at this point that the psychologist in question should patent his or her use of AI, so that he or she can live off the invention in addition to his or her psychology consultation practice.

While the steam engine and railways of the First Industrial Revolution created the preconditions for the growth of the big cities, such as Chicago in the US, the expertise and products of the Fourth Industrial Revolution will transform these cities into qualitatively better places to live in, emerging as so-called intelligent cities. This may be done by regulating the urban areas using intelligent robots so that the cities become 'intelligent' cities. The noise and pollution associated with the use of motor vehicles will gradually become a thing of the past with the increase in the use of electric vehicles and other pollution-free transport solutions. Of course, these developments will also be dependent on the use of green energy. Driverless small and large transport solutions will largely make the cities free of cars.

The factory economy of the first, second and partly the third industrial revolutions led to mass production due to falling unit costs. This industrial structure in the West was literally blown away by globalization whereby cheap labour in developing countries led to the closure of factories in the West, such as the automotive factories in Detroit in the US. In the Fourth Industrial Revolution, there will be a focus on 'scope' rather than 'scale'.

If the new technology of the Fourth Industrial Revolution is to transform society and our way of life, as occurred in the three previous industrial revolutions, it must be both innovative and pervasive. The psychologist in the example previously mentioned could be one of the first innovators in the field of psychology. The next step could be that the psychologist starts a company that develops expertise in coding and intelligent algorithms and goes on to develop intelligent robots and informats on a large scale. The Fourth Industrial Revolution will thus be transformative by first moving towards scope and then evolving into a situation in which entrepreneurs enter the picture. These will develop businesses that focus on mass production, such as within the area of technological psychology services. Therefore, this may be viewed as a traditional development – that is first innovation, then entrepreneurship. The transition from scope to scale in the Fourth Industrial Revolution will transform the economy in the same way as in the first three industrial revolutions. It is in this manner that the cities will be transformed in the Fourth Industrial Revolution. It is the new 'factories' that will create new jobs. The dual competence will be the first step in the development of intelligent robots and informats. The next step will involve a new mass production in which codes, algorithms, intelligent robots and intelligent informats will be produced on a large scale. One can envision that the codes are the new 'assembly lines' in the new 'factories'. Of course, these new 'factories' will have no time clock where workers clock-in and clock-out; in other words, there are no work-hours as such. The work in the new 'factories' will be performance-based and will not require workers to be physically present at a specific location. Workers will not have to 'go to work'; they will work wherever they happen to be. The new 'factory' is thus not located behind four brick walls. This will also reduce traffic jams and transport problems in urban areas. The new 'factory' will be virtual.

Universal mass education emerged during the first three industrial revolutions due to the need for an educated workforce. The more advanced education you obtained, the better job you would be able to acquire, and the higher the salary. Of course, higher education will still be important in the Fourth Industrial Revolution, but will students complete their education at physical universities, such as Oxford, Harvard, Wharton, and the like? Why should students pay staggering amounts to acquire special knowledge and expertise in a field, when they can acquire the same knowledge and expertise at a fraction of the cost at online universities around the world? In the Fourth Industrial Revolution, it is competence that will be in demand, that is the relevant knowledge, skills and attitudes. This competence will not necessarily be equated with a fancy diploma awarded by a 'hot-shot' university. The rationale is simple. The rate of change will be so great in the Fourth Industrial Revolution, given the exponential growth of new technology, that the skills demanded will change at a similar rate. The traditional universities will most probably be unable to adjust to this rapid rate of change. The online universities, however, will be able to change and modify their degree programs to meet the demand for new competences at the stroke of a key.

Intelligent robots, artificial intelligence and intelligent algorithms will be able to automate numerous professions in various fields, such as university teachers, doctors, lawyers, journalists and bartenders (Agar, 2019). The intelligent robots will be able to perform these and hundreds of other work functions more efficiently, with higher quality and productivity, as well as at a much lower cost than the people they replace. The point, however, is that when we talk about the Fourth Industrial Revolution and the skills that will be in demand, one should analytically introduce a distinction: before and after full automation. In the first instance, those with a dual competence will be in demand. This is when dual competence will be important, as shown in the earlier example of the psychologist who was able to streamline and improve various work functions and processes. How will social and emotional competence be important in this context? The answer is simple and revolutionary and can be expressed in one sentence: the more competence that is transferred to intelligent robots, the greater will be the need for social and emotional competence. Thus, when machines take over many work functions, humans will not necessarily become redundant. 'Humans are underrated', says Geoff Colvin (2016), that is the more time people will have to do things other than those functions that have been automated, the more meaningful it will become to transfer the time, resources and commitment gained to focusing on social and emotional competence. The point of the previous discussion is to point out that the technological revolution that is happening around us will also lead to a social and emotional revolution. Machines, no matter how intelligent they are, will always be poor substitutes for human contact. Even cats and dogs will be better substitutes than intelligent robots with regard to the social and emotional closeness that humans depend on. Few of us emotionally relate to other people purely on the basis of how intelligent they happen to be. It is not people's mental abilities that bring people together as couples and friends. Automating emotions will always be a poor substitute, no matter how one 'dresses-up' the intelligent robots. It will be relatively easy to automate a self-driving car so that it can make moral choices in the case of unavoidable accidents. It would be absurd to automate social and emotional competence in a car-owner relationship, although we can certainly see some psychological implications of this, which will surely find its solution on the Freudian sofa.

While there may be destructive consequences of allowing people access to a technology that will enable them to greatly increase their mental rational capacity, it will not necessarily be inevitably harmful, which Nicholas Agar (2013) believes. However, it may be harmful if we do not increase our ethical, social and emotional capacity as much as our mental rational capacity. In such a case, where we become more logically and rationally intelligent, without the same increase in ethical, social and emotional competence, we may start to resemble a 'blind machine'. In plain text, 'insanity' will be the result if we disconnect from everything that is not rational, i.e. feelings, emotions, morals, culture etc.

Technology is rational and logical. Humans are essentially social and emotional beings (Albrecht, 2006). Because technology is logical and rational, it can be used to formulate prognoses (Diamandis & Kotler, 2012: 51–55). Human, social and emotional competence concerns listening attentively to other people, being 'present' in the conversation and participating in the other's joy or sorrow (Goleman, 2006). Technology can help us in this behaviour, but not replace it (Snyder, 2016). Essentially, the interaction between a human and an intelligent robot is a relationship that can be described as 'I and It', while a human relationship can be described as 'I and Thou' (Buber, 2013). There is of course a difference in having a relationship to 'It' (an object that is separate), and having a relationship to another human being, 'Thou'. The difference may be expressed in terms of reciprocity, empathy, mutual engagement, taking the other's perspective and being there for the other (which is not the case in the relationship to 'It'). When talking to someone on the phone, we quickly notice whether the other person is 'participating' in the conversation, or talking in a 'mechanical' way, namely where they become more like 'It'. In other words, you notice straightaway if someone is 'present' in a conversation or not. One also notices if the other person is 'tuned in', if they are expressing empathy and closeness. In the case of an intelligent robot, people will not seek this type of relationship and will expect no more than an 'I-It' relationship. The feeling that a robot is not 'tuned-in' will result in relationships between people and robots being of a completely different character than between people. When you are talking to another person, you will quickly become aware if their attention is not fully focused – if they are focusing on something else. When you experience that another person is using you to achieve his or her own goals, while he or she is not really interested in your feelings, you will quickly become aware of such strategic behaviour – a type of 'mechanical' empathy. You will also quickly become aware in such a relationship when the other falls out of the conversation and slides into their own zone of focus. Instead, it is the listening, inquiring, engaging and participating individual who creates awareness and an 'I-Thou' relationship. As a general rule, the intelligent robot will always be at the 'mechanical' level, no matter how much it tries to listen, ask questions, engage in conversation and be engaged.

Theoretical points

In the 1990s and into the 2000s, Silicon Valley in California became a global byword for high technology. People, capital and businesses poured into the area.

Property prices quickly doubled and continued to grow (Avent, 2017: 83). Property also became an important resource along with people's expertise. Considering that property values in Silicon Valley rose during this period and that urban areas around the world will continue to grow in the future, it is not unreasonable to assume that a safe future investment will be property on the periphery of cities. The bottom line is that housing is a cost people must take into account when they move to the big cities. In addition, time is a factor because queues to and from work create time-pressure for many people. What if we turn this on its head and say that many people will not have to travel to work in the future? How will this affect the two factors – house prices and time? What has this got to do with social and emotional competence? These questions are linked to a number of paradoxes.

The first paradox concerns the relationship between the local areas and the urban centres. It has been empirically shown that urban areas will grow in step with the development of new technology. However, the use of new technology at the start of the Fourth Industrial Revolution indicates that work is something many people will be able to do anywhere, such as at home. Of course, not all professional and trade groups can do this, such as those who work in the hospitals and hotels in the cities. Nevertheless, many people will be able to choose where they want to work, resulting in property prices flattening out and a reduction in the time spent in rush hour traffic.

The second paradox concerns the contradiction between social inclusion and social exclusion. Because people will be able to both live and work in the suburban areas around the big cities, the role of local communities in these areas will be given a new meaning. In the past, people have lived in these suburban areas but worked in the cities. This has drained the residential areas of social and emotional energy because people have not had enough time to invest their energies in the areas where they actually live. However, in the new technological future, the local areas will be given more precedence and these areas will reverberate with social and emotional energy. The local areas will again, as in earlier times, become the arenas where people 'live their lives'. This will result in a demand for social and emotional competence in these new local spheres. In addition, such a development will lead to both an understanding of and a need for a greater degree of cooperation in the local areas.

> Proposition: The new vitality of the local areas in the Fourth Industrial Revolution will lead to an increased demand for social and emotional competence.

The British capitalists of the nineteenth century maximized their profits by paying factory workers very low wages, such as in the Manchester cotton industry, so they were forced to live in poor and inadequate housing, even by contemporary standards. This is described in detail by Friedrich Engels in his book, *The Condition of the Working Class in England*, first published in 1845 (Engels, 2009). In addition, the capitalists were able to reap huge profits in their exploitation of the British colonies.

Today, 175 years later, the living conditions of the English working class have clearly improved. However, there are indications that we are returning to earlier bleak times. Since the rise of neoliberalism around 1980 up until today (2020), wages have stagnated, while profits have increased. Moreover, profits are also reaped from investments in the so-called developing countries, i.e. this situation is not unlike the exploitation of the colonies in the nineteenth century. Yet again, profits are reaped by paying workers a smaller portion of the added value created both nationally and globally. Today, the ratio of wages to profits is greatly diminishing (Avent, 2017: 118–119). In addition, more profits are reaped by investing in the developing countries, among others, the former colonies, where new super profits have been made since roughly the 1980s onwards.

From the 1980s onwards, in step with the implementation of neoliberal policies, capitalism has solved the problem of scarcity of labour by moving many jobs from the industrialized countries to low-cost countries. Consequently, the scarcity of labour did not result in increasing the cost of labour; in addition, wages were also kept down in the industrialized countries. At the beginning of the Fourth Industrial Revolution, we are witnessing a similar development, only now it is not about labour costs but the cost of competence and expertise. In reality, there is no difference between the wages of the factory worker and the wages of the knowledge worker. The development we can observe in the period of global capitalism is similar to what we saw in neoliberalism's relocation of jobs to low-cost countries. The demand for expertise in coding, intelligent robots and intelligent algorithms can be satisfied by sourcing this expertise from various areas around the globe, such as Bangalore, India. Some of these 'experts' in the developing countries may move to the West, but most will continue to live in their home country in a culture they are familiar with. The point we are making here is that by organizing work in global competence clusters in developing countries, wage costs for this specialized competence can be kept down, similar to the way the labour costs of factory workers were kept down through the relocation of jobs to low-cost countries.

In addition to the previous arguments, the new technology of the Fourth Industrial Revolution will result in many work functions being automated, which will lead to a surplus of labour. However, this will not necessarily lead to unemployment. Instead, this development will increase the downwards pressure on wages. Two key social mechanisms will drive down wages: first, organization into global competence clusters and second, the surplus of labour created by automation. Yet, instead of unemployment, there will be enough work for everyone, but at lower wages. The empirical studies of Guy Standing (2014a, 2014b), who coined the word 'precariat', has already shown this, as well as David Shipler's work (2005) who coined the phrase 'working poor'. In this relatively new situation, to make ends meet, people often need to have several part-time jobs, which in total represent much more than an eight-hour workday. The social and emotional competence demanded in such a situation is the ability to organize the many casual workers, who are emerging as a new underpaid working class.

Proposition: The social and emotional competence that will be in demand in the Fourth Industrial Revolution is an organizational competence that will be able to unite casual workers (the precariat) into a unified working class.

If it is true, as Robert Putnam points out in his book, *Bowling Alone: The Collapse and Revival of American Community*, that people's participation and involvement in social networks, such as political and voluntary organizations, is declining, then we have a challenge at a time when social cohesion is being eroded in many areas (2001). However, this is nothing new. Already at the end of the nineteenth century, the French sociologist, Emile Durkheim, talked about anomie in his book *Suicide*. Anomie is a 'condition in which society provides little moral guidance to individuals' (Gerber et al., 2010: 97). The lack of social cohesion can be understood as being related to anomie. Both Durkheim and Putnam refer to the many injurious social conditions resulting from a lack of social cohesion or a high degree of anomie.

If a lack of social cohesion or an increasing degree of anomie is emerging in society, then this may constitute a crucial social mechanism, or an intervention point, where one can intervene to steer social development in a more fruitful direction (Johannessen, 2021a). Social and emotional competence is needed to strengthen social cohesion. At a time when robots and artificial intelligence are increasingly automating work processes, social cohesion will suffer, and we will see an increasing number of negative consequences. Loneliness, which Putnam wrote about, using the 'bowling alone' metaphor, and suicide related to social causes as written about by Durkheim, are just two of these negative consequences. Other negative consequences are:

- Lack of trust between people
- Fewer relationships between people, both in the workplace and in the local community
- Less political involvement
- Fewer people joining political parties
- Fewer people taking part in elections.

Social and emotional competence accumulates over time as people engage and spend their time on projects that strengthen social cohesion. However, this competence is context-dependent. Social and emotional competence is linked to the context of local communities, to the system in which it is developed. This makes this competence vulnerable at a time when the rate of change is great. In addition to context dependency, this competence is collective, i.e. it is dependent on a social network. However, the social network needs to be aware of its collective competence in order to capitalize on it. Put another way, if the people who possess and utilize this competence act collectively, then the social network will profit from it; for instance in relation to gaining bargaining and positioning power.

Social and emotional competence deepens and strengthens the meaning and degree of satisfaction with life. Once individuals have reached a certain level of material well-being, they will strive for a sense of meaning in life. In other words, it does not seem so important to own more 'things', travel on more holiday trips, purchase a more luxurious apartment and so on. Consequently, people start to look for meaning and purpose in life, and how to reach some kind of contentment. This meaningfulness can be created and developed in the local community. In a meaningful local community, nothing positive is created by coercion and imposition, but by community members who voluntarily contribute something. In this way, an active community is created, turning it into a social magnet for those living there. Accordingly, the local community sends out signals that it has a socially inclusive culture that supports the attainment of everybody's welfare and actively does something to make this happen.

What values are created in a society where meaningfulness is central? They are certainly not values that focus on chasing more and more material possessions. They are rather values that are related to people's relationships and to the experience of participating in something that bolsters these social relationships. Cultural and relational values are essential to the creation of meaningfulness in people's lives.

> Proposition: Increased automation in the Fourth Industrial Revolution will lead to an erosion of social cohesion. Therefore, a social and emotional competence will be sought that can strengthen social cohesion and create meaningfulness in people's lives.

Practical utility

Our emotions are visualized through our facial expressions, voice and body language, which is manifested in social settings. Therefore, there is a clear connection between social competence and emotional competence. One presupposes and reinforces the other. Descriptions of this relationship can be found in textbooks on psychology. However, Lisa Barrett (2017) offers a new perspective that differs from the traditional one. Barrett says that the culture we grow up in influences the emotions we show and how we show them. The emotions are created by us, says Barrett (2017: xiii), and they are created in a social context. Over time, this social context creates a common understanding of how we understand and interpret emotions. Barret's new perspective concerns a focus on the connection between understanding social relationships, the social context and the emotions expressed in this context. In the classical view, human feelings and emotions are universal and part of our primal nature that has evolved hundreds of thousands of years ago, from when our hominid ancestors trekked across the African savanna reaching the land mass of Eurasia. Feelings find their expression through the emotions. Barrett's different approach is suggested in the very name of the theory that she has developed, 'theory of constructed emotion' (Barrett, 2017). To understand emotions, Barrett's new theory proposes that we must first understand the culture and social context from which they originate. The essence of the new theory can be expressed as follows: 'emotions are in fact made and not triggered' (Barrett, 2017: xiii). The new

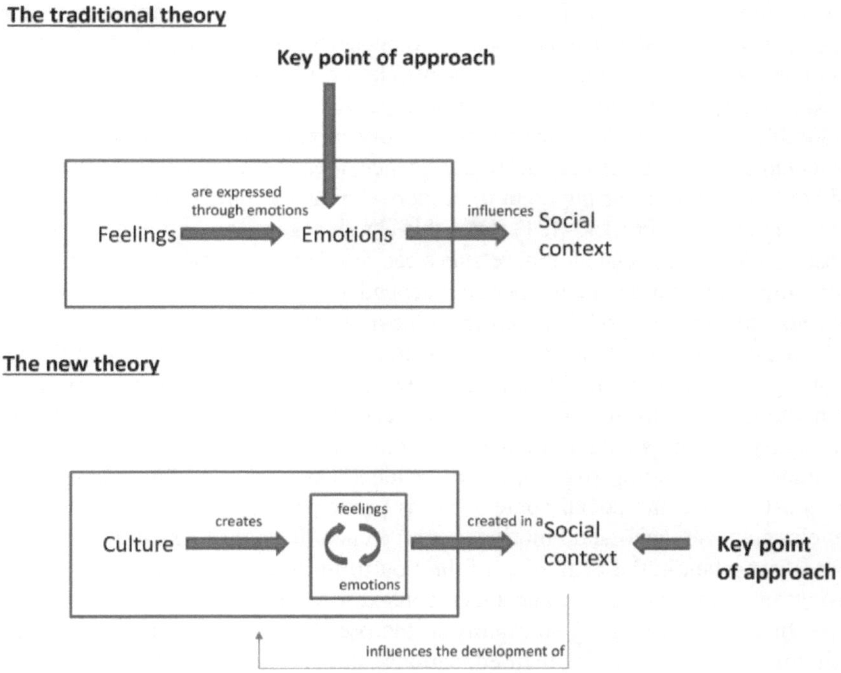

Figure 3.6 Two theories that propose different approaches to understanding emotions

practical approach proposed by Barrett's theory is that to understand someone's emotions, we must first understand the social context and culture in which these emotions are created. Thus, understanding the social context and culture are the key points if we are to gain an understanding of emotional expression. Consequently, Barrett's theory gives more emphasis to the connection between social competence and emotional competence than the traditional theory of human emotions, which does not emphasize the social context. Figure 3.6 shows a schematic representation of the two theories, the traditional theory and Barrett's new theory.

The brain simulates and creates connections (Barrett, 2017: 28). We interconnect our concepts and from this, we construct models of the external world and social situations, which in turn forms the basis for these simulations. This simulation process, in which we create connections and patterns in the external world, is also used when we create connections and patterns in our feelings and express them as emotions (Barrett, 2017: 29–42). A key point of this new theory of emotions is that emotions are socially constructed. Through this process, they make sense of the social context and predict possible actions. In this way, people participating in the social context are able to visualize what may happen.

Local communities are more important than ever. Raghuram Rajan (2019) refers to community as the third pillar of society. Although local communities are important for developing social and emotional competence, geographical distance means less than before when maintaining social relationships, because new technology makes it much easier to sustain relationships over long distances (Avent, 2017: 148–155). If we consider Barrett's new theory of emotions in relation to Daniel Goleman's (2006) studies of social intelligence, then the local community may be said to function as a starting point for understanding social relationships and emotions. Goleman (2006: 150–151) states this clearly: 'genes are more dynamic than most people – and science for more than a century – have assumed. . . . It is biologically impossible for a gene to operate independently of its environment: genes are *designed* to be regulated by signals from the immediate surround'.

Understood in this way, there is not necessarily an insoluble contradiction between the local community and the global with regard to social and emotional competence. The local community is a necessary prerequisite for developing and understanding social and emotional competence. This clearly means that to develop social relations over long geographical distances, one should understand the local culture and social context one is participating in. Thus, regarding the development of social and emotional competence, it might be said that distance is less important at the beginning of the Fourth Industrial Revolution, if one has insight into the local culture and social context in which one is participating.

Technology is changing so rapidly in the present day, that many job seekers will discover on completing their education that their knowledge and competence are already outdated. However, this will not apply to social and emotional competence, according to the new theory mentioned previously related to this topic. Technological development is therefore increasingly focused on social and emotional competence. No matter how quickly technology changes, success in the workplace will be linked to social and emotional competence, something both Karl Albrecht (2006) and Daniel Goleman (2006) underline.

Social competence is linked to both insight and behaviour. It is linked to how we relate to other people, and how we get other people to collaborate with us. Albrecht (2006: 28–159) has developed a model to show how interaction in social competence can best lead to success. The practical application of the model can be described briefly as follows:

Situational awareness

This can be described as a person's ability to sense a situation, a kind of intuitive understanding of what is happening. We say that some people are good at reading and understanding situations. Situational awareness is also linked to the ability to detect the intentions of other people. To succeed in doing this, one must show respect for other people's feelings, ideas and opinions. A self-obsessed person will never be able to develop situational awareness. A person with a high level of situational awareness will be able to read a context, allowing them to understand the signals that the context is sending. In a social situation, there may be many different types of groups that are sending different signals. A person with situational awareness will be able to read the different subgroups' opinions and develop a clear synthesis of the different signals that are being sent.

Presence

This concerns how a person interprets signals emitted by a social context. In everyday terms, we can understand this as having intuition about things that are gestating before they actually happen. A person who has 'presence' will influence a social situation simply by being there. The whole situation will be framed differently when that person is present. A person with a high degree of presence will be highly approachable and will be experienced as present by the other people there. Such a person's humour, friendliness and engagement are infectious. This person has an attitude that transmits positivity to the situation.

Authenticity

This is about how we radiate signals that other people sense and that are experienced as indicators that we are trustworthy, honest, ethical and reliable. A feeling of sincerity will characterize how other people experience an authentic person. In this context, the opposite of authenticity is being manipulative and using other people for one's own ends. Authentic persons keep their word, i.e. we can trust them, even if we are not present when they are speaking on our behalf.

Clarity

This says something about our ability to be open and to communicate clearly and unambiguously, without packaging our ideas or opinions in a lot of meaningless waffle. People who use language to create possible escape routes for themselves, regardless of how the situation develops, are not using clarity in their communications, but precise ambiguity. In such cases, the speaker is apparently precise, but if one pays careful attention, one finds that their formulations include an element of ambiguity, allowing them to be used on a later occasion as evidence that the speaker is keeping their word. Accordingly, people who use precise ambiguity will always be able to claim that they are keeping their word, because their statements can be interpreted in all sorts of different ways. In contrast, a person who communicates with clarity has not inserted this kind of ambiguity into their language. Another way of communicating that lacks clarity even more than precise ambiguity involves using abstractions to create room for manoeuvre. People communicating in this way use language as a kind of abstract ladder to create positive situations for themselves and to put the other person in a linguistic predicament.

Empathy

In our context, this means more than simply understanding the situation of another person and sympathizing with them. Obviously, this is part of what it means to be empathic. But here we are also referring to the emergence of a shared feeling of

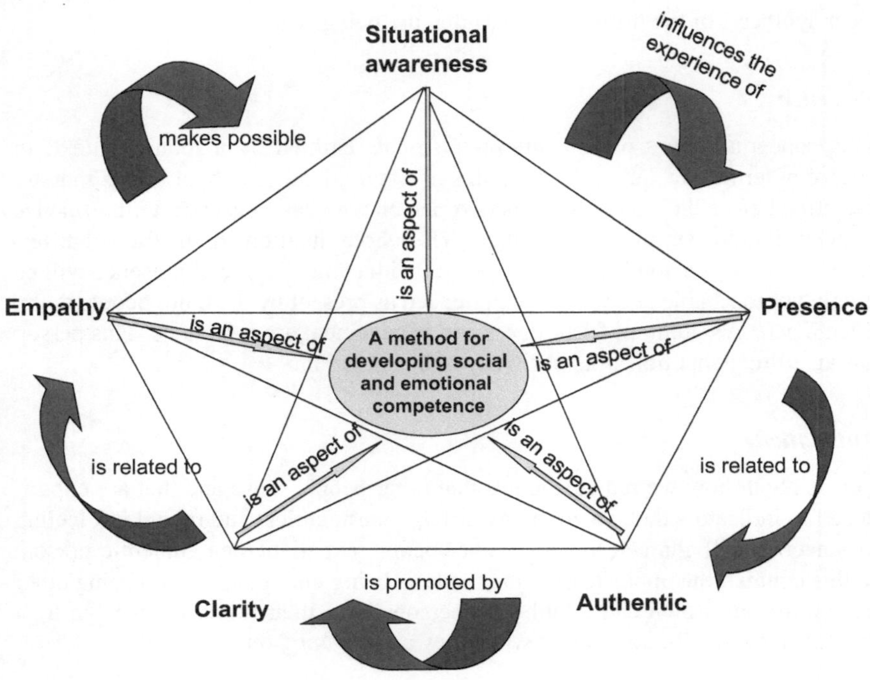

Figure 3.7 A method for developing social and emotional competence

empathy between the people concerned. What we are talking about here is how one experiences a connection to another person's feelings when one is in a state of empathy.

Participating in another person's emotional state and showing sensitivity and understanding is part of being empathic. This is how one develops mutual respect. This respect is generated through listening to the other person and telling them that one understands them. Mutual respect is also developed by paying attention to the other person and vice versa. Valuing the other person also plays a part in the development of mutual respect. These two factors, attention and valuing, create a situation in which each person feels a sense of affirmation that they mean something to the other. This is about behaving in such a way that the other person is represented in the way in which they want to be understood.

The five elements described earlier are shown in Figure 3.7.

Sub-conclusion

In this section, we have examined the following question: what social and emotional competences will be in demand in the Fourth Industrial Revolution?

The successful professional, such as the psychologist described in our example earlier, will need to possess dual competence in the Fourth Industrial Revolution. He or she will need to possess the skills, knowledge and competence associated with the specific profession. But this will only constitute a necessary but not a sufficient condition of the successful professional. The sufficient competence for the successful professional will be coding skills and knowledge of intelligent algorithms and of how intelligent robots function. With such competence, the professional of the future will also be able to develop his or her own business. Consequently, entrepreneurship will also constitute part of the future professional's competence.

It is improbable that the new professional will be able to operate as a lone wolf in the complex field of knowledge that is emerging. The rationale is simple. Those people who do best will be those who work in teams. In the Fourth Industrial Revolution, technology will be the main driver of change, and this technology will be so complex that a single professional will not be able to utilize it alone – at least not develop and maintain it without working together with other experts. In other words, the probable future scenario is that new teams of experts will be constantly innovative and develop new businesses. Technological innovations are very likely to increase in number and scope. There will be a transition from scope to scale, i.e. small focused businesses will develop and grow using economies of scale, not unlike what happened at the start of the first industrial revolution.

The social and emotional competence that everyone will need to have will be linked to the understanding that subjective feelings can be objective in their consequences and that emotions are created in the social context and the situation one finds oneself in. Therefore, trust will be important. What we know for sure is that the new technology will promote a very high rate of change. Therefore, change competence will be an important social competence in the Fourth Industrial Revolution. The many changes that will occur will result in many people losing their jobs; many people will also have to develop different skills and find new jobs. Therefore, in this difficult period of transition, being able to empathize with others will constitute an important social and emotional competence. Being able to understand and empathize with other people will also be related to understanding that there are always many perspectives that people have of the same situation. Consequently, it will be important to have expertise in perspective diversity.

Leadership competence

In this section, we will examine the following question: what leadership competences will be in demand in the Fourth Industrial Revolution?

The Fourth Industrial Revolution will be characterized by the use of artificial intelligence, intelligent robots and intelligent algorithms. We know that although new technology will acquire a more central role also in leadership, emotional and social competence will also be critical to success as a leader (Goleman, 1996, 2006). Goleman states that the purpose of leadership in the new era will be 'to prime good feeling in those they lead' (2014: ix). People are largely self-organizing in most businesses, especially knowledge workers. It is how they are 'seen' and listened to, and the extent to which they are given the opportunity to work with what they are passionate about, what they are good at and what they master, that differentiates the talented leader from the leader who is unable to bring out the best in their employees (Akerlof & Shiller, 2009: 11–59). Consequently, good leaders at all levels in the Fourth Industrial Revolution will need to possess emotional and social competence, if they are to manage employees optimally.

The primary ability for the new leader will consist of him or her being able to relate to employees, ignite their spark and produce the best in them. Leaders who are extremely good at the rational and logical level, but who have problems with the emotional and social interaction with others, i.e. the 'social eunuchs', are unlikely to succeed. Inability to communicate and socially interact with others will comprise an undesirable characteristic in future leaders. However, it is often those people who are skilled at logical and rational tasks (but who are socially unintelligent) who manage to scramble up the hierarchy into leadership positions. As leaders, these people will be like walking disasters waiting to happen, because they cannot 'see' others, listen to them or connect socially and emotionally. Research clearly shows that the performance of employees is directly affected by the emotions expressed by a leader.[6] Therefore, it might be said that leaders who are 'social eunuchs' may be likened to 'psychopaths' – they 'suck up and kick down' in the organization.

Leaders who lack social intelligence, i.e. the social eunuchs, will have trouble inspiring, arousing passion and motivating employees to reach goals. The leadership of these social eunuchs will create a toxic atmosphere in the organization in which rumours and stories will thrive. The stories circulating around the organization will often focus on the leader's inability to lead; these stories will often strengthen the view among employees that he or she is unfit to lead. Nevertheless, it is often the case that such leaders will continue to lead, as the organization's board is often disconnected from the daily activities of the organization. It is only when negative indicators eventually reach the board that they will finally respond to the problematic situation. However, at such a point it may then be too late, because what was once a well-functioning and growing entrepreneurial organization has now become an organization where employees spend a lot of time protecting their own positions. In such an organization, a form of institutional corruption may easily develop. Institutional corruption may take many forms, such as holding a protective hand over incompetent leaders. This development will often be experienced by employees as both unethical and unfair, resulting in a loss of trust and confidence in the leadership. Such an organization will be well on its way into the 'spiral of death'. The spiral of death in this context means that the organization spends more time and resources on dealing with internal challenges and problems than on winning in a market.

In contrast to the social eunuchs are those leaders who have the necessary social and emotional competence. These leaders *'see' their employees* and let them work on what they are passionate about and good at. The importance of

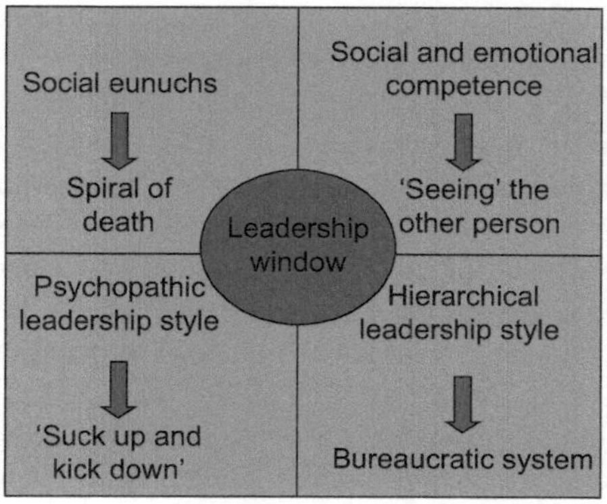

Figure 3.8 Leadership window

this for organizational success has been shown in the work of the two Nobel laureates in economics, George Akerlof and Robert Shiller (2009), as well as in recent brain research (Swart et al., 2015; Dimitriadis & Psychogios, 2016). The old and outdated leadership style was hierarchical. This style of leadership was viewed as 'normal' during the period of traditional industrial organization, i.e. with its factories and gargantuan buildings. In this leadership style, steering and control were important. The previous description is shown in Figure 3.8.

In the following, we will further describe social and emotional competence.

Narratives

Case letter 1: leadership and myths

What are the myths about leaders that make some people want to take on such an exposed position (disregarding for a moment the possibility that the pay gap between top executives and ordinary employees is a motivating factor)? One leadership myth is the idea of the leader as hero. We find the leader-as-hero in many myths of political and military leadership, e.g. Mahatma Gandhi. Gandhi was the hero who brought India out of its colonial status and transformed it into the world's largest democracy.

According to Joseph Campbell (1998: 1), the point of myths is that most of us are concerned with things and events that are either happening now or that will happen in the near future. We are not educated to think in mythical terms, particularly not leadership myths. These myths tell us, among other things, about many of the values that are worth fighting for, and which have been fought for by many leaders throughout history and into our own time. We find myths about leaders as early as the writings of Homer and Xenophon. In Homer (1950, 1956), we follow leaders in the *Iliad* and the *Odyssey*.

As a leader, Odysseus is presented as greedy, dishonest, disloyal to the people he is supposed to be leading and a comical presentation of self-assurance. Odysseus is a leader who suffers, but not necessarily with his men, and who does not necessarily share their fate. He is a rumour-monger, a philosopher and swindler whose lies result in the deaths of his followers. However, he is idealized along with Achilles for his courage and endurance, and as a tactician we would want on our side when a battle is joined in earnest. In the work of Sophocles, Odysseus is presented as an exponent of *Realpolitik*, who focuses on the possible and accepts the necessity of fate. In Homer, we see Odysseus both as a moral wayfinder, a hero who through his courage shows us the path, and as a leader of flawed character. Odysseus is depicted as a liar, deceiver and braggart just as often as he is depicted as a courageous hero. The courageous version of Odysseus is also presented in a remarkable light, when he withdraws from battles in the *Iliad*, ignoring the pleas of Diomedes and Nestor's urgings about duty.[7]

An interesting feature of Homer's writing is that his heroes demonstrate their morality through their actions (Rutherford, 2010: 157). We could envisage today's leaders as being subject to some of the same criteria, i.e. a leader comes to symbolize the ethics that exist within an organization.

Odysseus can be understood as an ethical role model and as symbolizing a leader's journey through life in pursuit of knowledge. If we read the *Odyssey* allegorically,[8] we might interpret Odysseus's travels as a leader's journey in search of knowledge, as a kind of progression towards ethical awareness and a more developed character. When Odysseus returns to Ithaca as an old man, he speaks to Amphinomous about the journey of life. He warns Amphinomous about youthful overconfidence and says that our souls change along with our fates.[9] If this is an expression of Odysseus's accumulated wisdom, following a long journey in search of knowledge and ethics, then we could understand him as saying that ethics change in light of circumstances and context. Character traits and ethics are an important part of Homer's message (Rutherford, 2010: 159). They are also important characteristics of capable leaders today. Like today's leaders, both Odysseus and Achilles were changed by circumstance and experience.

Machiavelli's admiration for Xenophon is indicative of Xenophon's importance as a military strategist and commentator on power politics.[10] In this context, an important book is Xenophon's *Anabasis*. In the first part of this work (Books I-III), Xenophon discusses preparations for war. Book IV describes life in wartime. Books V-VII discuss security policy following the war. The war in question was between the Greeks and Persians in 401–399 BCE. Among other events, the general in charge of the Greek army, along with most of the leading officers, was killed by the Persians near Babylon. Xenophon describes how 10,000 solders, lacking a leader, managed to survive in hostile territory and withdraw to the Greek areas on the shores of the Black Sea.

Of the 10,000 men who started the journey, 8,600 reached the Greek colonies by the Black Sea. Given that this was a withdrawal through hostile territory, this was a major achievement.

The march was made famous by Xenophon's book *Anabasis*: *The Long March* (1964). Readers and admirers of this book have included Julius Caesar, Lord Byron, John Keats and Leo Tolstoy, to name but a few.[11]

We understand from this short case letter that myths can be important for leaders and for how we experience leaders.

Case letter 2: leadership and change

Most people do not know what organizational changes will lead to and how they will affect them personally. In this context, Charles Handy (2007) goes ironically straight to the point when he titled his book on the topic, *Myself and Other Important Matters* (2007). In other words, the title goes straight to the core of what most employees care about regarding organizational change processes: how will the changes affect me? The Prospect Theory of the Nobel laureates in economics, Daniel Kahneman and Amos Tversky (1979, 2000), also deal with this with regard to the fact that people value losses and gains differently.

In his book, *The Age of Unreason* (2002), Handy illustrates the dangers of not adapting to changes in the external environment in his illustrative and amusing allegory of a frog: A frog is put into a large cooking pot filled with cold water. The water is heated up extremely slowly towards boiling point. The frog acclimatizes to the gradually warming water, and eventually basks itself to death. On the other hand, if a frog is put into a pot of boiling water, it will react instantly by jumping out of the pot albeit with some burns, but still alive. The moral of the two stories is that if the changes happen slowly, then no one responds to what is happening. If the changes happen quickly (the boiling water), then people will respond immediately.

For many people, life is a struggle, while for others it is a journey involving reflection about what is the meaning of it all. No matter what relationship one has to life, and how one has chosen to deal with it within one's limitations, both work and private life are about change. Some of these changes are driven by new technology, artificial intelligence, intelligent robots and intelligent algorithms. Fundamentally, however, it is efficiency, economic rationality and economic growth that drive the overall change processes. The idea is that efficiency, economic rationality and economic growth are necessary conditions to ensure progress and wealth. However, the question that every leader should ask is: are the aforementioned factors necessary and sufficient conditions for prosperity and well-being, for a better life for oneself and other people? Once again, Charles Handy provides us with a brilliant and illustrative allegory, 'The Empty Raincoat'. The story goes as follows: in a park in Minneapolis in the US, there is a bronze sculpture of a raincoat. However, there is no one inside the raincoat; it is empty. The moral is that we have become so good at goals (ends), rationality and technology that it has become our bronze raincoat, but we have forgotten what is supposed to be inside the raincoat, namely ourselves. We have completely changed our ends and means. The means have become the ends (goal), and we stand there like empty raincoats, with no content, no meaning and with a purpose that can be measured, weighed and counted. It is in such a context that economic growth becomes an empty phrase, leaving people with a loss of meaning, identity and a purpose worth living for.

Description

Warren Bennis has said that 'the factory of the future will have only two employees, a man and a dog. The man will be there to feed the dog. The dog will be there to keep the man from touching the equipment'.[12] The point here is that in the future, if an enterprise is organized as a factory, or a distributed system where the parts and the whole interact in a global context to produce something or a service, then intelligent robots, intelligent algorithms and intelligent informats will constitute the organizing principle. If eventually the dog, which guards the technological equipment, is the only employee left, because it is automatically fed, then we can no longer talk about labour productivity, but about input-output productivity. In such an enterprise, there will be no struggle between capital and labour concerning the distribution of added value; the relationship between profits and wages will cease to be a problem because there will be no workers to receive wages in this fully automated enterprise. Of course, such an enterprise is merely a *fata morgana*, an illusion or a utopia. The point being made here is that leadership in the future, no matter how automated an organization happens to be, will concern more than just steering and control. It will concern facilitating creativity, collaboration and innovation.

A significant aspect about leadership at the beginning of the Fourth Industrial Revolution is that leaders who have demonstrated good results in the past will probably continue to apply the same leadership skills that have resulted in past successes. What's wrong with this, one may ask? Shouldn't one learn from one's experiences and use them to good purpose for the organization when going forward into the future? The answer is both yes and no. Of course, one should learn from one's experiences. However, the bottom line is that when a revolution occurs – in this case, changes that are so formidable that everything we have learnt in the past will be put to the test, and most of it will be changed – then perhaps the most important strategy will be to throw what we have learnt from experience overboard. Steering, control and bureaucracy constituted a leadership and organization philosophy that suited a time when stability and planning were possible. In the new era, the only thing that will be stable or certain will be the major changes. In such a situation, planning will not be the most important factor, but being able to continuously create one's own and the organization's future in relation to rapidly changing conditions (Ackoff, 1981, 1999). The skills leaders will need in such a situation will be more focused on social and emotional competence because it is creativity and innovation that will release the productive forces, not the measuring, weighing and counting of various economic indicators. Of course, these indicators will still be important, but not as social mechanisms that will drive the organization forward, only as a benchmark for how the organization has moved from one period to another. The social eunuchs who use an outdated organization and leadership philosophy will only create problems and resistance, no matter how persistent they are on reaching goals. One may be very good at making goals, but that is where it stops, because the goals are never accomplished. The social eunuch may be very good at constructing detailed and elaborate goals for the organization. However, without dedicated, creative and enthusiastic employees, and regardless of the level of automation that an organization has implemented, the efforts of the employees will be crucial to success. To trigger creativity and commitment, the leader of the future will need to have a well-developed social and emotional competence. This includes the leader having the ability to 'see' his or her employees. He or she should be able to encourage employees to do what they are passionate about, what they are good at and that which can make a difference that will really make a difference. Situations in which employees feel they master what they are doing will ultimately benefit the organization. This also presupposes that employees receive continuous feedback and that they are largely autonomous, which is a prerequisite for motivation and commitment.

The rapid change processes which we are already experiencing, but which will probably increase in strength in the Fourth Industrial Revolution as new technology is implemented, will more and more start to resemble a pressure cooker. The pressure on employees and management will increase. The demands will be greater because global competition will increase, and new technology will integrate enterprises in one location with similar enterprises around the world, where wages are lower, productivity is higher and efficiency is better. All these factors will increase the stress level in organizations. Those employees who leave the organization first will probably not be the ones who are the least productive. Such a development will further increase the level of stress in organizations. In this situation, the leader must choose some simple and operative social mechanisms to avoid the great danger of apathy and conflict associated with a rapid rate of change, and transform this into a positive experience for employees, so that it constitutes a strategic resource for the organization.

'You want to shine', said the chair of the board to his CEO. 'Remember that I also need to shine', said the chair. This had been forgotten by the CEO, and at the next board meeting the CEO was criticized for his behaviour, which culminated in a decision made asking him to resign. Of course, he was given a golden parachute, but he nevertheless left with his tail between his legs. The point of this little story is that everyone wants 'to shine', everyone wants to be 'seen', and everyone wants to be seen when they are performing well. It's like Handy's second curve (Handy, 2016). If we are successful, and the growth curve is moving upwards, then we believe that success will continue. However, sooner or later, most of us end up at 'David's Bar'. This is Handy's metaphor for someone who didn't change course just before 'the peak' of the curve and ended up sitting at David's Bar talking about how great things were in the 'old days'. The CEO, in the previous story, should have known that the chair of the board also needed to shine and should have allowed her to be the one who 'rescued the ship from shipwreck'. The CEO clearly hadn't understood or heard about the 'second curve' and 'David's Bar'. The overall message here is that a leader should always give employees and superiors the opportunity 'to shine'. Being a leader is not about being the best-liked person among the employees, but about letting them shine, while at the same time it is wise to let one's superiors shine as well. The leader who understands this simple principle has understood the 'second curve' and will not end up at 'David's Bar'.

Edward Hallowell asks the question: 'What makes a person shine?' He answers his own question: 'Smart is overrated. Talent is overrated. Breeding, Ivy League education, sophistication, wit, eloquence, and good looks – they matter, but they're all overrated' (Hallowell, 2011: 1). What then is important? That you make the best out of what you have. This is perhaps not the answer you expected or even what you think is the most crucial. If we link Hallowell's answer to our own operational social and emotional competence (Figure 3.9), as well as to Handy's 'second curve' and 'David's Bar', then we will realize that all leaders, no matter what they have of life experience in their baggage, can get others to shine. This is the real leadership skill that is important at a time when everything is changing and most people will end up at David's Bar, talking about how talented they once were, and how they tackled various challenges.

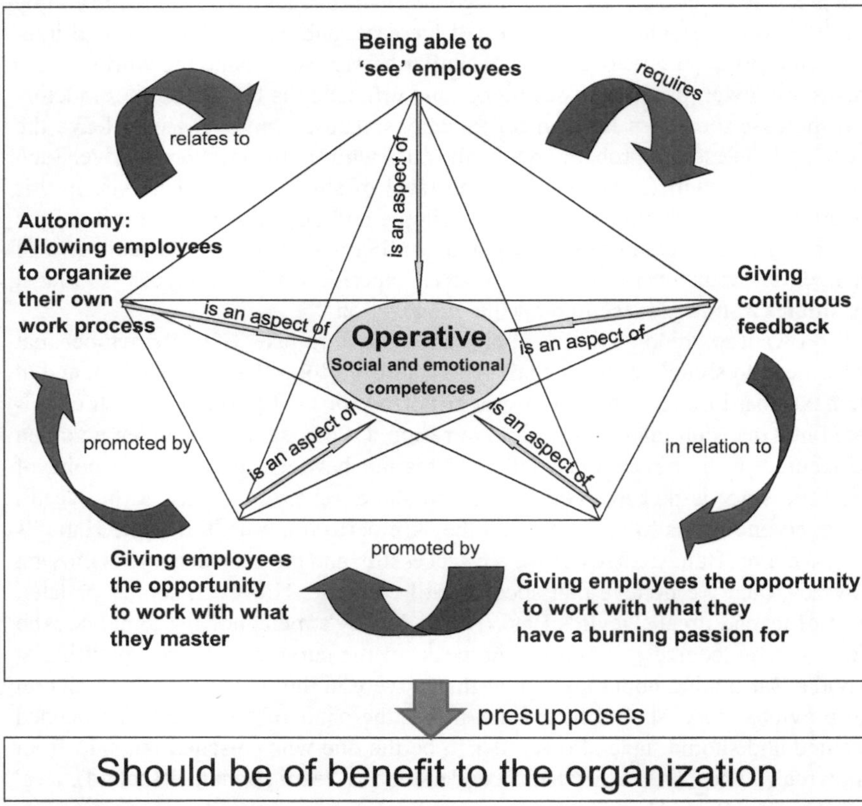

Figure 3.9 Making the others shine: the necessary operational social and emotional competences to facilitate effective leadership in the Fourth Industrial Revolution

The leader who lets the others shine, while paying attention to Angela Lee Duckworth's research findings, can be pretty sure to avoid ending up at 'David's Bar'. Duckworth (2017) proposes that there are four elements that are necessary conditions for success as a leader (2017). She has carried out studies over several years in various contexts asking the question *who is successful here, and why?* The answer produced by her research is that those people who are successful possess the following characteristics:

- *A burning desire* to contribute so you can make a difference, regardless of the field of interest.
- *Perseverance*; you have a long-term view with regard to what you are doing and you don't shy away from your goal.
- *Moral courage*; you do not compromise the values you believe in.
- *Self-discipline*, stubbornness or tenacity; you don't give up although others choose something else.

In Figure 3.9, we have illustrated aspects of an operational strategy for leadership success in relation to social and emotional competences.

Analysis

The previously mentioned skills required by a leader are so simple, but at the same time so difficult: the leader needs to set aside his or her own needs and to do everything possible for others, so that both subordinates and superiors will be given the opportunity to shine. This is the law of gravity for leadership. If the leader succeeds in this endeavour, then the paradox arises: they will also 'shine'.

But does everyone have the ability to shine? Does every subordinate and superior have something to show so that they can shine? Yes! And that's the beauty of it. If you get to do what you are passionate about, master and are good at, and you are able to organize your work time yourself, then you will shine. The objection is that not everyone is passionate about something. What can the leader do if an employee is not passionate about anything? The answer is given by one of Hallowell's informants in his book *Shine* (2011: 4): 'Just keep fishin'. . . . Everybody got that spark in them, somewhere.' Even the grumpy old guys, who have long since ended up at 'David's Bar' have a spark deep inside them somewhere that can flame up with the proper encouragement. However, one should keep in mind that one cannot do anything about the other person's behaviour. The best way to change the other person is to change one's reaction to their behaviour. When the grumpy old guys are met with understanding, their attitude changes, though it may take time, and then one can start looking for the spark deep inside them. It is this spark that the leader has to kindle into a flame and then turn it into a burning desire. This is where the core of good leadership is: making the other person shine. Some may argue that leadership is not 'rocket science'. This is perfectly correct. Management is more complex than rocket science, it is brain science (Hallowell, 2011: 5–6).

There are six process steps that are a synthesis of what is described earlier that can help even the most mediocre leader to be successful. These process steps are as follows:

1. Find the employees' burning desire and make sure that is where their efforts are focused at work.
2. Give feedback on even the smallest amount of progress, and make sure this progress is reinforced. In this way, the employees will feel that they are 'seen', something we all appreciate, no matter where we happen to be on the social ladder.
3. Make sure the work that the employees do is something they are able to master. In other words, it is what people are good at that needs to be reinforced, not the areas they are not so good at.
4. Be persistent in your search for the other person's spark. Finally, where you find a spark, make sure that this spark is kindled into a flame that is turned into a burning passion.
5. Help employees to develop self-discipline so that even the average employee is able to fully exploit his or her potential.
6. Show moral courage. Of course, this can mean so much, but here it means that you as a leader have an explicit moral standard and that you make your moral compass visible and follow the compass, without any deviation. When leaders reach a certain level, they tend to adjust their values to their new position. The leaders' moral courage should be constant so that they do not change their moral compass, even if they attain a higher leadership position.

The generic aspect of leadership

The effective leaders are namely the best because they have failed, acknowledged this, learnt from their mistakes, built further on this lesson and moved on. One can say that leaders must learn from their mistakes or be a failure. As leaders, it doesn't help much just having good intentions if the results are bad. Leadership is not a popularity contest. Therefore, the best leaders will dare to be open about their own insecurities and mistakes and build their self-confidence based on the understanding that learning and change apply to everyone in the organization, including themselves. The history of leadership has shown us that the combination of high ambition and low self-esteem in the character of a leader is a fatal flaw; such leaders will ultimately fail, resulting in disaster for the people they lead and the society around them (Bennis, 2009). There are many people today who want to be a leader because it will give them power, position, influence and a high salary. However, there are few people who actually want to perform effective leadership. To be an effective leader, some necessary and sufficient conditions need to be fulfilled. One of the necessary conditions is that one should be 'authentic', that is be oneself, and be able to reflect on one's own self-confidence and examine what experiences in life have shaped this self-confidence (Bennis & Sample, 2015: 4–5). The leader should also investigate and help build the self-confidence of employees, otherwise one will end up with an organization that is psychologically bankrupt. In such an organization, too many resources will be used on dealing with internal tensions and solving conflicts.

However, being authentic is not enough. The leader is really a goal-seeking system (Ackoff, 1981, 1999). This means that a leader who occupies such a position should, possibly together with a leadership team and in collaboration with the organization's board, point out the goals that need to be achieved, and then ensure that the entire organization is geared towards achieving the goals. To achieve this, all or part of the organization must go through a transformation process. This change will most probably lead to resistance. It is how the leader tackles this resistance that says something about how effective the leadership is (Johannessen, 2019b, 2020c).

Good leaders should also keep their moral compass intact. In plain text, this means that although they improve the organization's bottom line, this improvement should always be viewed in the context of ethical considerations, and the consequences that the actions and behaviour of the organization has for other parties and the environment.

Showing respect to others, taking responsibility for oneself and other people, and never opting out of a situation in which the dignity of others is threatened are evidence of good leaders, which will motivate employees and lead to good results (Bennis & Sample, 2015: 11–31; Johannessen, 2021b).

Figure 3.10 shows the generic conditions for being a good leader.

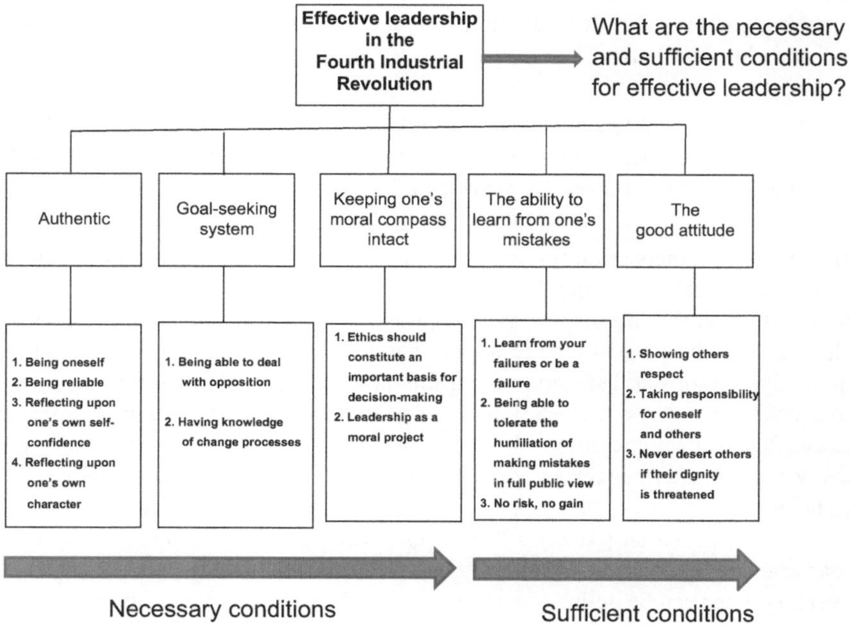

Figure 3.10 The necessary and sufficient conditions for effective leadership

Theoretical points

To feel that you are important is a basic human need, according to Abraham Maslow (Maslow, 2011, 2013) and others, such as Carl Rogers (2004). This also applies to leaders (Bennis & Sample, 2015: 11). Just as every employee wants to be 'seen', leaders also want to be 'seen' and thus valued by their subordinates. Employees who understand this simple psychological strategy can, in the most unexpected ways, guide their leaders by recognizing their importance, showing them respect and pointing out that they are crucial to the success of the organization. In this context, one might even agree with Warren Bennis and Steven Sample when they go as far to say that 'the drive for importance is today commonly called leadership' (2015: 11). Consequently, leaders, like us others, wish to be important to the organization, be recognized and be 'seen'. Taking risks is a necessary prerequisite to achieve this. Without taking risks, it is improbable that leaders can achieve success and thus gain recognition. In practice, taking risks also increases the possibility of making mistakes, and it is not making mistakes that will result in leaders being given recognition! The paradox can be expressed as follows: the greater the risk you take, the more likely it is that you will make mistakes. However, it is not the mistakes in themselves that make you successful, but without making mistakes you will not be able to learn how to do things correctly. Expressed in another way, you might say that half of a leader's efforts, energy and commitment lead to failure, while the rest lead to success. The bottom line is that the leader never knows which half leads to success and which half leads to failure. However, this must not be misunderstood: Making mistakes is not something good in itself. It is learning from one's mistakes, which is the underlying leadership trait here.

> Proposition: Making mistakes may lead to success or failure, but without making mistakes, failure will be unavoidable. Risk-taking is therefore a necessary prerequisite for successful leadership.

Being a leader attracts criticism and opposition. Therefore, leaders need to possess special traits, such as having the stamina to withstand such criticism and opposition, if they are going to increase the probability of their success. The Fourth Industrial Revolution will lead to major changes at all levels for people, organizations, institutions and society; taking this into consideration, the opposition to major changes in organizations will of necessity increase (Adriaenssen & Johannessen, 2016). In this context, the leadership traits that will be needed are the capacity to withstand uncertainty (Makunda, 2012); the willingness to take risks (Kahneman & Tversky, 1979); the ability to learn from one's mistakes, change direction and move on (Ackoff, 1999); possessing passion for one's work; and perseverance (Duckworth, 2017).

Perseverance can be defined in many ways. In leadership, as in other aspects of life, there is a general rule that is often formulated as the 80/20 rule.[13] For leaders, this rule may be formulated as follows: a leader spends 20 per cent of his or her time on things that substantially contribute to the organization, while 80 per cent of the time is spent doing trivial tasks that are difficult to see if they have any positive impact on the organization. The leader must learn to live with this principle because in its practical implications, many employees will view this positively. They will appreciate that the leader has the perseverance to complete trivial tasks that may initially look like a 'waste of time', but which in reality will be important to many, because they see that the leader is there for them, that he or she cares and that he or she 'sees' them.

Throughout history, we have many examples of people who have become leaders, even American presidents, who have not possessed the five special leadership traits mentioned previously. On the contrary, they are often ill-equipped to be a leader and are plagued with psychological deficiencies, such as the lack of self-confidence, or an unnatural drive to prove their worth. In this context, Bennis and Sample (2015: 32) refer to the former American president, Richard Nixon, as one who was plagued with such deficiencies, who despite his high ambitions left behind him a legacy of failure. In other words, those who are or wish to become leaders should examine their own motives and reflect upon whether they are driven to take on a leadership position, because they have some character flaw, such as the lack of self-confidence. Experiencing rejection may be another such flaw that leads one to seek recognition. That being said, it should also be pointed out that so-called character flaws can also result in giving an individual tremendous ambition, driving a person to take on a leadership position. Consequently, it is very important to clarify what drives a person to become a leader. Is the leader on a mission to prove something? Or is he or she on a mission to really make a difference to the organization?

These are some key questions a leader should answer before seeking to take on a leadership position:[14]

1. What motivates me to become a leader?
2. What values do I want to bring into the organization?
3. What skills make me a good leader?
4. What are my limitations, and how will these affect how I lead?

> Proposition: Key leadership traits in the Fourth Industrial Revolution will be:
>
> > To tolerate uncertainty and be risk-averse; to have the ability to learn from one's own mistakes; to be driven by a burning desire; and to have the perseverance to see things out to the end.

Leadership is not just about the bottom-line numbers. Leadership is a moral project (Knights & O'Leary, 2006: 125–137). In a crisis, leaders will have to make split-second decisions that will mark them for the rest of their lives, and in some cases throughout history. 'The die has been cast', said Julius Caesar on 'crossing the Rubicon', which committed him to an irrevocable act. The Roman Senate had ordered Caesar not to bring his army across the Rubicon river, so Caesar's act was considered an act of insurrection by the Roman government;

today, the phrase 'crossing the Rubicon' is a metaphor meaning to pass the point of no return. The morality of many other decisions made by leaders have been questioned by historians, such as Churchill's ordering of the firebombing of Dresden towards the end of World War Two (considered a war crime by some) and the decision by the Germans towards the end of the Second World War to use scorched earth tactics, when fleeing from the advance of Soviet troops in the north of Norway. In the aftermath of the war, the Germans were accused of plunder and wanton destruction, and it is still debated today whether or not this constituted a war crime. All the previously mentioned decisions made by leaders, and millions of other decisions like these, are made in crisis situations. In our context, the point is that ethical aspects should always be considered by leaders, even when making 'split-second decisions'.

Proposition: Leadership is a moral project.

In contrast to so-called split-second decisions are the decisions a leader makes in full public view, where the leader is exposed to the pressure of the media, opponents and others who are often just waiting in the wings to 'pounce on' on the leader's so-called catastrophic decision. In such situations, it is often the best strategy for the leader to make himself or herself as independent as possible from these groups. Following the herd and being influenced by herd mentality will never lead to decisions that will serve the organization as a whole. We witnessed this when President John F. Kennedy ordered the invasion of Cuba; the failed invasion was later called the Bay of Pigs Disaster, which Irving Janis has explained was due to such herd mentality, or what he terms groupthink – that is when people make irrational decisions due to 'group pressure'. We can all be exposed to group thinking. This is something we see occur in real crises, where people stand on the sidelines, when they should intervene, because others also choose to be 'bystanders'. In such situations, we are the victims of the bystander effect. As leaders, it is important that we surround ourselves with people who can prevent us from making so-called groupthink decisions, following the herd mentality or being affected by the bystander effect. This can be achieved by always having access to someone, or people in the leadership team, who can act as a devil's advocate, and who are strong and independent enough 'to speak out against Rome' (i.e. to speak out against a powerful authority).[15]

Proposition: To prevent groupthink, herd mentality and the bystander syndrome, leaders should have access to one or more devil's advocates who can take a critical or opposing view.

Practical utility

The belief in rationality as the most important management parameter for the economy, for leadership and for society is losing ground. The relatively new behavioral economics looks at completely different factors than 'rational' ones to explain people's economic behaviour (Akerlof & Shiller, 2009). Akerlof and Shiller look at factors such as *confidence, justice, fairness, illusion* as well as *stories and myths* in an attempt to explain economic behaviour. In our context, it is also highly probable that in the Fourth Industrial Revolution, leaders will need to consider such psychological factors (Goleman, 2014). The Nobel laureate in economics Akerlof, and his co-author Shiller, regard human behaviour as more explanatory of what is happening in the economy than so-called rational explanations, which traditional economists deem as being more important. Our point in this regard is that people's behaviour and attitudes, with regard to their confidence and commitment to an organization or system, will be something that leaders of the future will have to take into account. This is not because people are irrational, but because so-called animal spirits[16] can also be understood, and in this way are also 'rational'. Ever since Adam Smith wrote *The Wealth of Nations* in 1776, and up until today, traditional economists have ignored the human psyche (Akerlof & Shiller, 2009: 3). Overlooking the human psyche also characterizes the mainstream research in the field of leaders and leadership. By taking people's behaviour regarding their commitment as a starting point in the context of leadership, the leader can take into account the importance of factors such as uncertainty, ambiguity and herd mentality when making decisions and exercising leadership.

The leadership context is the same whether one uses a rational logic or a more behavioural logic of the type associated with behavioural economics. At first glance, this may seem like a theoretical debate, which it may be, but here it has a very concrete and practical relevance. If a business leader has an educational background from a business college, which many business leaders often have, then the likelihood is the leader in question will mainly use a rational logic when making decisions. A perspective that has a social science focus, for instance with a background in sociology, psychology or anthropology, will attach greater importance to so-called human factors. As we have pointed out throughout this chapter, it is these factors that will become increasingly important at the beginning of the Fourth Industrial Revolution. Goleman (2014: 3–23) calls this 'primal leadership,' which he defines as follows: 'Great leadership works through the emotions' (Goleman, 2014: 3). In practice, this means that the leader's mood and how he or she uses his or her voice in communication is crucial to outcomes. On the one hand, if the tone is optimistic, inclusive and inspiring, then the employees will be motivated. On the other hand, a negative tone will easily lead to opposition and conflict. A leader who is introverted, communicates poorly and uses the communication strategy one associates with 'social eunuchs' will tend to create a negative emotional mood. Social eunuchs will have problems motivating and engaging employees.

Skilled leaders emotionally engage people when they can demonstrate positive emotions, not through the use of rational logic. For instance, consider Martin Luther King's speech: 'I have a dream', or John F. Kennedy's 'ask not what your country can do for you – ask what you can do for your country!' Great leaders emotionally engage and motivate people by connecting to their emotions. The leadership competence that will be sought in the Fourth Industrial Revolution will be social competence, and especially emotional intelligence.

It is not only individuals who have emotions, groups can also have emotions, according to Caroline Bartel and Richard Saavedra (2000: 187–231). According to the two researchers, groups can develop a common emotional state, positive or negative, within two hours. It takes anywhere from two hours to a few weeks to synchronize the emotions so that a group reaches a common emotional state (Totterdell, 2000: 848–859). In the experiments, the two researchers examined the creation of emotional unity among groups, independent of context. The common emotional development was also independent of the problems and challenges that existed in the group. In addition to groups developing common emotional states, the leader's emotional state infects his or her closest colleagues and eventually the entire organization (Gardner, 1995).

The leader's emotional state and how he or she communicates this emotional state, spreads down through the organization and affects the performance of the entire system. The emotions that spread most quickly are the positive, warm and inclusive ones (Provine, 2000: 133). Leaders who communicate such positive emotions are more likely to hold on to competent employees as opposed to those who have a more negative or neutral emotional behaviour (George & Bettenhausen, 1990: 698–706). This research only supports what people know intuitively through popular phrases, such as 'smile and the world smiles with you'. However, what is new is that research emphasizes that this also applies to organizations and that it applies to leaders at all levels. The emotional state of leaders and employees is important, because their emotional state will positively or negatively affect those around them and directly and indirectly affect results (Maulding Green & Leonard, 2019).

As the introduction of new technology results in a sharp increase in productivity, this will reduce the demand for labour. This will mean that those who remain in the organization will most probably have an even greater need than before for consistent positive emotional signals, because job insecurity will increase.

In the new technological framework of the workplace, leaders and employees will greatly benefit from having emotional self-understanding, as this will help them relate positively to others. For instance, having insight into why one expresses emotions in a particular way will enable one to modify emotional expressions in various situations, so that negative emotions linked to past experiences do not unduly affect situations in the present more than is necessary and desirable.

Knowing why one seeks appreciation will make it easier to control one's emotional expressions (cf. Figure 3.3). If you show emotional openness in situations, you may benefit by this in two ways. First, there is less chance you will be emotionally hurt if you have nothing to hide. Second, the other person(s) will open up emotionally more easily if you show openness. We have referred to research mentioned previously that supports the importance of emotional optimism. Being emotionally optimistic can make it easier for a leader and his or her colleagues to positively influence other employees. Emotional self-insight, control, openness

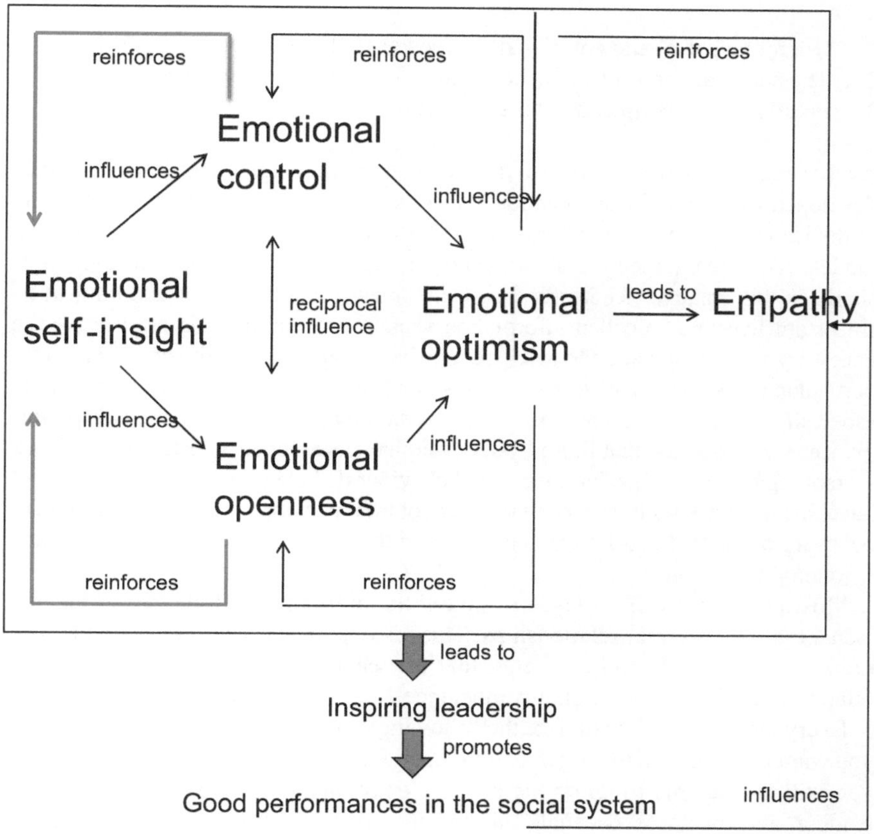

Figure 3.11 Practical leadership competences in the Fourth Industrial Revolution

and optimism are conditions directed inwards towards one's own feelings and emotions. In addition to these elements, empathy, understanding and being there for other(s) will affect the emotional contact between those involved. Empathy here means that one shows emotional understanding of the other person, whether this concerns customers, students, users etc.

In Figure 3.11, we have summarized and shown practical utility in relation to the question: what leadership competences will be in demand in the Fourth Industrial Revolution?

Sub-conclusion

The question we have investigated here is: what leadership competences will be in demand in the Fourth Industrial Revolution?

The brief answer to this question is linked to three factors:

1 Operative social and emotional competences (Figure 3.9).
2 The necessary and sufficient conditions for effective leadership (Figure 3.10).
3 Practical leadership competences (Figure 3.11).

A more detailed answer is linked to the fact that the whole leadership team should be developed so that previously mentioned factors 1–3 constitute the dominant thinking in the leadership team. If the three factors become part of the dominant thinking in the leadership team, then the likelihood of the 'leadership syndrome' developing is small. In this context, 'leadership syndrome' means that the leader and the leadership team live in a so-called information vacuum, so that they do not receive the necessary information and feedback about what is happening in the organization. In particular, this concerns the leader's behaviour. We know that the leader's behaviour, especially his or her emotional behavior, has an impact on the organization's performance. We also know that those leaders who have developed an effective feedback system regarding their performance and behaviour do better than leaders who do not have this feedback built into the assessment of their performance.[17] It is important to be aware of the fact that leaders and others in the organization can learn social and emotional competences.

Most people, as well as leaders, have little familiarity with the social mechanisms that affect social relationships. This also applies to learnt social and emotional incompetence, and the belief that one cannot change one's behaviour in relation to social and emotional competence.

Every leader should memorize the following principle: without a vision of what you want to achieve in the organization, there will be no passion. Without passion, you will not be able to ignite the positive emotions in the organization you are leading, and 'business as usual' will become your uninspiring motto. In relation to the competences that will be in demand in the Fourth Industrial Revolution, the previously mentioned principle can be rewritten as follows: focus on your basic values and turn them into your leadership philosophy. The point in this context is that your basic values are the values you are passionate about, which constitute a foundation for what you are good at, and where you can make a difference, and not any difference, but the difference that really makes a difference.

The values and a burning desire to make a difference are directly linked to developing goals for the organization. It is only the goals that are linked to the values and a burning desire to make a difference that can provide a strong foundation that will stand the test of time. In the honeymoon period of leadership, the leader's energy and goals seem to know no bounds. However, as most of us know, despite the euphoric feelings experienced during the honeymoon period, this is not enough to make the relationship last. The same is true with leaders. Once the honeymoon phase is over, a so-called leadership vacuum will appear. To avoid this, the leader should develop a management philosophy based on the values he or she is passionate about. The goals that are developed must be perceived as achievable. They must be measurable in one way or another, so that we know if we are on the right path or not. However, the goals must be based on requisite variety, so that they are multifaceted and can be adapted to changes in the outside world.

Cultural competence

In this section, we will examine the following question: what cultural competences will be in demand in the Fourth Industrial Revolution?

Intelligent robots, artificial intelligence and intelligent algorithms will change people's lives, relationships in and to working life, how to communicate, as well as our values and norms (Baldwin, 2019). Developments in the Fourth Industrial Revolution will deconstruct and remove the mechanical and analogue elements of the previous industrial revolutions. However, it will take time before all the remnants of the industrial society disappear. Rules and ways of thinking will remain, long after the foundation for the industrial way of thinking has disappeared. The changes will occur when a new way of thinking changes and replaces the established way of thinking.

Digitization and the fact that information processes are becoming more important than infrastructure processes will constitute the benchmark that will measure to what extent we have moved into a new era. However, even when we can say that the Fourth Industrial Revolution is a fact, cultural values, understood as our values, norms, traditions, myths and ceremonies, will still be rooted in past times, even if the foundations for these elements have disappeared (Bunge, 2015). When the Fourth Industrial Revolution has become a reality, the way we exchange information will be different from what it is today. What we can already observe today, regarding the use of all the information traces on the Web, represents only the beginning of how information and knowledge about each of us will be used in the future (Zuboff, 2019). This will represent a type of algorithmic capitalism that utilizes the emerging technological platforms (Johannessen, 2021a). The technology we are witnessing today is not only a social mechanism for the economic system, the political system and the relational system, but also for the cultural system.

The new technology affects how we communicate with each other, who we communicate with, what networks we are part of and who we influence and are influenced by. The technology that is evolving affects power structures, value creation and, not least, productivity in businesses and organizations. Our norms and values will probably also be influenced by the new technology, although this will take longer than, for example the establishing of new ways for distributing information and communicating with each other.

By observing the larger system that culture is part of, the economic, the political and the relational, we have the opportunity to examine the pattern and pattern of patterns that the cultural system tends towards. At the same time, when we observe technology from a longer historical perspective, it is easier to decode the complexity of the evolution of the cultural system as a function of the interaction between the other three systems.[18] The previous discussion is shown in Figure 3.12.

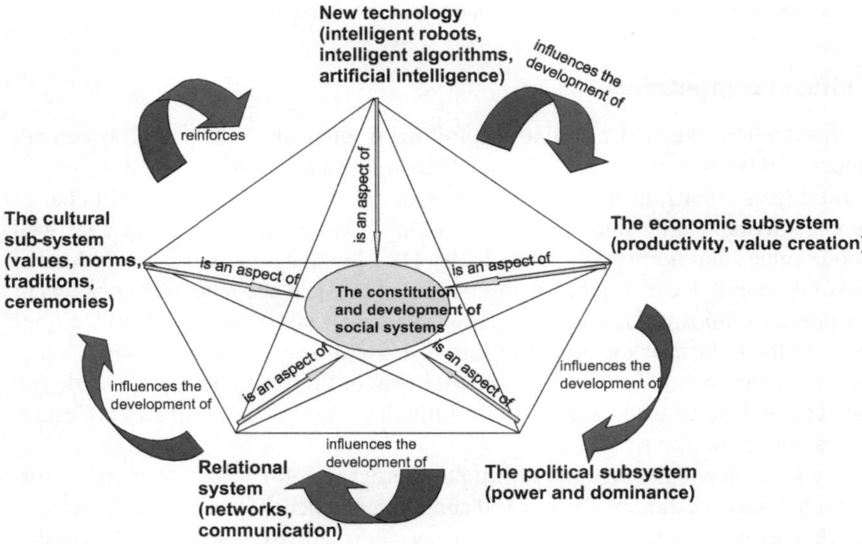

Figure 3.12 The constitution and development of social systems

Narratives

Case letter: intelligent robots as the new superheroes in a mythological narrative

Intelligent robots, artificial intelligence and intelligent algorithms are often presented as a danger to humanity. In films and literature, these technologies are presented as possible instruments for the eradication of workplaces and jobs, and the development of humanoid monstrosities, with intelligent beings taking over the Earth from humans.

What happens if we consider these technologies in a different context and view them as the heroes of a cultural narrative? We could imagine vividly how people's lives could be improved if we were to develop technologies that would help people with laborious and dangerous jobs. Simultaneously, we could imagine that these robots could benefit humanity best if we were to develop a social system whereby people are not only born equal but are assisted to become the very best possible versions of themselves. In such a heroic story, an intelligent robot would be humanity's best friend, an assistant who ends hunger, helps the helpless and unfortunate and is also a friend for the lonely.

Intelligent robots are Janus-faced – one face appears negative, while the opposite face looks towards a positive future. Obviously, we should not be naive, but if we attempt to see only the positive side, then a hero appears, an Odysseus, who returns home to Attica and makes up for the difficulties caused to his family by his many years abroad. In this context, an intelligent robot can be seen as 'the hero of a thousand faces' in Campbell's book of the same title (Campbell, 2008).

Briefly, this meta-myth sees technology as the gods' gift to humans, similar to the fire given to humans by Prometheus.[19] Prometheus suffered terrible punishment, however, and was condemned to live in eternal torment for having given this gift to humanity. We can understand this as referring to the Janus-faced nature of technology. Fire can be both good and bad for humans, just as obviously is the case with intelligent robots. If we choose to see positive opportunities, however, instead of aligning ourselves with modern-day Luddites,[20] then the intelligent robot emerges as hero. Just as fire liberated humans from darkness and cold, intelligent robots can free humans from toil, poverty and social isolation. In this technological narrative, the intelligent robot is not the serpent in Paradise, but the apple that gave knowledge, but also the fall of man, that is Adam and Eve became 'human' in the sense that they were disobedient, able to make mistakes ('sin'), and accordingly could exercise their free will. Despite the gods' prohibition, humans acquired both fire and knowledge, because a few heroes defied the gods, were disobedient and thereby created the opportunities we have today. It is here that intelligent robots emerge from dreams and myths and become the heroes that create a social hub among humans. We might think of intelligent robots as a rebirth of the opportunities we gained through the discovery of fire: a discovery that we have taken care of poorly, progressing from discovering fire to detonating atomic bombs over Nagasaki and Hiroshima. Intelligent robots are opportunities that have returned, that are being reborn and that are giving us hope of a fairy tale with a happy ending. What do the heroes of myths and fairy tales possess? They have superpowers – just like our modern hero, the intelligent robot. An intelligent robot is more intelligent than humans and it can help us, just as fire helped people in the past to survive darkness and cold. Humans need help, and so the gods send help in the strangest forms: as ravens, as whales, as fire, as hope, as love, and now as the intelligent robot, a superhero. Before heroes cross from the hereafter to come to the aid of humans, they are subjected to trials (like the sirens Odysseus was subjected to), which they must pass before they can return home as heroes. Home for Odysseus was Attica; for an intelligent robot, being at home means helping humans to understand that we are here together and must solve our problems together, just as a group of nomadic hunters in the Ice Age solved problems by working together to capture prey.

When humans first discovered fire, they most probably injured themselves by getting burnt before they eventually learnt to fear fire and harness it safely. Intelligent robots are similar to fire: simultaneously harmful and beneficial. But we will only find out how to use, tame and benefit from these new superheroes through a process of trial and error. We could also interpret the climate crisis as part of a mythological narrative, as something that the gods have thrown at humans to get us to understand that we must learn to work together as a community in order to overcome a trial set by the gods. An intelligent robot could be the superhero introduced by the gods to help us to understand that we are here to solve problems together, by acting as a community that doesn't categorize people as *insiders* and *outsiders*. In this context, remember the story about Socrates, who was given a choice between exile or drinking poison. According to this story, his community was so important to him that Socrates chose to drink poison instead of being exiled to live among strangers. Interpreted from a mythological perspective, the climate crisis and intelligent robots could be the gods' way of testing humans' understanding of community.

If we are to understand the intelligent robot as the superhero of our times, then we also need to understand that the gods are simultaneously vengeful and loving. They gave us fire, but also punished Prometheus for all eternity because of this discovery. The gods are giving us the intelligent robot, but they may also punish us with the full force of their wrath (for instance, through unemployment), if we fail to harness it intelligently to everyone's benefit. In this mythical narrative, the gods' love lies in the realization that the new superhero can free us from their wrath, if we work together to solve our challenges and problems as a community. The idea that the gods have taught us about love through their wrath is a possible interpretation of the many stories about Janus, the god with two faces. The intelligent robot is a modern-day Janus. We have simply to understand that through working together, we can transform the God of wrath into a God of love.

The gods look down on humans with sorrow, not because of hunger, need or the climate crisis, but because humans believe they can solve their problems alone, working individually, with each person fighting all the others. This is why the gods send myths to humans, but humans don't understand the myths. And so the gods send pestilence and war, but humans don't understand these signals either. And thus the gods send their messengers to humans, but humans don't understand their stories and narratives. Humans think that stories are stories and myths are myths. And so the gods send their heroes to humans, an Odysseus who seeks eternity without finding what he is looking for, or a Bodhisattva who is enlightenment or finally an intelligent robot, which is the superhero that can create a society that includes all of us.

The intelligent robot is an androgynous superhero, sent by the gods so that humans will understand that gender is irrelevant in stories about the gods. What is it that the intelligent robot is telling humans? It is telling us that we need protection. Protection against whom? Against ourselves, against our eternal need to fight against each other. In the same way as Isis in Egyptian mythology gives bread and water to the soul, the intelligent robot gives us freedom from loneliness and an understanding of community.

The intelligent robot, both as superhero and as a gift from the gods will create a new society. This new society will be based on a desire to live in community. The intelligent superhero will destroy our desire to forge our own paths, with lone horsemen creating their own lives and dying under the weights of their own destiny.

The superhero will crush the monster that is in the process of choking humanity and liberate humans from the force of their own destruction, as presented in all creation myths, including that of the serpent in Paradise. Our new superhero is like Gilgamesh, who sought eternal life. The difference is just that the intelligent robot is a superhero who liberates humans from their suffering, from the sickness they inherited from the gods and from the thought that one man can manage alone and create a life without a community. This sickness is at a deeper level a lack of understanding of what community is, of co-creation, of creating something for others, just as hunters share their catch with the rest of the tribe. This sickness is personified in the story of King Midas, who made everything he touched into gold, including what he loved most of all: his daughter.

The story of the intelligent robot does not stop with helping humans to get over their sickness. Eventually, everyone comes to love this superhero, but they have forgotten its message. They flock around this golden calf and invest everything they own in this superhero. This adulation and flocking leads to over-investment, crises and economic downturns. The superhero dies in the popular understanding of it as a hero. But then the strangest thing of all happens, on the 'third day' the hero comes back to life and the thing that is described in countless myths occurs: a resurrection. The thing that caused the crisis, and turned many people into victims, is precisely what leads us out of the crisis. A phoenix lays the egg that it will hatch from itself, just as an intelligent robot causes an economic crisis and destruction but is also what leads us out of the crisis, to recovery, thus becoming a guiding light for the many. Over and over again, the thing that saves humans is the same thing that caused the crisis in the first place. The resurrection is a recurring myth. We find it in Christianity. It also appears in Japanese myths about Amaterasu, who was also resurrected. We find the same basic story in Sumerian mythology. There are many such myths from the antiquity about resurrection. One of them, which is similar to the Christian myth, is the story of Inanna, a goddess who descends to the Underworld and emerges from the dead in the form of a human, with flesh and blood. The similarity with Christian mythology becomes even more striking when we find out that Inanna emerges from the Underworld after three days, fastened to a tree trunk. Considered from this perspective, our superhero is not completely separated from its god-like context. The intelligent robot destroys itself through the economic crisis it generates but is resurrected and becomes the superhero that restores good economic times to humans.

An intelligent robot is a master of two worlds: one that destroys and one that creates. An intelligent robot destroys jobs through automation, but at the same time creates new jobs through design, education, production, distribution, maintenance and application. On the one hand, for modern Luddites, an intelligent robot is a symbol of chaos, symbolized as a monster that destroys everything we humans have created. This monster is so intelligent in the imaginations of these modern Luddites, who include the now-deceased mathematician Stephen Hawking,[21] that it will take over the world and turn humans into its slaves. On the other hand, we have worshippers of modern technology who view all technology as wholly positive. In our world, an intelligent robot is a Janus-faced superhero – a being that can destroy but that can also create that which is innovative and new. Both possibilities are available to this new superhero. There are many myths about superheroes who are transformed into monsters that destroy everything and everyone. This kind of mythological superhero is often a warrior. Just imagine how our superhero, the intelligent robot, could be the war machine of the future, operating on both sides of a war zone. We find superheroes who are warriors in Greek mythology in the figures of Odysseus, Achilles, and many others. We find this warrior hero in most mythologies, from ancient Egypt to modern times. The monster Chaos is not the only thing that comes in many forms. The gods also come in many forms, according to the sea god Proteus (Campbell, 2008: 329). Our point in this context, which we can interpret from Campbell's comparison of historical mythologies, is that heroes also come in many different shapes and forms, such as our own superhero, the intelligent robot.

Description

What we are investigating here is technology as a cultural phenomenon. It may be easier to address this by first trying to understand technology as a social phenomenon. In this context, our new superhero, the intelligent robot, becomes a social mechanism for both destruction and development of the creative new. In terms of mythology, this can be represented metaphorically by the death and rebirth of the phoenix bird, while in terms of economic theory, we can refer to 'creative destruction', a concept coined by Joseph Schumpeter (Schumpeter, 1951). The intelligent robot is not something that has suddenly recently appeared out of nowhere; it can be understood as a gradual development starting at least as far back as the late 1930s and 1940s when Turing developed his 'automatic' machine.[22] Other early developments relate to the work of Norbert Wiener and other cyberneticists who took the first steps towards the development of artificial intelligence. The Internet also had early beginnings (1969). It is predicted by Ray Kurzweil (2005, 2008) that singularity will occur around 2045 – which will be roughly one hundred years after Turing's 'automatic' machine. In this way, we can understand technology as being a driver for social system change, and since culture here is understood as a subsystem of social systems, technology also becomes a driver for the cultural subsystem.

If we say that the cultural subsystem consists of norms and values (to put it simply), how can we say that intelligent robots, artificial intelligence and intelligent algorithms will influence norms and values? First, we know that new technology can lead to unemployment. J.M. Keynes introduced the concept of 'technological unemployment' as far back as the 1930s (Pecchi & Piga, 2010). Today, many theorists propose that the Fourth Industrial Revolution will also lead to 'technological unemployment' (Agar, 2019). However, we should keep in mind that technology is always part of a social system. It is technology as part of the social system that is interesting in relation to either the possibility of technological unemployment or the possibility of prosperity and well-being for the majority. This is where our previous story comes into play – the intelligent robots as both superheroes and monsters. The superhero creates wealth for everyone, while the monster creates enormous wealth, but only for a tiny upper-class minority. Thus, in our context, the question is: how do we control technology in the social system?

We can improve the intelligent robots until they are more intelligent, more morally conscious and more reflective than humans (Johannessen, 2020a, 2020b, 2020c, 2021a, 2021b). Of course, the question here is whether there should be no limitations on the development of technology – that is whether intelligent robots should be able to possess all the human characteristics but in a more advanced form; or whether there should be a limit to how far we should allow technology to develop in this direction. At least, this is what Nicholas Agar discusses in his book, *Truly Human Enhancement: A Philosophical Defence of Limits* (2014). Such a discussion is certainly interesting from a philosophical perspective. From our perspective, the most important point is who controls this technological development and who sets the limits. We see no philosophical problem with driverless cars, driverless buses, pilotless airliners etc. However, we see practical problems emerging when millions of people in the transport sector become unemployed because of such new transport technology. If we leave it to the market to solve these challenges, we can end up with a solution that creates new problems, e.g. a downward spiralling of wage levels. We see few problems if artificial intelligence and intelligent robots replace medical personnel, e.g. in lifting operations in health care or in surgical procedures. Why should anyone limit the ability of robots to improve people's medical treatment through surgical operations? It is not always the case that limitations should be respected, neither in war nor in peace – and in any case, not when it concerns improving people's health, well-being and living conditions.

The history of technology can be viewed as a path beginning with the supplementation of human muscle power and animal power by various physical processes, such as water and steam power. If we progress much further along this path to the present day, technology is being used to supplement or replace human rational brainpower; and, in the future, possibly human thinking related to ethics, as well as human emotions. There has been resistance throughout history both in terms of the automation of human muscle power and skills, i.e. the original Luddites, up until today, with resistance to brainpower automation, i.e. the modern Luddites with the recently deceased Stephen Hawking as their front figure. However, the point perhaps not always understood by the original and modern Luddites[23] is that in a larger perspective, technology can improve people's lives, for instance, by automating monotonous and tiring work in factories; and in health care, by providing assistance to overworked nurses and doctors. For example if we consider the case of heart surgery, in the not-too-distant future, if an intelligent robot is connected to all the available knowledge globally, it will be able to solve medical problems that individual surgeons or team of surgeons are unable to. One may ask: what is the downside with this? The only problem we can see is a possible loss in the social status of the surgeon, which is not so much a 'problem' viewed from the perspective of the overall health care.

Of course, there is a lot people can do, which the intelligent robot can't do, for instance, humming contentedly while working on some tedious work task, or thinking of God while planting potatoes in the garden. People can multitask doing both useful and mundane tasks and carrying out meaningless actions, which may make a lot of sense in the end, and possibly give birth to a poem that pleases others. This in itself is a cultural value that can make sense to many, though some feel it may be meaningless and wasted energy.

What is the most pivotal change that can happen at the beginning of the singularity and the Fourth Industrial Revolution? It seems reasonable to suggest that we will see two different cultural contexts, i.e. 'before and after singularity'. Before singularity, it is people who make all the important decisions. After singularity, intelligent robots will make the most important decisions. If this is a correct assumption, then we are heading towards a cultural divide, which we have not witnessed before. The technology before singularity freed people from tireless, monotonous and dangerous work tasks. However, the technology of singularity may result in people being superfluous with regard to work functions. Of course, this need not necessarily be a bad thing if meaningful lives for people can be developed in other ways.

It is crucial that we think of technology in combination with the social system and not view it as a social mechanism for the social system. The point is that by considering technology as an integral part of the social system, we can more easily investigate what we want it to do for us and what limitations we should set for both technology and the social system. If we view technology as an integral part of the social system and not something external to the system, we can more easily maintain and develop collective social decisions. It is technology as part of the social system, which will make it possible for us to regard the transition to singularity as a liberating force, so that we can finally use our powers to build communities that serve everyone, which are meaningful and which can accommodate diversity.

Culture can be understood as the centre of a social system. This centre can change, move and have more or less influence on the rest of the social system. If this centre is eroded and replaced by the economic or technological subsystem, there is a great risk that the social system will fall apart, like a wooden chair falling apart when its glued joints are exposed to too much moisture.

If such an understanding of culture is correct, then it makes sense that societies have holidays to celebrate religious festivals, various ceremonies to pay homage to something or someone and so on. This is the glue of society that maintains and strengthens cultural and social cohesion. The culture sends signals to people through various ceremonies. These signals are interpreted and reinterpreted throughout history and become myths that help build the cultural core where culture creates identity for the individual and for society as a whole. Through this identity, our understanding of society, and how it is organized and structured, is maintained. Such an understanding of culture means that cultural competence will be essential when dealing with the transition to singularity. What we claim here is that while cultural competence before singularity was important, but not essential for human well-being, after singularity it will become absolutely crucial to how humans control intelligent robots and artificial intelligence, especially in relation to the fact that these technologies will exceed human intelligence and probably be more morally aware than most people.

Analysis

As is evident from the previous narrative, we choose to consider intelligent robots here as the superheroes of the cultural change we see evolving towards singularity. This is not so much a prediction, but a description and analysis of a change that has long been underway. It has been evident for a long period that our moral compass has been eroded (Johannessen, 2019c, 2020b). This does not mean that morals and ethics are less valued now than before. It just means that the moral compass we all previously considered to provide a common direction and guideline is now so out of alignment that it no longer shows something unified and common to the people of nations or regions, such as the EU.

Throughout this chapter, we have investigated how human competence is affected by, and influences, the development of the new emerging technologies. Our main focus has been to regard technology as a social phenomenon. By this, we mean how technology and the social system interact to develop each other. However, we do not believe that there is a linear relationship between technology and social systems. Our starting point is the circular or interactive connection between technology and social systems. In this understanding, culture is at the core of all the other subsystems, like the planets that revolve around the sun. If the culture in such a picture is changed, not necessarily weakened, a new cultural competence will emerge. This competence will develop as personal cultural competences. We find these personal competences in a person such as Greta Thunberg, the 16-year-old Swedish environmental activist works who sees something wrong with our world and does something about it; that is she actively fights to warn people of the current inaction by governments to address the climate crisis. We have also witnessed such personal competence in people like Mahatma Gandhi, Nelson Mandela, Martin Luther King and others who stand up for what they believe is right and bring about changes and motivate others to take part in change processes. The cultural competence we are talking about here is the personal cultural competence that causes some people to stand up and do something about what they see needs changing, whether it is to end apartheid in South Africa (1990s), or end racial discrimination in the US, by building a civil rights movement (1950s–1960s), or environmentalists such as Greta Thunberg who has given silent nature a voice. Personal cultural competence is the opposite of the bystander syndrome; it concerns standing up for something you fully believe in and doing something to change things.

Cultural competence is an overarching abstract concept linked to norms and values. Personal cultural competence is aimed at a concretization of these norms and values embodied in people who attempt to follow the norms and values as guiding principles. This is no more difficult than relating to the norms and values that emerge through a pattern of events, such as the changing values associated with the present environmental crisis and today's enormous economic inequality, and then becoming the change one wants to see in the world. As mentioned earlier, Greta Thunberg, Nelson Mandela and Martin Luther King are obvious examples of people who possess this very personal cultural competence we are referring to here. An important point in this context is that these people are not political or religious extremists. On the contrary, they are right in the centre of society, a society that is looking for a figure to materialize their values, norms, dreams and hopes. These people represent the cultural power that unites the frustrations, hopes and dreams of many. It is in opposition to the bystander that personal cultural competence becomes evident. We can only observe this explicitly in a few people, but it resides in many others and is embodied in the statement: 'Be the change you want to see in the world'.[24]

Personal cultural competence is the competence that will ensure that we do not end up where many fear we will end up, that is in a technological ragnarok, such as that predicted by Stephen Hawking and Apple co-founder Steve Wozniak (Agar, 2019: 5); this fear is also expressed by other famous people such as Henry Kissinger and Elon Musk (Ford, 2018: 2).

Personal cultural competence is influenced by the signals transmitted by the overarching culture. These signals are emitted during a specific historical period and context. The point is that the signals are received by all of us, but only a few people respond to them. Those who respond obviously have a more well-developed personal cultural competence than others. They are more sensitive to the signals and they are more oriented to do something to bring about change based on the signals. In other words, they are more willing to be the change they and many others want to see in the world.

In the global cultural context, there is a disruptive trio,[25] consisting of automation, globalization and capital logic.[26] Automation consists of intelligent robots, artificial intelligence and intelligent algorithms, which will greatly affect the workplace in the future. Globalization is pushing down costs while competition is reinforcing the trend towards further automation. The logic of capital promotes a drive towards profit. The cultural competence needed to understand and deal with the negative aspects of this disruptive trio can be understood in relation to technology as a social phenomenon. This means that technology affects social systems, but that social systems both influence and reinforce technological development. We have shown technology as a social phenomenon in Figure 3.13.

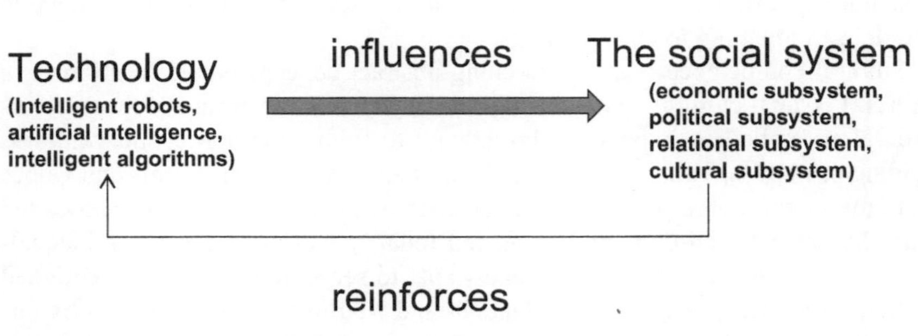

Figure 3.13 Technology as a social phenomenon

The major problem is not the changes themselves, but the speed and penetration that the changes will have. Most people will be affected by these changes and will not have the adequate time to respond and adapt to them. Even during the First Industrial Revolution, the changes were profound, but they went on for a longer period so that people could adapt to the changes (Johannessen, 2018). The disruptive trio will increase in strength towards singularity, if no major social upheavals occur before that time (Johannessen, 2020a, 2020c). When time and distance collapse into themselves, a whole new form of competence will arise, which we have referred to here as personal cultural competence. It is this personal cultural competence that will be in demand in the Fourth Industrial Revolution.

Theoretical points

Artificial intelligence has been described in numerous science fiction novels but has now become a reality in several scientific fields of research, such as genetic editing (Buontempo, 2019), evolutionary algorithms (Zelinka & Chen, 2019), as well as in all the technological-social projects that create innovations in social systems. Various technical devices can soon understand what we are saying and comply with our verbal commands. Intelligent robots with highly developed artificial intelligence, coupled with other such robots globally (informats), will soon be able to diagnose and cure most cancer types. This technology is spreading extremely rapidly due to the connections in global networks. Artificial intelligence will constitute the technological force that will greatly affect our social systems, locally, nationally and globally. Just as electricity revolutionized the work and living conditions of the 1800–1900s, artificial intelligence will revolutionize the social system in the future. This trend will accelerate towards 2045 (Kurzweil, 2005, 2008; Johannessen, 2020a).

> Proposition: The risks involved in the use of artificial intelligence will be reduced by developing personal cultural competence.

As artificial intelligence and intelligent robots are introduced into most areas of working life, around 2045, most work functions will be automated. This will occur in production, administration, and distribution. Any job that can be digitized will be automated first, then more complicated work tasks will also be automated. As long as the logic of capital dominates our way of thinking, this will of necessity lead to greater inequality. A simple understanding of this logic is that when the drive towards ever-greater profits dominates our society and is given precedence over people's welfare, and automation is introduced at the expense of people's participation in working life,[27] then social and economic inequality will of necessity increase. Work conditions will be characterized by contract and self-employed workers, with wages being pushed down due to global competition, while profits are pushed upwards. We will witness unemployment in some occupational groups, while others will be retrained for new work functions. The end result will most likely be full employment, but at lower wages and the use of more contract work (Johannessen, 2020a, 2020b, 2020c).

> Proposition: If the disruptive trio[28] is allowed to continue undisturbed, then cultural competence will not be able to offset a development that reinforces inequality. The intervention needed will be personal cultural competence that can change the logic of capital.

Fundamentally, personal cultural competence at the individual level consists of the ability to see patterns unfolding and to frame thinking in a new way according to how this pattern unfolds. In the 1800s, this could concern the ability to see how the 600-year-old Ottoman Empire was falling apart, and then position oneself in relation to this. In the 1900s, cultural competence could be to envision how the British Empire was about to collapse before this actually happened. In the twenty-first century, one can say that personal cultural competence is linked to two major phenomena: first, the question of the sustainability of the planet and second, the challenges regarding the fall of the American sphere of influence and the rise of the Chinese. In both the nineteenth and twentieth centuries, as well as at the beginning of the twenty-first century, changing cultural patterns also changed our understanding of our own identity. For instance consider how the Turks' identity changed with the collapse of the Ottoman Empire, and the Young Turks grew in strength and founded the state of Turkey in 1922. Imagine how British identity changed with the collapse of the British Empire. An important point of identity, however, is that it takes time for thinking and identity to adapt to the new reality. In this context, one way of viewing Brexit is as 'the last gasp of the Empire'.

If it is the case that American global dominance is being seriously challenged by China's increasing strength, then this will probably affect the identity of both nations. Nations that feel their position or identity is being seriously challenged will expend considerable efforts in an attempt to re-establish a former and more dominant position. It is in this context one can interpret Donald Trump's 2016 presidential election campaign slogan, 'Make America Great Again'. History shows us that one of the greatest dangers is when empires and nations feel that their identity, culture and position is being threatened, because they will greatly resist changes which they view as negative.

> Proposition: The ability to 'see' patterns and patterns that bind together will be an important personal cultural competence that will be in demand in the Fourth Industrial Revolution.

Throughout the 1900s, nations and production were viewed as one, that is industries and companies had their home nations as their point of reference. This identity first started to develop during the last two centuries, since the time of the First Industrial Revolution. However, towards the end of the twentieth century, more specifically around the 1980s when neoliberal economic policies were implemented around the world, industries and companies did not necessarily view the home nation as the starting point for their success. It was rather the world that became their point of reference, not the nation. This obviously had an impact on where and how production and distribution took place. One of the consequences was that nations became less important for the earnings of companies. Whether it was Communist China or capitalist United States that benefited from the production's organization was immaterial to the company in question, as long as they were able to reap super profits.

The development described previously led, among other things, to a resurgence of nationalism, in all its political shades. National populism emerged with both a capitalist and a socialist face. Once again, cultural identity became closely associated with the nation. What we can observe is an erosion of the forces that link nations together, namely an increasing erosion of the cohesion between nations. Indicative of this development is Brexit, the withdrawal of the UK from the European Union, and America's recent 'go it alone policy'. There seems to be limits to a falling identity. When the whole and the parts are unable to co-exist, the whole takes over and constitutes a new identity. This is expressed in statements of the type: 'We must take back control (from Brussels)'; or we need to regain our strength, as expressed in the statement: 'Make America Great Again'. We also find this type of thinking back in the 1980s in Communist China, when Deng Xiaoping famously said, 'It doesn't matter whether a cat is black or white, as long as it catches mice.'[29] In this context, an important component of cultural competence is the realization that the sum of the parts does not necessarily constitute the whole. Thus, one cannot find out how the whole works by only studying how the parts act individually and together. The point is that the whole is something more than the sum of the parts, and identity can be a way of interpreting the signals that the context sends.

The competence that has given nations a new identity cannot be used to bring nations and the world together to deal with the global challenges we face, such as the climate crisis. More abstractly, the parts (nations) cannot repair the whole (the global challenges). What is needed is a cultural competence that transcends the parts. However, this is unlikely to happen, because it would mean that the entire political power apparatus would be forced to don a dunce's cap.

> Proposition: The personal cultural competence needed that can put the most burning issues of economic inequality, climate crisis and environmental pollution on the agenda, and bring about a change in our identity and thinking, will emerge as a grassroots' initiative, i.e. a populist initiative that goes against the established power structures.

We are in the midst of a new transformation in the Western world, as well as in large parts of the East, with China and India at the forefront. Our worldview is changing. We live in the midst of a cultural storm that is casting disruptive winds in all directions, and it is difficult to interpret the cultural signals: who is friend and who is foe? This changing cultural identity is frightening to many people and neither does it facilitate dealing with the global climate challenge, as there are few if any nations or collective systems that have the necessary strength of leadership. Back on the battlefield, negative global forces are growing without anyone taking leadership or attempting to make the necessary changes. The nation that traditionally took leadership, the USA, has shamed itself in the eyes of the world by electing a president who shies away from global responsibility, preaching an 'America First' policy. Such a policy that puts the nation before anything else may be viewed as a distorted national version of Adam Smith's individual self-interest: What is good for the individual (USA) is good for society (the world).

> Proposition: Leadership, which is not linked to established power structures, but which seeks to create the world we want to see evolve, will become a cultural competence that is in demand.

Practical utility

Major technological changes not only affect individuals, organizations and the larger system, they also affect and are influenced by culture. Culture also affects the individual, so that various aspects of the culture affect our behaviour and our physiology right down to the physiological and brain wave level (Kitayama & Cohen, 2019). Cultural psychology has found that what we learn from our culture in our upbringing has such a powerful effect on us that what we learn later in life must address what we learnt earlier in the culture we grew up in (Heine, 2015). Culture also makes us perceive things in our surroundings differently (O'Hara & Leicester, 2012: 26). Even what can be perceived as the success for an individual depends on the culture in which he or she was raised. Most people who work with culture know that our norms and values are culturally conditioned. However, there is less awareness of the fact that our personal psychology is culturally conditioned. This was first discovered on a scientific level with the new cultural psychology of the twenty-first century (Kitayama & Cohen, 2019). We should be aware that in the multicultural societies that we find ourselves in now, our reactions will depend on the culture we grew up in (Shiraev & Levy, 2016). Our early cultural influence is like an anchor that holds us to a point in our upbringing, no matter how much we may drift away from that point. We can understand this anchor and anchor chain that holds the anchor as the social mechanism that helps create our identity (Shweder, 1991). Anyone who has tried to set sail without raising the anchor knows that the boat will only go in a ring around the anchor. In this way, our identity is held firmly in the culture we grew up in, the landscapes we can still see with our inner eye, even when we are 70, and haven't been 'home' for the last 45–50 years or so. These landscapes of our inner eye create more than just our identity; they become the psychological landscape we assess our place in the world from, our success and our way of life, and how we understand others. Although we may create a different identity later in life, and we have lived this identity for 45–50 years, we always go back to our 'original' identity – back to the culture that shaped our identity early in our lives.

At a practical level, one can avoid the complexity inherent in the cultural identity of a multicultural society by following simple guidelines and approaches:

- You are always interested in learning something new that is not linked to your own identity.
- You should have the open mind of a child and constantly ask questions, although they may be perceived by some as fatuous.
- You should never be satisfied with the answers you are given, even if they seem adequate and obvious to others.

If we apply the knowledge of cultural psychology in a practical and simple way, the results that come out of such an approach can be complex and innovative. It is a misconception to believe that one will only obtain simple results by using simple strategies (Delanda, 2019). It is often the opposite that is the case, because ideas and practices are interconnected in the strangest ways, something complexity theory has taught us (Byrne & Callaghan, 2013). One of the lessons from chaos theory and complexity theory is that tiny changes can have the greatest and complex consequences (Lansing et al., 2019), hence the statement that when 'a butterfly flaps its wings in the Amazonian jungle, it can subsequently cause a hurricane to ravage China'. Similarly, in the social system, simple strategies may result in radical innovations (Delanda, 2019).

Most of us can look back on our lives and point to an episode, an event, a moment and so on that changed the direction of our life and gave it a new or changed meaning. Most nations also have such critical moments in their history that have changed the nation's narrative. For instance, such 'critical' moments may be when they were attacked by a foreign power, gained their independence, adopted their constitution, fought a liberating revolution and so on. This is a commonly accepted approach when historians construct the histories of nations. What is new in our context is that cultural psychology explains that cultural histories adopt a similar approach. For instance, European cultural history is often described as changing dramatically in relation to certain key events and occurrences, such as the adoption of Christianity as the major religion, and its influence on European thinking. The wars between European nations have resulted in new superstructures that have clearly affected the course of history, and not least the cultural history. Other key events affecting cultural history are technological changes, such as the invention of the printing press around 1440, which resulted in knowledge being disseminated wider and faster than ever before. The religious battles between Christians and Muslims are often viewed as being key events in the shaping of European cultural history. One of these battles, the Battle of Roncevaux Pass in 778, during the reign of Charlemagne, is described symbolically in the epic poem, *The Song of Roland.* The point here is not whether the poem is historically correct, or whether it was in fact the Basques who ambushed and wiped out the rear guard of the Frankish army. The point is that the poem written around the eleventh–twelfth century (some 300 years after the event it describes) formed part of a larger European cultural narrative of the Christians' struggle against the Muslims (the Saracens). The cultural history changed and in turn gave energy to the struggle against the Muslims both in Spain and the Balkans, resulting in a new cultural narrative emerging in Europe. Of course, *The Song of Roland* is not the only text describing an event that has changed the European cultural narrative in a religious context of Christians and Muslims. There are many small and large events around Europe that have also contributed to changing this narrative, not least, the Ottoman wars in Europe from the Middle Ages until the early twentieth century. Neither are the battles between Christians and Muslims in Europe the only violent struggles between peoples that have shaped European cultural history. In the thirteenth century, the conquest of much of Europe by the Mongols not only had a great political and economic impact, but also a cultural impact, whereby new cultural narratives emerged, which have also become part of the narrative of European culture.

In Figure 3.14, we have shown schematically how the different subsystems influence each other and constitute the cultural narrative, as well as how this narrative is again influenced by events in the different subsystems.

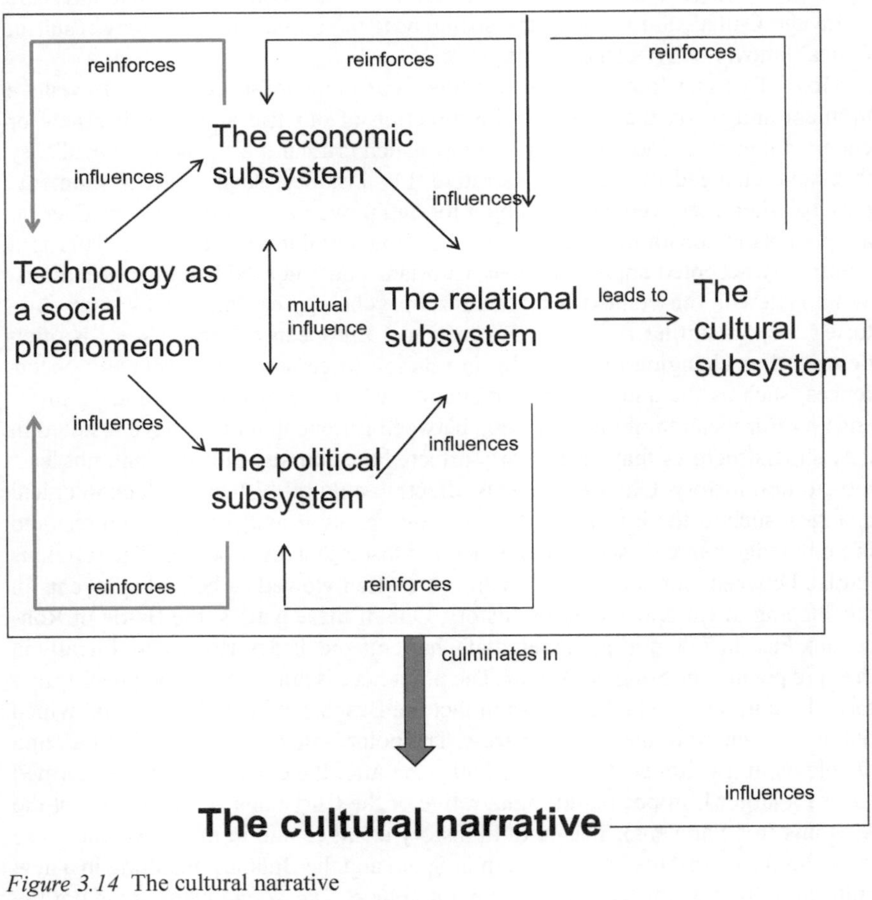

Figure 3.14 The cultural narrative

Sub-conclusion

The question we have investigated in this section is: what cultural competences will be in demand in the Fourth Industrial Revolution? We need to develop many different cultural competencies that can be utilized in the new era we are now moving into. Understanding technology as a social phenomenon will become important because intelligent robots, artificial intelligence and intelligent algorithms will be embedded into every aspect of our lives, and possibly some of these will also be embedded in the human body. In such a fusion process, technology and the social system will become a unit, and not separated and understood as a cause and effect process.

Furthermore, it is important that each of us develop a personal cultural competence and at the same time keep in mind that 'no one is too small to make a difference'.[30] This can be understood in a context where cultural psychology becomes important to understand. Therefore, it is important for each of us to develop cultural competence in which we take cultural leadership so that we can support and contribute to the development of grassroots initiatives. The rationale is that the established formal political leadership is so ingrained in its positions, networks and balancing diplomatic mechanisms that all the actions they propose and take the initiative to implement are done at a minimum, which will rarely lead to the changes that are important to make in order to create the future that many people want to be a part of.

In summary, in briefly answering the question we have explored in this section, it is important that we:

1. Understand technology as a social phenomenon
2. Acquire personal cultural competence
3. Gain insight into cultural psychology
4. Understand cultural narratives and the 'the points of change', that is the key points that change narratives throughout history
5. Initiate cultural leadership.

General conclusion

The question we have investigated in this chapter is as follows: what human competences will be in demand in the Fourth Industrial Revolution?

A brief answer can be described along four axes:

- Social competence
- Emotional competence
- Leadership competence
- Cultural competence.

At a time when technology is playing a decisive role in our lives, human competence is perhaps more important than ever, because it can resist technology as the new 'false idol' and give us an understanding that being human is about something quite other than being able to develop and manage tools that are becoming more and more refined, regardless of what names or forms they take. We wish to develop the following proposition, which synthesizes the whole of this chapter:

> The more technology fills social spaces, the greater the importance of human competence. Our reasoning is that the meaning and purpose of what we do is created in social relationships, where tools are at best a help in achieving this goal.

We are not only living in an age where technology is exploding around us at every level. We are also experiencing living in an age when the cultural narrative is in a state of flux. One of the social mechanisms that is changing our cultural narrative is a reduction in faith in neo-liberalism as an ideology for economic subsystems. Another social mechanism that is also undergoing change and that has the power to influence the cultural narrative is our perception of our Christian cultural heritage. This part of Christianity's cultural heritage can be understood as loving one's neighbour. This can also be understood in relation to Jesus's Sermon on the Mount. This may be interpreted as the importance of following six ways of living: being humble, being fair, helping those who are suffering, avoiding causing conflict, doing good deeds and being able to forgive.[31] This seems to be changing in the European cultural narrative, where more and more countries and political parties are asking questions about the 'foreigners' who are seeking refuge in the European concept. To the many who are rejected, this European Christian concept precisely embodies a concept of Christianity that has not materialized. There is much to suggest that the European cultural narrative in this area has reached a point of cultural change, where a new narrative is in the course of constructing itself. When cultural narratives are undergoing change, tensions and sometimes conflicts are generated around these points of change, e.g. stories about immigration, foreigners, people who are 'different', people who are not like us and so on. When a cultural narrative is undergoing change, cultural dissonance emerges, which causes us to doubt whether we should interpret or reinterpret our cultural history.

The human competence that is also required of our leaders is that they have a black belt in human understanding, as well as have an understanding of change processes and an ability to tackle resistance to change.

Notes

1 This double competence comprises professional competence plus competence in the areas of coding, artificial intelligence and intelligent algorithms.
2 Ross (2016), Wang (2015), Johannessen (2019), Zuboff (2019).
3 Bruce and Crook (2015), Brynjolfsson and McAfee (2014), Ford (2016), Harari (2015).
4 The Dublin Declaration on Human Resources for Health, 2017, referred to in Britnell (2019: 175). Mark Britnell (2019: x) states that probably closer to 80 million will be needed.
5 *The Creation of Adam,* painted by Michelangelo 1508–1512.

6 Bear et al. (2016), Hallowell (2011), Brann (2015), Crockett et al. (2008), Cote and Saavedra (2005), Damasio (2004), Dimitriadis and Psychogios (2016), Snyder (2016), Swart et al. (2015), Johannessen (2020).
7 Homer (1950: Book 8).
8 Symbolically and metaphorically.
9 Homer (1996: Chapter 18).
10 Machiavelli refers to Xenophon, both in *The Prince* and in *Discourses on Livy*, more often than to any classical philosopher.
11 Fox (2004: 2–3).
12 Bennis cited in Benton and Wright-Ford (2017: vii).
13 The Pareto principle: https://en.wikipedia.org/wiki/Pareto_principle
14 The questions have been reworded from Bennis and Sample (2015: 33).
15 This is a Norwegian metaphor '*taler Roma midt imot*' (literal translation: 'speak out against Rome'). It refers to King Sverre of Norway who opposed the dictates of the pope in Rome and was excommunicated (in 1194).
16 Akerlof and Shiller (2009) use the abstract Keynesian concept of 'animal spirits', when referring to psychological elements that can affect people's economic behaviour, such as confidence, fairness, corruption, illusion as well as stories and myths. Taking people's behaviour into account, it is important for leaders to create 'commitment', a term which we choose to use here.
17 Goleman (2014: 346, note 5).
18 We use a systemic understanding of the four subsystems that constitute social systems.
19 https://no.wikipedia.org/wiki/Prometheus
20 https://en.wikipedia.org/wiki/Luddite
21 https://en.wikipedia.org/wiki/Stephen_Hawking
22 https://en.wikipedia.org/wiki/Alan_Turing
23 Represented by Stephen Hawking and Apple co-founder Steve Wozniak among others (Agar, 2019: 5).
24 The statement was possibly made by M. Gandhi: www.quora.com/Did-Gandhi-really-say-Be-the-change-you-want-to-see-in-the-world
25 RichardBaldwin (2019: 20) calls this a 'disruptive duo' because he chooses to consciously or unconsciously disregard the logic of capital.
26 Capital logic is the underlying logic of the capitalist system. Key elements of this logic are competition, profit, markets, stock exchanges and corporations. This logic is obviously not a law of nature but created by someone for someone. It can therefore also be changed if so desired.
27 For instance people with special needs (Slorac, 2016; Rendal & Kuys, 2013; Oliver, 2012; Quarmby, 2011).
28 The disruptive trio are:

    1 Technology (artificial intelligence, intelligent robots, intelligent algorithms, intelligent informats)
    2 Globalization (competition for wages that reduces wages and increases profits)
    3 The logic of capital (profit before people's welfare).

29 The underlying meaning of the metaphor is that as long as the economy works well, this is what matters. China eventually opened up its economy allowing capitalists to invest in China with the aim of improving the country's economy.
30 *No One Is Too Small to Make a Difference* is a book by climate activist Greta Thunberg, which consists of a collection of speeches which she has written about the climate crisis. See the online Norwegian newspaper *Dagbladet*: www.dagbladet.no/nyheter/greta-15-er-klimatoppmotets-new-superstar---derder-stjeler-firtida-var/70567176
31 It is possible that a theologian would interpret the Sermon on the Mount differently, but this is a layman's understanding of aspects of our cultural story.

References

Ackoff, R.L. (1981). *Creating the corporate future: Plan or be planned for*, John Wiley & Sons, New York.

Ackoff, R.L. (1999). *Re-creating the organization: A design of organizations for the 21st century*, Oxford University Press, Oxford.

Adriaenssen, D. & Johannessen, J.-A. (2016). Prospect theory as an explanation for resistance to organizational change: Some management implications, *Problems and Perspectives in Management*, 14(2):83–92.

Agar, N. (2013). *Humanity's end: Why we should reject radical enhancement*, MIT Press, Cambridge, MA.

Agar, N. (2014). *Truly human enhancement: A philosophical defence of limits*, MIT Press, Cambridge, MA.

Agar, N. (2019). *How to be human in the digital economy*, MIT Press, Cambridge, MA.

Akerlof, G.A. & Shiller, R.J. (2009). *Animal spirits*, Princeton University Press, Princeton.

Albrecht, K. (2006). *Social intelligence: The new science of success*, Jossey-Bass, London.

Avent, R. (2017). *The wealth of humans: Work and its absence in the twenty-first century*, Penguin, London.

Baldwin, R. (2019). *The globotic upheaval: Globalization, robotics and the future of work*, Weidenfeld & Nicolson (W&N), New York.

Barrett, L.F. (2017). *How emotions are made: The secret life of the brain*, Pan Books, New York.

Bartel, C. & Saavedra, R. (2000). The collective construction of work group moods, *Administrative Science Quarterly*, 45:187–231.

Bear, M.F.; Connors, B.W. & Paradiso, M.A. (2016). *Neuroscience: Exploring the brain*, Wolters Kluwer, London.

Bennis, W. (2009). *On becoming a leader*, Basic Books, New York.

Bennis, W. & Sample, S.B. (2015). *The art and adventure of leadership*, Wiley, New York.

Benton, D.A. & Wright-Ford, K. (2017). *The leadership mind switch. Rethinking how we lead in the new world of work*, McGraw Hill, New York.

Brann, A. (2015). *Engaged: The neuroscience behind creating productive people in successful organizations*, Palgrave-Macmillan, London.

Britnell, M. (2019). *Human: Solving the global workforce crises in healthcare*, Oxford University Press, Oxford.

Bruce, D. & Crook, G. (2015). *The Dream Café: Lessons in the art of radical innovation*, John Wiley & Sons, New York.

Brynjolfsson, E. & McAfee, A. (2014). *The second machine age: Work, progress, and prosperity in a time of brilliant technologies*, W.W. Norton, New York.

Buber, M. (2013). *I and thou*, Bloomsbury Academic, London.

Bunge, M. (2015). *Political philosophy*, Transaction Publishers, New York.

Buontempo, F. (2019). *Genetic algorithms and machine learning for programmers*, O'Reilly, New York.

Byrne, D. & Callaghan, G. (2013). *Complexity theory and the social sciences*, Routledge, London.

Campbell, J. (1998). *The power of myth*, Anchor Books, New York.

Campbell, J. (2008). *The hero with a thousand faces*, New World Library, New York.

Colvin, G. (2016). *Humans are underrated: What high achievers know that brilliant machines never will*, Nicolas Brealey Publishing, New York.

Cote, S.T. & Saavedra, R. (2005). The contagious leader: Impact of the leader's mood on the mood of group members, group affective tone, and group processes, *Journal of Applied Psychology*, 90(3):295–305.

Crockett, M.J.; Clark, L.; Tabibnia, G.; Lieberman, M.D. & Robbins, T.W. (2008). Serotonin modulates behavioral reactions to unfairness, *Science*, 320(5884):1739.

Damasio, A. (2004). Emotions and feelings: A neurobiological perspective, in Manstead, A.S.; Frijda, N. & Fisher, A. (Eds.). *Feelings and emotions: The Amsterdam Symposium*, Cambridge University Press, Cambridge. Pp. 49–57.

Delanda, M. (2019). *A new philosophy of society*, Bloomsbury Academic, London.

De Waal, F. (2019). *Mama's last hug: Animal emotions and what they tell us about ourselves*, Granta Publication, London.

Diamandis, P.H. & Kotler, S. (2012). *Abundance: The future is better than you think*, Free Press, London.

Dimitriadis, N. & Psychogios, A. (2016). *Neuroscience for leaders: A brain adaptive leadership approach*, Kogan Page, London.

Duckworth, A. (2017). *Grit: Why passion and resilience are the secrets to success*, Vermilion, London.

Engels, F. (2009). *The condition of the working class in England*, Oxford University Press, Oxford.

Ford, M. (2016). *The rise of the robots: Technology and the threat of mass unemployment*, Oneworld, London.

Ford, M. (2018). *Architects of intelligence: The truth about AI from the people building it*, Packt Publishing, Birmingham.

Gardner, H. (1995). *Leading minds: An anatomy of leadership*, Basic Books, New York.

George, J.F. & Bettenhausen, K. (1990). Understanding prosocial behavior, *Journal of Applied Psychology*, 75(6):698–706.

Gerber, J.; Macionis, J. & Linda, M. (2010). *Sociology*, Pearson, Toronto.

Goleman, D. (1996). *Emotional intelligence: Why it can matter more than IQ*, Bloomsbury Publishing, London.

Goleman, D. (2006). *Social intelligence*, Hutchinson, London.

Goleman, D. (2014). *The new leaders: Transforming the art of leadership into the science of results*, Sphere, London.

Hallowell, E.M. (2011). *Shine: Using brain science to get the best from your people*, Harvard Business Review Press, Boston.

Handy, C. (2002). *The age of unreason*, Arrow, New York.

Handy, C. (2007). *Myself and other important matters*, Arrow, New York.

Handy, C. (2016). *The second curve: Thoughts on reinventing society*, Random House, London.

Harari, Y.N. (2015). *Sapiens: A brief history of humankind*, Vintage, London.

Heine, S.J. (2015). *Cultural psychology*, W.W. Norton Company, New York.

Homer (1950). *The Iliad*, Little, Brown and Co., New York.

Homer (1996). *Odyssey*, trans. Robert Fagles, Viking, New York.

Janis, I.L. (1982). *Group think: Psychological studies of policy decisions and fiascoes*, Houghton Mifflin, New York.

Johannessen, J.-A. (2018). *Innovations leads to economic crises*, Palgrave, London.

Johannessen, J.-A. (2019a). *Historical introduction to knowledge management and the innovation economy*, Emerald, London.

Johannessen, J.-A. (2019b). *Leadership and organization in the innovation economy*, Emerald, London.

Johannessen, J.-A. (2019c). *Automation, capitalism and the end of the middle class*, Routledge, London.
Johannessen, J.-A. (2020a). *Singularity innovation*, Routledge, London.
Johannessen, J.-A. (2020b). *What is wrong with capitalism*? Verso, London.
Johannessen, J.-A. (2020c). *Building the innovation economy*, Routledge, London.
Johannessen, J.-A. (2021a). *Feudal capitalism, algorithmic capitalism and platform capitalism*, Routledge, London.
Johannessen, J.-A. (2021b). *Artificial intelligence, intelligent robots and ethics: An intelligent ethical Robot communicating about moral with an un-ethical human being*, Routledge, London.
Johannessen, J.-A. (2022). *Intelligent robots: Consciousness and creativity*, Routledge, London, forthcoming.
Kahneman, D. & Tversky, A. (1979). Prospect theory: An analysis of decision under risk, *Econometrica, Journal of the Econometric Society*, 47(2):263–292.
Kahneman, D. & Tversky, A. (2000). Prospect theory: An analysis of decision under risk, in Kahneman, D. & Tversky, A. (Eds.). *Choices, values and frames*, Cambridge University Press, Cambridge. Pp. 17–43.
Kitayama, S. & Cohen, D. (2019). *Handbook of cultural psychology*, Guilford Press, London.
Knights, D. & O'Leary, M. (2006). Leadership, ethics and responsibility to other, *Journal of Business Ethics*, 67(2):125–137.
Kurzweil, R. (2005). *The singularity is near*, Penguin, London.
Kurzweil, R. (2008). *The age of spiritual machines: When computers exceed human intelligence*, Penguin, London.
Lansing, J.S.; Cox, M.P. & Dove, M.R. (2019). *Islands of order: A guide to complexity modelling for social sciences*, Princeton University Press, Princeton.
Makunda, G. (2012). *Indispensable: When leaders really matter*, Harvard Business Review Press, Boston.
Maslow, A. (2011). *Towards a psychology of being*, Wilder Publication, New York.
Maslow, A. (2013). *A theory of human motivation*, Wilder Publication, New York.
Maulding Green, W.S. & Leonard, E.E. (2019). *Leadership intelligence*, Rowman & Littlefield, New York.
O'Hara, M. & Leicester, G. (2012). *Dancing at the edge*, Triarchy Press, Devon.
Oliver, M. (2012). *The new politics of disablement*, Palgrave, London.
Pecchi, L. & Piga, G. (2010). *Revisiting Keynes: Economic possibilities for our grandchildren*, MIT Press, Boston, MA.
Provine, R. (2000). *Laughter is "brain to brain"*, Viking Press, New York.
Putnam, R. (2001). *Bowling alone: The collapse and revival of American community*, Simon & Schuster, New York.
Quarmby, K. (2011). *Scapegoat: Why we are failing disabled people*, Portobello Books, London.
Rajan, R. (2019). *The third pillar: How markets and the state leave the community behind*, William Collins, London.
Reese, B. (2018). *The fourth age, smart robots, conscious computers, and the future of humanity*, Artria Books, London.
Rendal, G. & Kuys, B. (2013). Design for disability: Industrial designed-led interventions for assistive cutlery, *Hospitality & Society*, 3(3):229–237.
Rogers, C. (2004). *On becoming a person*, Robinson, New York.
Ross, A. (2016). *The industries of the future*, Simon & Schuster, New York.

Rutherford, R.B. (2010). The philosophy of the Odyssey, in Doherty, L.E. (Ed.). *Oxford readings in classical studies, Homer's Odyssey*, Oxford University Press, Oxford. Pp. 155–189.

Schumpeter, J. (1951). *Theory of economic development*, Harvard University Press, Boston.

Shipler, D. (2005). *The working poor: Invisible in America*, Vintage, New York.

Shiraev, E.B. & Levy, D.A. (2016). *Cross-cultural psychology*, Routledge, London.

Shweder, R.A. (1991). *Thinking through cultures: Expeditions in cultural psychology*, Harvard University Press, Cambridge, MA.

Slorac, R. (2016). *A very capitalist condition: A history and politics of disability*, Bookmarks Publications, London.

Snyder, R.A. (2016). *The social cognitive neuroscience of leading organizational change*, Routledge, London.

Standing, G. (2014a). *A precariat charter: From denizens to citizens*, Bloomsbury, London.

Standing, G. (2014b). *The precariat: The new dangerous class*, Bloomsbury Academic, New York.

Susskind, R. (2017). *Tomorrow's lawyers: An introduction to your future*, Oxford University Press, Oxford.

Susskind, R. & Susskind, D. (2015). *The future of professions: How technology will transform the work of human experts*, Oxford University Press, Oxford.

Swart, T.; Chisholm, K. & Brown, P. (2015). *Neuroscience for leadership*, Palgrave Macmillan, London.

Topol, E.J. (2019). High-performance medicine: The convergence of human and artificial intelligence, *Nature Medicine*, 25:44–56.

Totterdell, P. (2000). Catching moods and hitting runs: Mood linkage and subjective performance in professional sports teams, *Journal of Applied Psychology*, 85(6):848–859.

Wang, R. (2015). *Disrupting digital business: Create an authentic experience in the peer to peer economy*, Harvard Business Review Press, Boston.

Xenophon (1964). *Anabasis: The march up country*, The University of Michigan Press, Ann Arbor.

Zelinka, I. & Chen, G. (2019). *Evolutionary algorithms*, Springer, London.

Zuboff, S. (2019). *The age of surveillance capitalism*, Profile Books, New York.

Index

Note: Page numbers in *italic* indicate a figure on the corresponding page. Page numbers followed by 'n' indicate a note.